WOMEN IN THE VIKING AGE

A szüleimnek

WOMEN IN THE VIKING AGE

Judith Jesch

THE BOYDELL PRESS

First published 1991 by The Boydell Press, Woodbridge
Reprinted in hardback and paperback 1994, 1995,
1996 (paperback)

The Boydell Press is an imprint of Boydell & Brewer Ltd
PO Box 9, Woodbridge, Suffolk IP12 3DF, UK
and of Boydell & Brewer Inc.
PO Box 41026, Rochester, NY 14604-4126, USA

ISBN 0 85115 278 3 hardback
ISBN 0 85115 360 7 paperback

British Library Cataloguing-in-Publication Data
Jesch, Judith
  Women in the Viking age.
  I. Title
  940.1082
  ISBN 0–85115–278–3
  ISBN 0–85115–360–7 pbk

Library of Congress Catalog Card Number: 91–16402

This publication is printed on acid-free paper

Printed in Great Britain by
St Edmundsbury Press Ltd, Bury St Edmunds, Suffolk

Contents

List of Illustrations

List of illustrations

The author and publishers are grateful to the following for permission to reproduce the illustrations listed below:

Antikvarisk-Topografiska Arkivet (ATA), Stockholm   22 (bottom, 23 (top), 23 (bottom), 56, 57, 65, 67, 129, 131

Copenhagen National Museum   26 (top)

Forhistorisk Museum, Moesgård, Højbjerg   41

Helge Ingstad, Oslo   183

Historisk Museum, Universitet i Bergen   11 (bottom), 20 (top), 137

Kulturen, Lund   47

Manx Museum   26 (bottom), 73 (right)

National Museum of Iceland   201

Orla Svendsen, Højbjerg   18

Stofnun Árna Magnússonar, Reykjavik   145

Tromsø Museum   16 (top)

Trustees of the National Museums of Scotland   11 (top)

Universitets Oldsaksamling, Oslo   20 (bottom), 30, 31, 32, 33, 47, 73 (left), 125, 132, 163

Vikingeskibshallen i Roskilde   153

Introduction

Vikings are irredeemably male in the popular imagination. Fierce bands of bearded and helmeted warriors emerge suddenly and inexplicably from the countries of the far north, descending on the peace-loving and vulnerable inhabitants of Christian Europe in their fast ships. They maim and murder, rob, pillage and destroy, rape and enslave, venting their fury on defenceless monks and women in particular.

That, at any rate, is the historical myth. Like most such myths, there is more than a grain of truth to it, and it has a respectable pedigree. Our modern idea of viking raids is not very different from that of the Northumbrian scholar Alcuin, writing home from the safety of the Frankish court, soon after the raid in 793 on the monastery of Lindisfarne:

> never before has such terror appeared in Britain as we have now suffered from a pagan race, nor was it thought that such an inroad from the sea could be made. Behold, the church of St Cuthbert spattered with the blood of the priests of God, despoiled of all its ornaments;

The natural consequence of such a view is to brand all vikings as male. Historically, women have had little opportunity to participate in war, murder, rape and robbery; such activities have usually been the prerogative of members of the male sex. If a 'viking' is a marauding pagan warrior, then a 'viking woman' is logically impossible.

However, myths tend to simplify, and a concentration on bloodthirsty vikings ignores the more complex historical pattern. Scandinavian scholars have always emphasised the northern background to the viking raids; in recent years, interest in the Scandinavian culture that produced the raiders has led to modifications in the historical myth. Thus, 'vikings' are defined, not just as roving bands of warriors, but as Scandinavians, or people of Scandinavian origin, during the 'Viking Age', the period when shipborne warriors from Scandinavia had such an impact on the rest of the world. The time span of the Viking Age is defined broadly, as 793–1066, or in round figures 800–1100, covering not just the raids of the late eighth and the ninth centuries, but also Scandinavian

1

settlement abroad, and the gradual opening up of Scandinavia to medieval, Christian Europe. A seminal book called *The Viking achievement*, first published in 1970, had the subtitle 'The society and culture of early medieval Scandinavia' and hardly mentioned raiding activities abroad. Ten years later, an important international exhibition assembled by the British Museum aimed to 'redress the balance' after the 'bad press' given vikings, whose 'activities are equated with rape and pillage' and whose 'reputation for brutality is second only to that of the Huns and the Goths'. In the preface to the exhibition catalogue, the Director of the Museum, Sir David Wilson, wrote, 'In a brutal age the Vikings were brutal, but their brutality was no worse than that of their contemporaries.' He pointed out that vikings were 'administrators as well as pirates, merchants as well as robbers' and noted their achievement in fields such as law, culture, the discovery of America, the acceptance of Christianity, the creation of nation-states and the government of colonies.

A spurt in archaeological activity in the 1970s and 1980s has contributed to this much broader definition of 'vikings'. In Scandinavia itself, excavations at Birka, Hedeby and Kaupang had already shown the industrial and commercial side of the Viking Age: the people who lived and worked in these places were rich merchants and traders with wide-ranging international contacts. The scope of these contacts was further illuminated by new archaeological evidence from cities such as York, Lincoln and Dublin. The development and prosperity of these urban centres in the Viking Age appear to have been a direct consequence of 'viking' activity and Scandinavian connections.

New methods of presenting such archaeological discoveries are well on their way to changing the popular image of vikings and to creating a new historical myth to replace the old one. At the Jorvik Viking Centre in York, tourists can see models of the Viking Age denizens of the city, merchants and craftspeople revealed in all their domestic intimacy. This new view of peaceful, urban vikings, based mainly on archaeological finds, presents images of women and children as well as men. Vikings are now people. Is it possible, then, that there is such a thing as a 'viking woman'?

Every man is born of a woman, and most also have sisters, lovers, wives or daughters. Even the bad old warriors who terrorised Europe had females in the family, like the more domesticated traders and craftsmen who, we are told, represent the other, pleasanter, side of viking activities. Yet, in all the books written about the Viking Age, there is little mention of these females who undoubtedly existed (and the tendency in such books that do mention women to lump them together with children in a subchapter just reinforces the impression that 'vikings' were adult males). If historians' emphasis on vikings as warriors made invisible the women in the background, then it is not always clear where the more visible female counterparts of the new urban vikings have come from. Women's history has penetrated many areas, but is only just beginning to have an impact on viking studies. This book is an attempt to bring into prominence the invisible women of the Viking Age. And it was written out of a belief that, even if we choose to retain a narrow definition of 'vikings' as murderous, roving males, we cannot possibly study them without an understanding of the whole of the historical period during which they operated, and of both the culture that they came from and those which they, to a greater or lesser degree, affected. For the study of such a substantial period of time and such a variety of cultures to ignore the experiences of half the population would be a nonsense.

Since there has as yet been no book-length study in English of women in the Viking Age, this book has had to concentrate on basics. I believe I am the first to have brought together such a broad range of material in this subject, and so my discourse is more descriptive than analytical, although I hope not uncritical. The field of viking studies is a truly interdisciplinary one and it is almost impossible to say anything about the Viking Age without taking into account the wide variety of evidence from sources archaeological, art historical, linguistic, historical and literary (to name just the most obvious ones). The student of the Viking Age is constantly comparing, contrasting, weighing up against one another these different types of material, and using one to interpret another. Such a procedure, however, carries within it the danger of circular arguments. For this reason, and because the sources are often complementary rather than overlapping, I have chosen to structure the book around these categories of sources, rather than relegating discussion of them to one chapter called 'The sources' somewhere near the beginning of the book and then ignoring their difficulties later on. Although it is impossible to enforce a rigid distinction between the source-types, my aim has been to foreground the differences between them, and to make a virtue of their variety. The information from these different types of sources adds up to a total picture of women in the Viking Age that is greater than the sum of its parts, but I do not pretend that this is anywhere near a complete picture, even if such a thing were possible.

Thus, I begin with surveys of two rich bodies of material which are from the Viking Age itself, the archaeological evidence which is both dateable and concrete, and constantly increasing (ch. I), and the evidence of runic inscriptions, the only texts produced by 'vikings' themselves that still survive in their original form (ch. II). The evidence of names, of both people and places, that originate in the Viking Age (even if only preserved in later sources) is also invaluable, if limited (ch. III). Chapter IV is devoted to texts which present a non-Scandinavian view of vikings, written, as it were, by their 'victims'. Some of these are contemporary and therefore rank with the material in the first chapters, others are later and of doubtful value, but they share the characteristic of presenting vikings through foreign, and sometimes uncomprehending, eyes. The last two chapters tackle the most copious, and most difficult, body of material, the visual and verbal artworks of early Scandinavia. Much of the poetry and the mythology described in ch. V must have its origins in the Viking Age, but since the texts are preserved in the forms in which they were written down by antiquarian Icelanders in the 13th century, they cannot be taken purely as the authentic voice of vikings, but also embody the attitudes of those medieval Icelanders, and disentangling the two is no easy matter. While the visual arts of the Viking Age are a contemporary expression of viking culture, they belong in this chapter because they cannot be interpreted except with reference to the Icelandic recordings of mythological narratives. Finally, I have not been able to avoid a brief consideration of the Icelandic sagas dealing with the Viking Age (ch. VI). Long thought to have been based on genuine historical traditions, these sagas now tend to be regarded as imaginative products of the thirteenth century; even those who admit their origins in oral traditions do not give much credence to the historical truth of those traditions. But I have chosen to look at these sagas, not for whatever kernel of genuine history they may or may not contain, but because our modern view of the Viking Age is so utterly entangled with our knowledge of the sagas. No other source is so colourful, so detailed, so seductive in its realism. The sagas speak to us more directly than the dry bones of archaeology or the terse statements on runestones. They are primarily responsible for the widespread view that women in the Viking Age were forceful, independent and powerful, and for the efforts of modern scholars to demonstrate this in the other sources.

This arrangement may seem to imply a hierarchy of sources, from the 'reliable' and concrete evidence of archaeology to the 'unreliable' romantic mythologising of the Icelandic sagas. There is certainly a continuum and the different sources give different types of information

4

about the Viking Age, but I do not necessarily subscribe to the view that 'only archaeology can reveal the truth'. Archaeological evidence must also be interpreted, just like other, more nebulous, material, and verbal artefacts can also give us some kinds of information about the Viking Age, even if this cannot be measured in centimetres or subjected to dendrochronology.

A word must be said about those sources *not* included in this survey, for there are several important ones. Thus, I have avoided discussing the legal position of women in the Viking Age, because I believe we know very little, if anything, about it. The medieval Scandinavian laws were, like the Icelandic sagas, long thought to preserve older elements, deriving from the Viking Age, handed down in oral tradition. Nowadays, however, many legal historians would doubt whether these laws reflect any society other than the high medieval, Christian ones that produced them, if, indeed, essentially normative laws do reflect society.

In discussing Icelandic sagas, I have concentrated on Sagas of Icelanders (*Íslendingasögur*) and have ignored the heroic and mythical sagas (*fornaldarsögur*) which also present a medieval view of the viking past, and one that is radically different from that of the Sagas of Icelanders. Here again we are in the realms of medieval mythmaking and, since the *fornaldarsögur* have been less influential in forming modern views of the Viking Age, I felt that considering them would make me stray too far from the main theme of the book. I have also omitted any discussion of the kings' sagas (*konungasögur*). While they may embody more genuine traditions about the Viking Age than any other type of saga, there are so few female characters in them that such an analysis hardly seemed worth doing (although this very rarity of female characters is significant in itself!). However, it must not be forgotten that most of the skaldic poetry discussed in ch. V is in fact preserved in the kings' sagas.

Even the categories of source material that I have included are not treated exhaustively. Chapter I does not give a full survey of the archaeology of the Viking Age (which I, as a non-archaeologist, would in any case feel trepidatious in attempting), but only of those aspects of the archaeological evidence which seemed to me to be particularly illuminating for the study of women. (A detailed survey of the archaeology of daily life in the Viking Age would indeed tell us much about the lives of women, but I prefer to leave such a survey to the specialist archaeologist.)

Similarly, the discussion of Eddic poetry in ch. V is not exhaustive, but concentrates on some texts which I believe are most likely to have their origins (preferably in form, but sometimes only in content) in the Viking Age, a perilous procedure, since no two scholars can be found who agree on the dating and the history of the poems of the *Edda*.

In short, this book presents a selective and, it must be admitted, personal account of the history of women in the Viking Age, but I hope that others will be inspired to do more work and to fill in the outline sketched here.

While agreeing with Winifred Holtby (*Women*, 1934) that 'the only adequate history of women would be a history of humanity and its adventure upon a changing globe', I have resisted the temptation to try and do two things at once by writing a general history of the Viking Age while exploring the role of women in it. Thus, readers will find it helpful to have at least skimmed through one of the many general books available, for an outline of the main events and characteristics of the age. However, I hope the book is nevertheless comprehensible to those readers who are completely new to the subject, and that the notes and bibliography will provide them with some ideas for further reading.

Writing about the Viking Age is a linguistic nightmare. Not only must such an undertaking be based on texts written in a variety of languages (some in other alphabets which need to be transliterated), which often have little orthographic consistency even within themselves, but there is the added problem of how to present both names and specialist terms to an English-speaking audience. While complete consistency is impossible, I have tried to follow these principles:

— Names of places in Scandinavia and Western Europe are given the form most commonly used today in the country in question (e.g. Breiðafjörður, Stiklestad, Angers), except where a common anglicised form exists (Norway, Jutland, Copenhagen).
— Names of both persons and places taken from texts written originally in Russian or Arabic follow the principles of transliteration used, respectively, in Cross and Sherbowitz-Wetzor (1953), and the *Encyclopaedia of Islam* (somewhat modified). However, some inconsistencies may have arisen in quotations from sources using other systems of transliteration.
— Names of historical and fictional characters known from Old Norse texts are generally given in the normalised Old Norse form. In a few cases where the names are very well known (e.g. the gods Thor and Odin), I have used the anglicised forms when referring to

them in a general way, but reverted to the Old Norse forms (Þórr, Óðinn) when closely following or translating an Old Norse text. Readers unfamiliar with Old Norse or Icelandic should note, in particular, the following special characters:

    Þ, þ = Modern English 'th', as in *think*
    Ð, ð = Modern English 'th', as in *father*

— Names in runic inscriptions present their own special problems, for (1) normalised Old Norse (based mainly on Icelandic) is not entirely appropriate for texts from mainland Scandinavia (2) runic orthography is too varied to be normalised across the whole range of Danish, Manx, Norwegian and Swedish inscriptions (3) the Scandinavian practice of giving the modern Swedish (or Danish, or Norwegian) forms of the names is not appropriate for English-language readers. Yet, while none of these three methods is entirely appropriate, they all have some value, so I have attempted an uneasy compromise between them, entirely of my own devising. The forms of names given should thus enable the student of Old Icelandic to recognise their normalised Old Norse equivalents, and should help those familiar with the Scandinavian languages to recognise their modern descendants, while also giving some hint of the runic orthography.

It goes without saying that further inconsistency is introduced when, quoting from a modern translation or a secondary work, I have had to follow whatever orthography is used by its author!

All texts are given in Modern English translation, but in a few cases I have also given the original text. This is done in quotations from runic inscriptions (in transliterated form) and skaldic verse (in normalised Old Norse) where the text may originally have been composed by a woman, thus enabling the modern reader to hear the authentic voice of Viking Age women. Translations from Old Norse texts, including runic inscriptions, are my own, with just one or two exceptions. For texts in other languages, I have made use of published translations, or made my own summaries where no English translation exists. All published translations used in this way are acknowledged in the *Notes*.

People in the Viking Age were necessarily polyglot. I have not tried to conceal the linguistic difficulties of dealing with the period, because anyone seriously interested in viking studies will eventually have to become acquainted with at least some of the many languages in which vikings speak to us.

Finally, a note on the word 'viking'. The history and meaning of this noun, in its Old and Modern English, as well as Old Norse, forms have been extensively discussed. Modern dictionaries give meanings ranging from the very specific 'one of the pirate Northmen plundering the coasts of Europe in the eighth to tenth centuries' to the very general 'Scandinavian'. My own use of the word is as follows:

— Wherever possible, I use the term 'Viking Age' (thus, 'art of the Viking Age' instead of 'Viking art'), referring to the historical period ca 800–1100 AD, especially in Scandinavia and in other countries with a significant presence of people of Scandinavian origins.

— I use the term 'viking' or 'vikings' about people of Scandinavian origins, in the Viking Age, mainly when they are engaged in activities characteristic of the Viking Age, i.e. raiding, trading or settling outside mainland Scandinavia. In this sense, the word is not capitalised, just as I would not capitalise 'pirates' or 'businessmen'.

— For stay-at-home Scandinavians during the Viking Age, I tend to use the term 'Scandinavian(s)'.

As with everything else, complete consistency is not possible!

Friends and colleagues have given generously of their advice and knowledge while I was writing this book. I would particularly like to thank Christine Fell, Richard Perkins and Else Roesdahl for their informed perusal of parts of the text. Despite their efforts, mistakes and infelicities doubtless remain in the book, but the only person who should be blamed for them is its author.

The book could not have been written without the patient diligence with which Deborah Bragan-Turner and all her colleagues at the Hallward Library, University of Nottingham, dealt with my seemingly insatiable appetite for inter-library loans, store requests and bibliographical information.

The book is dedicated to my parents, who taught me to love the North.

Nottingham
January 1991

CHAPTER I

Life and Death – the Evidence
of Archaeology

THE WESTNESS WOMAN

In October 1963 the people on the farm at Westness, on the island of
Rousay in Orkney, went out to bury a cow by the seashore. While
digging the pit, they unexpectedly found the skeletons of a young
woman in her twenties and a newborn child. These were not recent
murder victims on a peaceful Orkney island: they had died naturally
over a thousand years earlier and had been buried according to the
custom of that time in what was then the island's cemetery. The dead
woman had been provided with articles she had used in this life and
which might come in handy in the next. These included domestic implements: a pair of wool combs, a weaving batten, a bronze basin, a knife
and a pair of shears. Outdoor work was represented by a sickle. Yet the
young woman had been no drudge – she was adorned with fashionable
jewellery: a pair of bronze oval brooches, a string of about 40 beads,
mostly of glass, and a silver ringed pin inset with gold panels of wire
filigree patterns, amber studs and red glass. This pin is of a Celtic type
found in both Ireland and Scotland in the eighth century, but the woman
in whose grave it was found was not a Celt and she lived in the ninth or
early tenth century. The extensive grave goods show that she was a
heathen, not a Christian. The characteristic oval brooches indicate beyond doubt that she was a Norse woman. The worn condition of the
Celtic pin (the filigree was damaged and it had lost most of its glass
insets by the time it came to be buried with her) shows that she was not
its first owner.

The Scandinavian character of the Westness burial is apparent if we compare it with female graves in Norway. Thus, a typical ninth-century female grave at Bjørke, innermost in the Hjørundfjord, Sunnmøre, contained, like Westness, a mixture of jewellery and practical items: two bronze oval brooches, two bronze arm rings, some glass beads and an iron weaving batten. The grave also contained an Anglo-Saxon bronze mount which may have been used as a pendant. Such insular objects (originating in the British Isles) are interpreted as viking loot, plunder that male raiders took home to their wives and girlfriends, as many of them were found in women's graves. In excavations of Scandinavian trading centres such as Kaupang, so many insular objects of such variety have been found that it is likely there was also a regular secondhand trade in them. Then these small decorated metal objects, originally mounts for books, shrines or chests, were fashioned into women's jewellery which was buried with its owner, surviving to be dug up in modern times.

We may wish we knew more about the young woman of Westness, but she has already provided us with important information about the lot of women in the Viking Age. The very fact that a young Norse woman was buried in Orkney, her newborn child at her side, and the everyday nature of the implements buried with her, show another side to viking life than the stereotypes of that turbulent age. Warriors did descend unexpectedly from their ships, plundering, burning and terrorising ill-defended Christian countries, but at the same time many vikings went abroad as pioneers, wanting, for whatever reasons, to make new lives for themselves and their families. The Westness grave also illustrates the contribution that the archaeological investigation of burials can make to our understanding of the Viking Age. Without the knowledge gained from thousands of graves excavated in Scandinavia and elsewhere, we would know much less about the everyday life or the death of people in the Viking Age.

THE ARCHAEOLOGY OF BURIALS

Burying the dead in the Viking Age

Before their conversion to Christianity, the heathen peoples of Scandinavia practised forms of burial of the dead that are of great value to archaeologists. With the advent of Christianity, it became the custom to bury the dead shrouded simply in a sheet: the trappings of this life were

Celtic-style ringed pin from
the Westness burial.

Gilt-bronze mount of Anglo-Saxon origin found
in a female grave of the Early Viking Period at
Bjørke, Møre og Romsdal, Norway.

considered irrelevant in the next. But before this minimalist approach was introduced by the Church, the heathen Scandinavians would send off their dead fully dressed, with personal adornments, and often accompanied by the implements and utensils of daily life. Such grave goods were intended to equip the dead for the next world, which was imagined as very like this one. Sometimes the dead were accompanied by their horses or dogs and there is some evidence that slaves were sacrificed to attend their masters or mistresses in the next life. Other grave goods had a more symbolic function: burials with boats, wagons or horses represent the journey to the next life. Sometimes, as in the spectacular women's burial of Oseberg, whole ships and wagons were used. Sometimes the ship is represented symbolically by a boat-shaped stone setting, or only part of a wagon is used. The most common form of burial was inhumation of the corpse (possibly, but not necessarily, in some kind of coffin or, more elaborately, in a chamber), but cremation was also practised. Even in cremation graves, the dead could be accompanied by grave goods, but these can be more difficult to recover archaeologically because of their damaged condition.

Although we may not always know what specific burial customs meant to the individual heathen Scandinavian, their practice of accompanied burials is a boon to the archaeologist, and the archaeology of burials is most valuable as a source of information about many aspects of that period. The objects found in Viking Age graves, properly studied, can tell us a lot about what people wore, how they adorned themselves, what implements they used in their daily activities and hence what those activities were, and even what they ate. The presence in graves of objects of foreign origin reveal which areas of the world the Scandinavians were in contact with. The finds of typically Scandinavian objects in burials outside Scandinavia give us an idea of the geographical spread of the viking expansion and of the areas that had contact with Scandinavians. These contacts with the outside world undoubtedly led the Scandinavians eventually to adopt Christianity and this process can be traced in the burials, too. Both burial customs and grave goods can provide indications of the social status of the dead, and even of their surviving relatives. Finally, an overall picture of Viking Age burials reminds us to look for similarities as well as differences. Despite regional differences between the areas of Scandinavia, between the homeland and viking colonies, between rural and urban areas, there is enough of a common denominator for us to be able to identify many Scandinavian graves in places as far apart as Greenland and Russia.

How to identify the grave of a woman

The first question an archaeologist, having identified a Viking Age burial, will ask is 'was the deceased male or female?' Unfortunately, this question is often difficult to answer. There are two approaches to determining the sex of the buried person or persons: by analysis of the human remains or by investigation of the grave goods. Often, archaeologists have to use a bit of both, as the finds are rarely so clear as to permit conclusions to be reached on the basis of one of these methods only.

Identifying the sex of human remains is often hampered by the absence of those remains or of any traces of them in the grave. Depending on the conditions of preservation of the burial and on the circumstances of its discovery, there may be no skeleton at all. If it is a cremation grave then there will be only a pile of burnt bone. When there are bones remaining, they may not add up to a complete skeleton. Even with a complete set of bones, there are no traits on any individual skeleton that unequivocally determine its sex, although there are strong indications: men tend to be more robust and larger than women, there are certain differences in the skull, and the shape of the pelvis also tends to be distinctive. Osteological analysis can also indicate roughly the age at time of death and demonstrate the presence of certain diseases and injuries.

A recent study of Iron Age skeletal remains found in Denmark during the last century and a half identified 320 Viking Age individuals that could be analysed in this way. Of these 85 were males, 73 females and 162 could not be determined as to sex. The average stature of these individuals was 172.6 cm for the males and 158.1 cm for the females. The interesting thing about the female group, compared to earlier groups of female skeletons examined in the study, was that 75% of the females were over thirty-five when they died. This was a dramatic reduction in the numbers of female deaths occurring in the twenty to thirty-five age group compared with the pre-Viking period. At the same time, the Viking Age females had a low average stature compared to earlier periods.

In the absence of adequate skeletal remains, it has long been common practice to determine the sex of the dead on the basis of their grave goods. In the Scandinavian context this has meant identifying skeletons buried with weapons and certain tools as male, and those buried with jewellery and domestic implements as female. The Danish study compared the grave goods with the results arrived at by skeletal analysis to determine what relationship there was between sex and grave goods. The results showed that there was a high correlation between the sex of the dead person and the character of some of the objects buried with them. The objects which could be used to distinguish men's and women's graves in Viking Age Denmark were as follows (although any one grave would contain only a selection):

> Men: weapons (sword, spear), axes, spurs, riding equipment (stirrups, bits), blacksmith's tools (shears, hammer, tongs, file), penannular brooches.

> Women: (pairs of) oval brooches, disc brooches, trefoil buckles, arm rings, necklaces, caskets, spindle whorls.

But some types of grave goods were common to both sexes:

> buckles, combs, clay pots, wooden vessels, knives, whetstones, coins, beads.

Since very similar objects appear in other Viking Age graves, it is reasonable to assume that this pattern, with variations, applies throughout Scandinavia and the viking world. Thus, women are distinguished largely by their jewellery and accessories, and men by their weapons and other accoutrements appropriate to a warrior. In parts of the viking world, e.g. Norway, where the dead were more commonly buried with objects of everyday use, it is also possible to detect a distinction between the sexes based on their roles in daily life. The implements most characteristic of women's graves are those used in the production of textiles, such as spindle whorls, wool combs and weaving battens.

What women's graves contain

Jewellery and clothing

The jewellery worn by women is thus an important diagnostic feature in identifying their graves. The presence of typically female jewellery can in fact make women's graves easier to identify than those of men, which are not so consistent in their grave goods. Thus, Anne-Sofie Gräslund, who studied 1100 burials from the Swedish trading centre of Birka, came to the following conclusions: less than half of these (415, or 308 inhumations and 107 cremations) could be sex determined. Of the inhumations, 180 (or 58%), and of the cremations, 66 (or 61%), were female. However, rather than indicating a preponderance of women in Birka, this may just mean that their graves are easier to identify.

The most characteristic items of female jewellery are the pairs of oval brooches (sometimes called tortoise brooches, from their shape), usually made of bronze, found in many female graves from the Viking Age. The graves in both Westness and Bjørke contained such brooches, and so did large numbers of other female graves, particularly from the ninth and first half of the tenth centuries. These brooches must not be thought of as purely decorative objects, they served the highly practical purpose of keeping a woman's dress up! In fact, apart from their diagnostic value in identifying female graves, oval brooches can tell us a great deal about the dress of Viking Age women, when they and the textile remains preserved around them are subjected to detailed archaeological ana-lysis. Were it not for the brooches, we would in fact know very little about what the well-dressed woman wore in this period.

Textiles do not normally survive very well in the ground, unless there are very special conditions. However, there are quite large numbers of textile fragments found in association with the oval brooches and other metal objects. Some are still attached to the brooch and have been pro-tected from disintegration by its proximity. In other cases, the textile has disappeared but has left an impression on the metal of the brooch. Painstaking research, particularly by Agnes Geijer and Inga Hägg on the textiles of Birka, has helped to establish what fabrics the brooches were attached to. On this basis, it has been possible to reconstruct the entire habit of the women of Birka, even though no whole dress is preserved. Finds from elsewhere, particularly Hedeby, confirm that fashions were essentially the same throughout the viking world.

Normally, a woman would wear an outfit consisting of two or three layers. First, a shift or underdress was worn. This could be of linen or wool, had sleeves, and was sometimes pleated and gathered at the neck. The neck opening was usually held together by a small disc brooch. Over the shift, the woman wore a strapped gown, or overdress. This was basically a rectangular piece of material (usually wool) wrapped around the woman's body and reaching to her armpits. Holding the gown up were looped straps over the woman's shoulders which were sewn on at the back and which were joined to smaller loops sewn on to the front by means of the two oval brooches, the pins of which passed through the loops. Thus, the term 'brooch' is something of a misnomer,

Set of bronze ornaments from an Early Viking Period
female grave at Loppasanden, Finnmark, Norway.

Reverse of an oval brooch from Birka showing textile remains.

since their function was more like that of a buckle. The strings of beads found in many women's graves could be hung between the oval brooches. Pendants of amber, jet or silver could also be strung between the beads at intervals: this is where the woman from Bjørke may have hung her Anglo-Saxon book mount. Here also the woman newly converted to Christianity could wear a small silver cross. Useful implements, like scissors and knives, could also hang from the brooches on straps or rings.

Another garment which could be worn in addition to the basic shift and gown was a tunic worn between them, known from Birka and clearly of oriental inspiration. The better-dressed woman would have her tunic decorated with bands of tablet-woven braid of linen or silk, often with a metal weft for a particularly luxurious effect. Over all these garments, for outdoors, a woman might wear a sleeved caftan or a cloak, also held together by a brooch or pin. There was more variation in this fastening, it could be a disc brooch, a trefoil brooch, an equal-armed brooch, or even a refashioned metal souvenir from the British Isles.

Although the garments were of simple design, they were carefully made. In a study of textile fragments from twenty-five women's graves in the west of Norway, Inger-Marie Holm-Olsen found evidence of stitching, hems, sewn-on cord, loops and pleating. The women of Birka, whose clothing has been studied in most detail, were however not representative. As members of a rich trading community with wide international contacts, they did not have to make do with homespun. In fact most of the textiles at Birka appear to have been imported, at least those used for women's clothing and studied in connection with the grave finds. It is also likely that women were buried in their best clothing. They undoubtedly had simpler textiles for everyday wear that are not preserved in burials.

While burials tend to give us information about clothing worn by the higher levels of society, new archaeological techniques can indicate what kind of clothes were worn by poorer people in the Viking Age, often from unexpected sources. Thus, the largest collection of Viking Age textiles comes from the underwater excavation in 1979–80 of the harbour at Haithabu (Hedeby), the southernmost emporium of Viking Age Scandinavia, now in Germany near the Danish border. These textile fragments were all discarded clothing which had been torn up into rags and used in shipbuilding, either for tarring the outside of a ship, or for stuffing into cracks to make it watertight.

The simplest clothes found at Haithabu were made of the roughest

Female dress with finely pleated shift, over-dress and oval brooches. Reconstruction.

woollen fabric, suggesting that these were the clothes of slaves, servants and the poor, or the daily dress of the better-off. The women's garments consisted of very simple ankle-length, long-sleeved dresses, cut loose to enable freedom of movement at work, and possibly a simple wrap or shawl.

Better-quality clothing was also found in the rags of Haithabu and here the finds are similar to those of the clothing from Birka and elsewhere in Scandinavia: over a linen shift, women wore an overdress of fine woollen fabric, held up by the ubiquitous pair of brooches. However, whereas elsewhere the overdress has always been reconstructed as a straight garment, the Haithabu finds indicate that there at least it was tailored at the waist. Tucks and decorative braid running vertically further emphasised the wearer's shape. Outdoors, the better-off women of Haithabu wore an ankle-length coat, again quite wide at the bottom. These coats were made of high-quality dyed wool that had been felted to make it weather-resistant, and were lined, and often quilted with down or feathers for added warmth.

Domestic utensils

The presence of jewellery in the female graves of the Viking Age can be explained by the fact that women were normally buried fully dressed with a complete set of accessories and that the jewellery had a function in their costume. But often they were also buried with objects that they did not normally wear or carry about their person. Unlike the almost obligatory jewellery, there is greater variation in which of these objects, if any, were buried with them. The objects reflect the rank and status of the dead woman, or the tasks she had undertaken in this life and thus the tasks it was expected she would undertake in the next. However, the choice of objects may simply represent a local or temporary fashion in grave goods. There is variation in grave goods from region to region and in different periods of the Viking Age and it is not always possible to tell the cause of such variation (beyond changes in fashion), although sometimes we can guess. Thus, the general falling away of the practice of burying grave goods with the dead in the latter part of the tenth century was not because people were poorer and could ill afford to bury expensive objects, but is thought to be a reflection of the increasing influence of Christianity, which frowned on such practices. Yet the tasks of daily life in the late tenth century cannot have been much different from those of the early tenth century, even though they are not so well represented by implements in burials.

It is thus more difficult to generalise about women's lives and work from grave goods than it is to generalise about their habits of dress from their jewellery. Yet it is possible to draw some conclusions about the nature of work considered normal for women in the Viking Age from these additional grave goods, although they cannot tell the whole story. The most common implements found in graves are those used in the making of textiles: wool combs, spindle whorls, loom weights, weaving battens, weaving tablets, needles and various implements used in smoothing cloth. Then we find implements that could be used in a variety of working contexts: knives and shears, whetstones for sharpening them, and containers of various types and materials. Cooking equipment is not widely represented in female graves, but we do find a few roasting spits and some soapstone vessels. There are also some agricultural implements, especially sickles.

Although it is true that many of these objects, particularly the textile-working implements, are characteristic of women's graves, none of them are exclusive to female burials. We can find most of the implements listed above in male graves, although not necessarily in the same numbers. In a study of Viking Age graves in western Norway, Liv Helga Dommasnes found that there was cooking equipment in 26% of the

Wool-comb from a female grave at Vangen, Sogn og Fjordane, Norway.

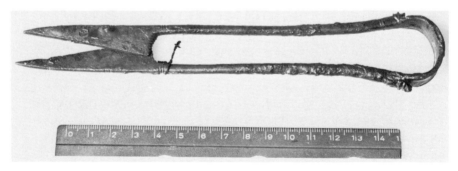

Iron shears from an Early Viking Period female cremation burial at
Ås, Akershus, Norway.

female and 16% of the male graves. Agricultural equipment was found in 50% of the female and 36% of the male graves. However there was an important distinction: the women had only small sickles, while the male graves had a wider variety of implements.

Tools and implements

As far as tools are concerned, about the only implements found exclusively in the graves of one sex are blacksmith's tools in male graves. Even weapons, hunting equipment and carpentry tools, found mainly in male burials, can be found in the odd female grave. At the great market town of Birka, weights and balances have been found in female graves, suggesting that women could engage in trade. However we need to consider whether grave goods really represent the former lives of the dead, or whether some of them could not in fact have more of a symbolic function. The presence of weights in children's graves does not necessarily mean that they engaged in trading activities too.

Not all grave goods were practical implements used in daily work. This is particularly obvious with the weapons (swords, shields, spears) found in male graves. Their deposition must have been at least partly symbolic. The weapons can be seen as reflecting the man's status in society as well as helping him defend himself in the next life. Because of this partly symbolic function, we must remain open to the possibility that women were buried with weapons as well. However, the small number of female burials with weapons recorded are mainly chance finds from before the days of systematic and scientific archaeology, and are therefore very uncertain. For instance, in 1867 a skeleton was discovered at Santon Downham, Norfolk, seemingly buried with an iron sword and two oval brooches. Rather than jumping to conclusions about the presence of brooches in a male grave or a sword in a female grave, archaeologists nowadays are inclined to think it was a double burial of a man and a woman, in spite of the absence of a second skeleton, which may simply not have been noticed in 1867 (it has even been suggested that the 'sword' was in fact a weaving batten). More recently, however, the discovery of a female skeleton at Gerdrup, in Denmark, buried with a needle case and a spear suggests that the possibility of a woman being buried with a weapon should not be ruled out. Other weapons crop up in female graves, for instance small axes and arrowheads in some female graves at Kaupang. The axes in particular could of course simply be practical implements, for chopping firewood, for instance. And even burial with a real weapon does not necessarily imply that the woman knew how to use it in real life – we should again recall the possible symbolic functions of grave goods.

Although they do not present a complete or uniform picture of daily work in the Viking Age, grave goods do indicate the tasks most commonly associated with women. Not unexpectedly, these are the domestic, indoor tasks involving the preparation of food and clothing. But women could also do outdoor work on the farm, do carpentry and leather-work, and engage in trade. At the same time, we must remember that there are many types of work which leave no trace in the archaeological record, whether in burials or elsewhere. Many of these are jobs traditionally done by women, the bringing up of children or the care of the elderly and the sick, and the Viking Age was no different from later ages in this respect.

Burial customs

Burials and religion

Although grave goods can tell us much about people's everyday lives, there is also important information to be deduced from other aspects of burials, although they can be difficult to interpret. Thus, burial of the dead is essentially a religious ceremony, yet trying to deduce something about religious beliefs from the variations in burial practices discoverable by archaeologists is not always straightforward.

Accompanied burials of the type considered here are a heathen custom, yet it is possible to see the transition to Christianity in some graves. Of the 1100 graves at Birka studied by Gräslund, ten were found to contain silver cross-shaped pendants and nine of these were the graves of women. (The tenth was a double burial of a man and a woman, containing both a Thor's hammer and a cross pendant.) Of these, six contained no other grave goods than the woman's jewellery and accessories. We know that missionaries were active at Birka and it is likely that this small group of graves represents some of the converts to Christianity in Birka. The pendants are not just mere trinkets to be hung on a woman's necklace, without religious significance, as the lack of other grave goods suggests Christian influence on burial customs. The fact that these crosses were found overwhelmingly in female graves does not necessarily mean that women took to Christianity more readily than men: it may simply mean that women were more likely to wear a pendant.

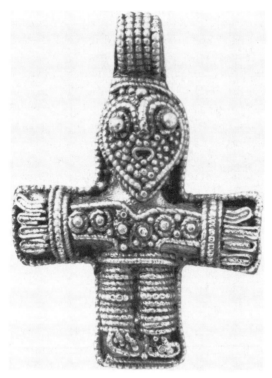

Silver crucifix pendant from a Middle Viking
Period female grave at Birka.

Cross pendant from Birka.

In contrast to the graves containing crosses, there were twenty-seven graves at Birka containing Thor's hammer pendants. Such pendants are also known from elsewhere in Scandinavia. Most of them are fairly late (tenth century), and it is thought that the use of a Thor's hammer pendant was a pagan response to the spread of Christianity, a heathen equivalent to the sign of the cross. Other traces of religious beliefs in Viking Age burials are more difficult to interpret. Apart from the belief in a life hereafter implied by the provision of food, clothing and equipment for the dead, burials are more easily interpreted in terms of social and occupational status than as religious rites, although some grave goods may have a religious significance that we cannot recognise.

Sacrifice

The feeling that burials ought to reflect religious beliefs and practices has led archaeologists to seek for evidence of one of the more sensational practices, sacrifice. The sacrifice of animals such as horses and dogs, presumably so they could continue serving their master or mistress in the next life, is fairly common in Viking Age burials. The practice seems to have been particularly popular in Iceland, where a large proportion of graves contain both horse and hound, but such graves are found throughout the viking world, at Pierowall in Orkney, at Birka in Sweden and quite commonly in Norway. In Denmark, some women were buried with small dogs that must have been lapdogs rather than working dogs. More emotive is the question of whether humans were also sacrificed. After all, if a man needed his horse in the next world, might he not also need his slave, or his wife? Influenced by Arab accounts of the sacrifice of slaves, both male and female, among the Rūs, probably Swedish vikings based in Russia, archaeologists have looked for evidence of the custom in Scandinavia itself.

To establish whether or not human sacrifice took place, we need to look at instances of double burials, where more than one person was buried at the same time. As we have already seen, it can be difficult to identify a double burial: if no skeleton, or only one skeleton, is preserved, are grave goods alone enough? Many burials were discovered in the last century, or early in this century, when archaeological techniques were not sophisticated enough to cope with these problems and archaeologists were perhaps too quick to assume that a double burial must mean human sacrifice. More recent excavations, done with modern techniques, can show that the second person may have been buried very soon after the first, yet not at the same time. For instance, a mound containing two cremation burials at Hestehagen in Østfold, Norway, is thought to be that of a couple who died within a few years of each other. In her comprehensive study of the graves at Birka, Gräslund found evidence of secondary burials in chamber graves. The men's remains showed signs of having been moved into a corner, suggesting the burial of a widow in her husband's grave. The usual pattern for double graves at Birka, however, was for the skeletons to be on the same level, suggesting that they were buried at the same time. But even where it can be shown that a man and a woman were buried simultaneously, there can be an innocent explanation – they might both have been carried off by the same disease.

More significant is if the second skeleton shows signs of having been maltreated. A number of Danish graves of the ninth and tenth centuries demonstrate human sacrifice. The clearest example is from the old royal centre of Lejre, where a grave contained two adult male skeletons, the lower one well-equipped, above him a man who had been decapitated and buried with hands and feet tied. At Dråby, the burial of a housewife (identified by her keys) was accompanied by a decapitated male skeleton, possibly her slave killed to serve her in the next life. The woman buried at Gerdrup, who was around forty when she died in the early ninth century, was buried together with a man of about the same age whose feet had been tied and whose neck had been broken. Thus, it seems that males could also be sacrificed to accompany females into the next world.

Three rich warrior graves have been found in the Isle of Man and two of these also contained female skeletons without any grave goods. One of these, from a grave at Ballateare, was a young woman in her twenties, with a large hole in the top of her skull. Unfortunately, it is not possible to determine whether this blow caused her death or whether it was inflicted soon after it. The excavators at any rate were cautious about interpreting this as a possible case of suttee – the remains are simply not well enough preserved.

The archaeological evidence for human sacrifice is thus not extensive. However, it is more substantial than the literary evidence, although archaeologists often use the literary evidence to bolster their interpretations of unusual burials. Human sacrifice did take place in the Viking Age, but only rarely, and it could happen to both men and women. Sacrifice cannot be said to have been a central tenet of the heathen

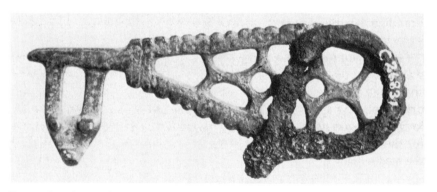

Bronze key from a female burial at Dråby, Sjælland, Denmark.

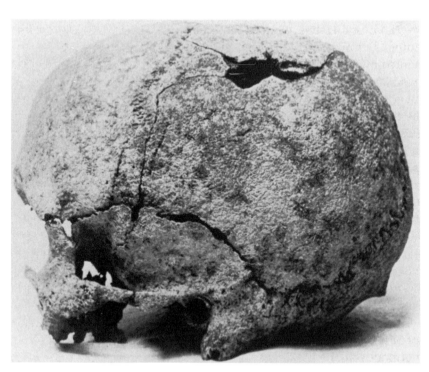

Slashed skull of a young female whose skeleton accompanied a Middle Viking Period male burial at Ballateare, Isle of Man.

Scandinavian religion and the average free woman can have had no expectations of ending her life as a victim of suttee.

Nor, it seems, did the average man have great expectations of being waited on in the next life. Some male graves contain cooking equipment, soapstone cooking pots, blackened by fire from previous use, iron cauldrons, roasting spits, meat forks or griddles. Men away from home for long periods on raiding or trading expeditions had to learn how to cater for themselves. They clearly expected to do the same on the journey to the next world.

Graves and status

Types of burial

The Viking Age covers such a long period of time and such a wide geographical expanse that it is not surprising to find a variety of burial customs and practices. Both cremation and inhumation burial were practised, sometimes apparently simultaneously in the same community. Burials could be placed in a mound, a ship setting, or be unmarked on the surface. Inhumation burials are further subdivided into those where the corpse was put directly into the ground, with or without a coffin (usually specially made, occasionally a re-used wooden chest), and those where the corpse was buried in a specially constructed chamber, or in a boat or wagon. There was also variation in the number and type of grave goods deposited with any individual. Many of these variations were probably no more than changes in fashion and some may have had to do with religious beliefs. It is likely, however, that a large number of them were indications of the social and economic status of the deceased or, perhaps, of their survivors. These social signals of Viking Age burials are the most difficult to interpret, not least because so many factors are involved. The sort of status reflected in a burial might depend on the age, sex, parentage, wealth or skills of the individual in life, or of their survivors, and these factors might be accorded different degrees of importance in different cases.

The few obviously royal burials that we have, such as Oseberg, cannot be mistaken for anything other than the monuments of persons with enormous status, wealth and power. Although they share characteristics with other Viking Age burials, they are really in a class of their own. Apart from them, however, it is difficult to determine the correlations between type of burial, character of grave goods, and social and economic status. To get an idea of what indicators of social status were involved in burials, we need to compare a fairly wide range of them to get an overall picture. This is particularly true if we want to make relative deductions about the status accorded to men and women, both in life and in death. The girl from Ballateare and the queen buried at Oseberg may have had very different views of their own status in a man's world, yet both belong to a full picture of women in the Viking Age.

Even if we concentrate on a selection of graves limited in space and time, the indications of status are difficult to judge. Thus, the 1100 graves of the trading town of Birka, covering less than two centuries, divide almost equally into inhumation and cremation graves. Of the 544 inhumation graves, 119 are the more elaborate chamber graves. We might expect these to be indicative of the high status of the deceased because of the work and expense involved in constructing the chamber. This is further suggested by the fact that horses are found in 18 of these chamber graves, but not in any other type of burial at Birka. Yet the chamber graves are poorer in grave goods than the other sorts of burial, both inhumation and cremation, which can give the impression of great wealth. We might wish to make a distinction between social standing implied by the elaborateness of the chamber graves and economic status implied by the wealth of the grave goods in other burials, but the matter is clearly not a straightforward one. It is also worth noting that, while women form an overall majority among those graves which can be determined for sex in Birka (over 59%), their share of the chamber graves is lower (44% of single burials).

Birka, with its concentrated population, is the exception rather than the rule in Viking Age Scandinavia. Normally people lived in small rural communities, often isolated farmsteads, but there, too, we find that burial customs raise more questions than they answer. A particularly interesting problem of the relative status of men and women is raised by the cemeteries of Valsgärde and Tuna i Badelunda, both in east central Sweden.

Some powerful women?

East central Sweden is one of the richest areas of Scandinavia, its importance going back to well before the Viking Age. This area, covering roughly the later provinces of Uppland and Västmanland, is rich in antiquities from the seventh century (and sometimes earlier) right through to the eleventh century. It is by far the richest area for rune-stones and has a large number of important cemeteries with elaborate boat burials in mounds. Many of these cemeteries were in unbroken use for centuries, going back to 300 AD in some cases, although the practice of boat burials seems to have started around 600 AD. Some of the most spectacular finds date to this period just before the Viking Age, the Vendel period, named after one of the cemeteries. In a settled, rich, rural area with such continuity of traditions we would expect differences of wealth, rank and status to be clearly marked. We might also expect gender roles in such a community to be rather rigid. But the information we get from the cemeteries is difficult to interpret: who were these rich Swedes and where did they get their wealth from? The grave goods from the cemeteries show that they must have traded extensively abroad and they were perhaps the precursors of the Viking Age merchants of Birka.

An interesting problem emerges when we compare the cemeteries of Valsgärde and Tuna. Valsgärde is unique among the central Swedish cemeteries in never having been disturbed or robbed, so that we have the complete sequence of graves. The 800-year history of this cemetery comprises a series of 25 chieftain's graves, representing probably one leader per generation, buried at first in small chamber graves and then in boat graves. These are all inhumations, whereas during the same period, in the same cemetery, there is a series of about 50 cremation graves, almost exclusively of women. Seventy kilometres away, in Tuna, the pattern is reversed, although there the site had been disturbed so that it is not absolutely certain that the cemetery was in continuous use. There are approximately 70 graves identified, mainly male cremation graves from the Viking Age, but there are also eight boat burials, all of them of women and richly furnished. The male cremations, on the other hand, were very simple. Before this Viking Age sequence, the oldest burial in Tuna is a richly furnished female grave from about 300 AD. It has been suggested that she was the first head of a matriarchal clan and that her successors were buried in the boat graves. Certainly, if we view the boat graves of Vendel and Valsgärde as representing lines of hereditary chieftains, the cemetery at Tuna appears to be analogous, except that the important individuals selected for boat burial were all female.

While it is unlikely that matriarchy was widely practised in Viking

The Oseberg ship.

Age Scandinavia, if indeed at all, there is other evidence that some women could attain high standing in the rural community, at least as far as we can deduce from the archaeology of burials.

In her studies of 68 Iron Age burials in Sogn, in western Norway, Liv Helga Dommasnes found that female graves were in a minority (19, or 28%). With such a small sample, the distribution could be due to chance, but there were other indications that women had to achieve a relatively higher social status than men in the same community to be given the kind of burial that shows up in the archaeological record. Thus, the female graves were richly furnished with a wide variety of grave goods, they were concentrated in the ninth and tenth centuries, and they tended to be found in the longest-established agricultural districts with the biggest farms. At one farm (Hopperstad), six out of the nine graves found were female and some of them contained artefacts normally associated with male graves. Finds from this farm showed connections with the British Isles and Dommasnes concluded that these women might have achieved importance and status by managing the farm while their male relatives were away on viking expeditions.

The Oseberg wagon.

A royal burial

The royal mound of Oseberg, in southeastern Norway, shows the pin-nacle of status women could reach in Viking Age Scandinavia. Oseberg is undoubtedly the richest and most sumptuous burial known from the Viking Age and the woman who was buried in it must have had great power and influence, as well as wealth, in her lifetime.The graceful lines of the Oseberg ship are familiar to all visitors to Norway and appear regularly in literature about the Viking Age. This ship was discovered in 1904, when the huge burial mound of Oseberg, in the outer Oslofjord, was excavated by Gabriel Gustafson. The mound, built up of stones and clay, and covered with turf, had been so well built that it was almost hermetically sealed. Thus its contents, even those of wood, leather and textiles which would normally have disintegrated, remained very well preserved in the moist blue clay for over a thousand years. The weight of the mound had pressed down on the ship and the grave goods, breaking many of them into small pieces. Further disturbance had been caused when the grave was once robbed, no one knows quite when. This made an enormous task of reconstruction necessary: the ship alone

A selection of vessels from the Oseberg burial.

was a puzzle of a couple of thousand pieces. Despite this, it was immediately clear that only a queen could have had a burial such as at Oseberg.

She must have died at some time in the first half of the ninth century. For her burial chamber, a great ship, 21.6 m long and 5 m wide, made of oak with elaborately carved fore- and after-stems, was placed into a large hole in the ground. A wooden burial chamber was built onto its deck and in it were laid two women, one young, in her twenties, the other about fifty, with very bad arthritis. Everything these two women could possibly want on their long journey was put into the ship with them. The ship itself was provided with a baler and a landing plank. If the ship should prove not to be the right mode of transport to the realm of the dead, there were a cart and four sledges, all with the most beautiful and elaborate carvings, and a saddle, and twelve horses were sacrificed. For the women's comfort during the journey there were three beds (with traces of bedding), a chair and two lamps. Three oak chests with iron fittings and some tapestries completed the furniture. For their culinary needs the women were provided with buckets, pails, troughs, bowls, knives, ladles, two iron cauldrons (one with a chain to hang it up

The Oseberg weaving tablets.

on, the other with a tripod) and an iron frying pan. Food was also provided: two oxen, bread-dough in the trough, apples in one of the wooden buckets, spices to keep it all fresh. To keep the women occupied there were four looms and a variety of implements for spinning and weaving. A set of tablets for tablet weaving still contained an unfinished length of braid. Traces of ready-made textiles were also found of wool and silk, the linen ones having totally disintegrated. The textiles found in the grave were of the finest quality and many were red in colour, otherwise unknown in Norwegian finds. Finally, there was a variety of personal belongings, including combs and two pairs of specially made shoes for the swollen arthritic feet of the older woman. The women's jewellery had unfortunately disappeared when the grave was robbed, but it must also have been splendid.

The dead woman's family, as well as being rich, were clearly patrons of the arts. The wood-carving found on the ship, the wagon and the sledges, and on five decorated posts of maple whose function is unclear, is of a superb quality. The artistry of the wood-carvings has been studied in detail and scholars have identified the different carvers and their stylistic development. The carving seems to have been done over a period of about 50 years, so the pieces were not carved specially for the burial, but were presumably family heirlooms. Yet who these two women given such a splendid burial were remains a mystery. Even if we assume that one was a queen and the other her servant, we do not know which was which, nor can we be sure if they died at the same time, or if one was possibly sacrificed to accompany the other. The special shoes made for the older woman's arthritically deformed feet were of a very fine calfskin, beautifully hand-stitched. But this need not mean that she was the queen: presumably even a young woman of the rank of the one buried at Oseberg could afford two pairs of fine shoes for her old nurse.

We have no contemporary documents that can tell us reliably who were the rulers of Vestfold, in eastern Norway, in the ninth century. We do however have Icelandic traditions first written down in the thirteenth century which tell us who later generations thought they were. Snorri Sturluson's history of the kings of Norway, *Heimskringla*, mentions two women, Álfhildr and Ása, who were successively married to a king in Vestfold called Guðrøðr. These two have usually been the favourite candidates for the queen in the burial mound, especially the latter, since there might be a connection between her name and the place-name Oseberg (ON *Ásuberg*). But Snorri tells us not much more than their names, except for a fanciful legend that Ása arranged the murder of her husband.

The Oseberg burial is not unique, only the most splendid of a group of roughly contemporary burials from ninth-century Vestfold, all of which can be seen together at the Viking Ship Museum in Oslo. Twenty-five kilometres south of Oseberg is the mound of Gokstad, another ship burial, this time of a sixty-year-old man. His ship was larger (and more seaworthy) than that of Oseberg and he was also very well equipped for his last journey, if not quite as lavishly as the lady of Oseberg. Slightly to the north of Oseberg, at Borre, and at Tune, directly across the Oslofjord from it, two further ship burials were found, but they were not very well preserved. Whatever the names of the people who were buried in these mounds, there is no doubt that they belonged to the chieftain class who controlled the Oslofjord and hence southeastern Norway in the ninth century. If Ása was indeed the lady buried at Oseberg, her grandson, Haraldr Finehair, surpassed even the power she had. According to Icelandic traditions written down in the thirteenth century, he was the first king to take Norway under his control by conquering the other chieftains who ruled the different districts. Thus Ása may have been the grandmother of the Norwegian nation.

But such splendid burials are the exception rather than the rule: most people in the Viking Age probably had no wealth, or power, or influence. The contrast is vividly illustrated at Haithabu. Here, there is also a rich chamber grave for a woman of very high social status: she was buried in the body of a wagon (1 x 2 m) placed inside an enormous wooden chamber (3.4 x 2.6 m) with grave goods that include the richest collection of precious metals yet found in a Scandinavian grave. At the same time, 95% of the 1500 graves excavated at Haithabu contained only insignificant grave goods or none at all. These must have been the graves of those who did the work on which Haithabu's prosperity depended.

Travelling women in the Viking Age

Our picture of women in the Viking Age is very often a static one. We imagine a solid housewife, left at home in charge of the farm while her husband and sons go out on raiding and trading expeditions, her reward a pretty trinket from England or Ireland when they return. While this picture has some truth in it, there is plenty of evidence that it is not the whole truth. The literary sources suggest that women did go on some of these expeditions, but the archaeological evidence is even clearer. The evidence of burials shows that Scandinavian women (identified largely by their jewellery) reached places as far apart as Greenland and Russia. In fact we can find typically Scandinavian female burials in almost all the areas of the world in which we know that the Scandinavians were active, indicating that women also had their part to play in the viking expansion.

Of course this part varied and in many areas of the world there is very little evidence that women accompanied Scandinavian men on what must have been largely military expeditions. Thus there are no Scandinavian burials found in southern Europe or North Africa and very few in the northern half of the continent (including, in Normandy, the only female burial). There may of course be many reasons for this: archaeologists in those countries may not necessarily recognise a Scandinavian burial, the Scandinavians may have adopted local burial customs so that they cannot be identified, or it is simply a matter of chance that nothing has yet been found. But as there is very little other evidence that Scandinavian women went to continental Europe in any great numbers, we may conclude that the lack of archaeological evidence of their presence gives us a reasonably accurate picture.

Where the Scandinavian presence involved trading as much as raiding, however, the picture is quite different. The great rivers of Russia leading eventually to Byzantium were an important multinational trading area where Swedish vikings played their part. Among the burials of clear Scandinavian type near the large trading centres of Staraya Ladoga, Yaroslavl', Smolensk, Chernigov and Kiev we find a considerable number of women's graves. These trading bases supported regular Scandinavian communities, where the families of the merchants lived while they themselves went on their long trading journeys. A study by Anne Stalsberg of 99 Scandinavian graves dating from the late ninth to the late eleventh century in Russia reveals that 60% contained women, while 55% contained men (some contained both). Even allowing for the fact that women's burials are easier to identify than those of men, this indicates a significant proportion of Scandinavian women throughout the period. And this in turn suggests long-term, peaceful settlement in the region. Moreover, the fact that at least 19% of the weights and balances found in Scandinavian burials belonged to women suggests that women were involved in the trading activities that took place.

Although the first Scandinavian voyages to the British Isles were purely military expeditions on which there were probably no women, the presence of relatively large numbers of female burials in these islands shows that this viking movement soon became one of settlement. Most of the Scandinavian settlers in the British Isles became converted to Christianity within a short period of time and gave up their traditional burial customs, so that pagan Scandinavian graves mostly belong to the very earliest settlement phase, in the ninth, or early tenth, century. The picture is least clear in England, where comparatively few pagan Scandinavian burials are known and where there has long been controversy among scholars on the extent of Scandinavian settlement. If, as some historians have believed, the Scandinavian settlement of eastern England was largely a matter of a few viking leaders taking over local estates, there are not likely to have been many, if any, women involved in this settlement. However, both place-name and linguistic evidence suggest large scale Scandinavian immigration, at least in parts of eastern England, probably as a secondary migration after the initial land-taking. This could hardly have happened without the presence of female settlers. But this sizeable immigrant population has left little archaeological trace. The small number of burials (both male and female) suggests that they were very soon converted to Christianity and abandoned their heathen burial customs.

In less densely populated areas of the British Isles, the proportion of settlers was greater and they presumably took longer to become Christians. Thus, Scandinavian burials in the Northern and Western Isles of Scotland give a clear picture of significant immigration. The picture is clearest in Orkney, where the Norse element is so strong that some scholars have believed the immigrants totally displaced the native Picts. One viking cemetery there is that of Pierowall, on the island of Westray. Of seventeen burials, six contained the diagnostic pair of oval brooches indicating women, and three had so few or no grave-goods that the sex of the dead is impossible to determine. With the two sexes equally represented in burials in this way, we are justified in talking of a regular migration.

The Isle of Man, on the other hand, is quite different. It lives up to its name in that, despite the 20–30 viking burials found there, only one is of a Scandinavian woman. The female skeleton found in the Ballateare grave, who may have been sacrificed, was buried with no grave goods, so that it is impossible to establish her ethnicity or, indeed, her religion. However, a richly equipped pagan burial found in excavations at Peel Castle in 1984 is probably of a Scandinavian woman, even though she lacks the characteristic pair of oval brooches: such brooches go out of fashion in the mid-tenth century, which is probably when she was buried.

Finally, the viking colonies of the Faroes, Iceland and Greenland can be considered as a part of Scandinavia from the point of view of the population. The archaeological evidence supports that of the later historical sources that the Scandinavian settlers arrived *en famille*. The Faroes and Iceland were uninhabited, virgin lands when settled by the Scandinavians and in Greenland there seems to have been little contact between the native Eskimos (who lived further north then) and the incoming settlers. These countries became officially Christian in the decades around the year 1000 AD. Greenland had not been settled long then, so we have no pagan burials there, but a Christian cemetery, dating from the early eleventh century, shows a fairly equal distribution of male and female skeletons, as well as a number of children. Iceland has a large number of pagan burials dateable mainly to the tenth century, which are very similar to contemporary ones in Norway and the British Isles, and in which women are fully represented. The custom of burying the dead with horse or dog was popular in Iceland, although found elsewhere in Scandinavia. There are instances of this in female burials everywhere, but whereas they are relatively rare in mainland Scandinavia, the custom was practised quite frequently in Iceland.

WOMAN IN HER HOME ENVIRONMENT

Settlement archaeology

Town and country

In the last fifty years, we have greatly increased our knowledge of the conditions in which people of the Viking Age lived. Single farms and agricultural villages (the latter mainly in Denmark) have been excavated in mainland Scandinavia, in the British Isles, in the Faroes, Iceland and Greenland, but the most spectacular results have come from the excavation of the great trading centres of the Viking Age: Birka in Sweden, Kaupang in Norway, Ribe in Denmark, Haithabu/Hedeby in Denmark (now in Germany), York and Lincoln in England, Dublin in Ireland. We know the kinds of houses people lived in, the activities that went on in those houses, about furniture, crafts, hygiene and diet. There is even an archaeology of insects which can trace the movements of people and animals by the six-legged friends they unwittingly and unwillingly carried with them.

Trading centres

The Viking Age coincided with the development and expansion of markets and towns throughout Europe. Thus in Scandinavia we have great trading and manufacturing centres in the Viking Age such as Birka, Haithabu and Kaupang. Excavation continues at Birka and none of the three is fully published yet, but the nature of the communities that lived in them in the Viking Age is reasonably clear. Both Haithabu and Birka became large, fortified settlements in the tenth century. Although we know little yet about the layout of Birka, Haithabu consisted of regular-sized building plots, with rectangular wooden houses, built at right angles to planked 'streets', providing both dwellings and workshops for craftsmen and merchants. The layout is so regular, it appears to have been planned. The houses had from one to three rooms and measured between 3.5 x 17 m and 7 x 17.5 m. Kaupang was smaller and not fortified, and only seasonally occupied, but it was also an important international market.

The three trading centres specialised in different articles of trade from different sources. Thus Haithabu controlled trade to the Baltic from both the North Sea and Western Europe (and vice versa), in luxuries such as wines, pottery and glass, and Frisian cloth. Birka was the main centre for the Eastern trade, as shown by the many Eastern imports found there, although westward contacts were not neglected. It specialised in the export of furs and the import of such goods as silks and spices. Kaupang was the first staging post for the export of goods from the north of Norway, furs, skins, down and walrus products, as well as the usual imports of luxuries. All these trading centres also had manufacturing activities: practical objects of metal, bone, antler, wood and leather were crafted in the workshops, some for local use, some for export both far and near. Glass-bead-making and amber-working provided more frivolous items for sale and use. Kaupang specialised in the export of cooking and storage vessels made of soapstone, a form of stone available almost exclusively in Norway, and produced in the region.

As we have seen from the burials associated with these trading centres, women formed a normal proportion of their population and took a full part in their life. There is some evidence (such as the finds of weights and balances in female graves at Birka) that women took part in the trading activities of the town. Given the physical structure of the towns, the dwelling houses with their associated workshops, it is likely that most merchants and craftsmen ran small family businesses in which their wives played an active part.

Very similar trading and manufacturing centres can be found outside Scandinavia, such as York and Lincoln in England, or Dublin in Ireland. Both York and Lincoln had urban roots going back to the Roman period, yet it is clear that they were revitalised at the time of the Scandinavian settlement of England, while Dublin owed its origins to the arrival of the Scandinavians. The arrangement of the houses and the types of objects manufactured and traded in these towns are similar to the Scandinavian settlements, and there is no doubt that the Scandinavian towns of the British Isles were in close contact with the trading centres of the homelands. It is however difficult to unravel the exact Scandinavian contribution to towns such as York and Lincoln. The period of Scandinavian political control of such towns was brief, the populations could never have been entirely Scandinavian and their Christian culture could not have been threatened for very long. Given that such trading towns were basically cosmopolitan, albeit heavily influenced from Scandinavia, it is impossible to determine to what extent that urbanity included Scandinavian women. However, both York and Lincoln were located in those areas of England which had the densest Scandinavian population.

Rural settlements

Although some of the greatest achievements of the Viking Age are characterised by these wealthy and cosmopolitan trading centres, most
people in fact still lived a rural life based on farming. This was true not
only of the Danes, Norwegians and Swedes who stayed at home, but
also of those who settled in the North Atlantic colonies of Iceland, the
Faroes and Greenland, or in Scandinavian settlements in Scotland, England or Normandy. Of course, the distinction between farming and trading is not always so easy to make. The inhabitants of Kaupang, for
instance, were primarily farmers and engaged in trade on a seasonal
basis. At the other end of Norway, beyond the Arctic Circle, the large
chieftain's farm excavated at Borg in Lofoten shows evidence of long-
distance trading contacts in the finds of high-quality pottery and glass.

The type of agriculture practised and the community in which people
lived were of course determined by geography. Thus, many Danes lived
in nucleated villages and those who emigrated to England found a
similar pattern there. Elsewhere in the viking world, the isolated farm
run by an extended family group was the norm. In Norway, only 3% of
the land area is arable, so the Norwegians had to rely on animal hus-
bandry and on the exploitation of natural resources such as timber and
iron, and on hunting and fishing. Possibilities were even more limited in
a place like Iceland, whereas Denmark, England and parts of southern
Sweden were suitable for the growing of a variety of crops.

Despite this variety of landscape, climate and resources, there was
some similarity in the houses in which people lived. They could of
course vary in size, according to the amount of wealth available, and in
building techniques, depending on local materials, but most people in
the Viking Age lived in the same basic type of house. The main dwelling
house often incorporated a byre and a typical house with a byre, such as
the Viking Age farmhouse excavated at Vorbasse in Denmark, could be
32 m long. The walls could be of wood, turf or wattle, according to the
materials available locally, but each house was rectangular or boat-
shaped, the floor was of trampled earth, and warmth and light were
provided by a fire on a slightly raised central hearth. There was no
chimney and the smoke had to find its own way out through a hole in
the roof. Raised platforms along the long walls of the house provided
both seating and sleeping accommodation near the fire and out of the
draught. Only the largest houses had more than one living room, although occasionally a sleeping alcove provided the head of the house-

Interior of a house from Haithabu, as reconstructed at Moesgård, Denmark.

hold and his wife with some privacy and there could be a separate dairy. Trestle tables were used for eating, otherwise there was not much furniture apart from chests for storage and a loom. Richer members of society might have carved panels or tapestries on their walls, both as decoration and to keep out draughts!

In this narrow smoky space, all indoor activities took place. Women living in rural areas in the Viking Age spent most of their time in the triangle of byre, dairy and living quarters, providing their families with food and clothing. To discover whether women's horizons ever extended beyond the butter-churn or the spindle, however, we need to look beyond the archaeological evidence to other types of sources.

CHAPTER II

Women's Lives in Runic Texts

RUNIC INSCRIPTIONS

Runes and writing

Like the archaeological evidence, runic inscriptions bring us into direct contact with Viking Age women. This contact may not be quite as immediate as when we come face to face with the skeleton of a woman, undisturbed since she was laid in her grave a millennium or so ago. On the other hand, the runic evidence can often be more informative about the lives of women than the mute objects that come out of archaeological investigations about which we can only guess whether, how and when they were used by women. Runic inscriptions rank alongside archaeological evidence in that they are strictly contemporary evidence, and come from within the culture we are studying rather than being the biased or partial view of an outsider. Yet the inscriptions are superior to the archaeological evidence in that they enable us to identify real people and learn something about them: their names, their family relationships and, occasionally, some of the facts about their lives and deaths. In a limited sense, most runic inscriptions are narratives, and it is narrative that we need in order to fill out the concrete picture we get from the archaeological sources.

Today the descendants of vikings living in Scandinavia read and write using the Roman alphabet. Although the first inhabitants of Scandinavia had contacts with the Roman Empire from a very early stage, this alphabet was not introduced into the North until much later, after the conversion of the Scandinavian peoples to the Christian religion, when it came as part of a package along with the new beliefs and customs introduced mainly in the eleventh century. The Church brought its own language, Latin, for both administrative and theological purposes, and with it an alphabet and a new technology of writing in books made up of vellum leaves, with a quill pen and ink. Both the alphabet and the technology were soon adapted to writing the vernacular languages of Scandinavia as well as Latin and this is what led to the eventual triumph of the Roman alphabet. But the Scandinavians had not been illiterate before their introduction to the writing techniques of Rome: they had been writing their own language since at least the late second century AD in the runic alphabet, known as the *fuþark* from its first six characters. During the whole of the Viking Age, this was the only alphabet used in Scandinavia and by Scandinavians.

Runes were never restricted to Scandinavia. The distribution of early inscriptions correlates fairly closely with the known distribution of peoples speaking a Germanic language, from Scandinavia in the north through England and down to central Europe as far south as present-day Romania. Thus the runic alphabet is essentially a Germanic phenomenon, although the greatest number of surviving inscriptions by far comes from the area of present-day Scandinavia. If runes were ever used to any great extent on the Continent (inscriptions from there are very few in number), this petered out with the conversion of the Germanic tribes to Christianity. In England, the Anglo-Saxons, speaking a Germanic language, were also converted to Christianity fairly early, by the seventh century AD. They too had known the runic alphabet before the change of religion, but here its use continued after the conversion and we can find runic characters used alongside Roman letters in a variety of epigraphic contexts, including explicitly Christian ones. But the most widespread use of runes was in Denmark, Norway and Sweden, starting with the very earliest inscriptions from about 200 AD, right through to the full flowering of runes as the script of the Viking Age. Many of the runic inscriptions we have are even later, from the medieval period and, indeed, in some remote areas of Scandinavia, runes were occasionally used well into modern times.

In spite of the thousands of known runic inscriptions of all kinds, the actual volume of text (and therefore information) in these inscriptions is not as great as we might think. Runes and the technology used to produce them were never designed for long texts. Runes were scratched or cut into wood, metal or stone. The laboriousness of this process meant that the messages were kept relatively short. However, within these limitations, runes could be used for any purpose in which a permanent or semi-permanent written text was required: to record the name, maker, donor or owner of a prized object, such as a spearhead or a brooch; for inscriptions on coins; to write a charm or curse; to mark a memorial to a dead person; to send messages; and to inscribe casual graffiti.

Both the Anglo-Saxon and the Scandinavian versions of the runic alphabet were developments from an original set of twenty-four characters. In England further runes were added to this alphabet, while the Scandinavians went the other way and reduced it to sixteen runes. This major change in the Scandinavian *fuþark* coincides roughly with the beginning of the Viking Age. The reduction of the runic alphabet reflects great linguistic changes that seem to have been complete by the eighth century, so that all runic inscriptions relevant to viking history are in this peculiarly Scandinavian runic alphabet known as 'the younger *fuþark*'. The runic alphabet continued to develop throughout and even after the Viking Age, increasingly influenced by the Roman alphabet. Indeed some of the most interesting inscriptions found on Scandinavian soil, particularly finds made in the 1960s during major excavations in the trading centre of Bergen, belong to the medieval period, rather than to the Viking Age.

Viking Age runes

Runic inscriptions are found from Norway, Sweden and Denmark throughout the whole of the Viking Age, 800–1100. In addition, we find runic inscriptions from many of the areas outside Scandinavia that we know were visited by vikings, places as far apart as Greenland and Istanbul, with the largest number in the British Isles and Ireland. Not all of these extra-Scandinavian inscriptions are actually from the Viking Age. The runic stone found at Kingigtorssuaq in Greenland (72° 55′ N) is from the early fourteenth century and most of the inscriptions from places such as Iceland and Orkney are medieval. Of runic inscriptions from outside Scandinavia, the most important are the 30-odd from the Isle of Man, although these include some medieval ones.

Although we have inscriptions from most of the areas associated with vikings and from the whole of the Viking Age, the distribution of these inscriptions is not regular. Runic inscriptions cannot give us a complete history of the Viking Age in all the countries inhabited and visited by Scandinavians. But what they do give us are snapshots (of varying degrees of clarity) of different places at different times. The most obvious example of this is the collection of more than 2,000 memorial stones with runic inscriptions from certain parts of eleventh-century Sweden which overshadow all other groups of inscriptions by their number alone. Although we are still in the Viking Age with these Swedish stones, it is very much the late Viking Age, the moment of transition to Christian, medieval Scandinavia, and many of the stones have obviously Christian characteristics. Other groups of inscriptions, being much smaller, give us even more restricted views of particular places at particular times. But as women are represented in all types of inscriptions, the runic sources are invaluable for a study of their history.

OBJECTS WITH RUNES

Objects of personal and domestic use or personal adornment found in archaeological contexts can be attributed to women either through direct association with a female skeleton in a grave, or through assumptions made by archaeologists and others about the types of objects likely to have belonged to and been used by women in daily life. Occasionally, an object will carry a brief inscription in runes which will give us further cause to associate that object with women's work or female dress. Such inscriptions are not usually an integral part of the object, but were scratched or carved on it later. Therefore we cannot assume that the object in question was always owned by the particular woman named, or indeed by any woman.

The number of such objects is fairly small and the inscriptions on them are not especially informative. Names scratched onto small objects do not tell us whether they are those of the owners or not, although we may imagine that ownership was the most likely reason for scratching a name on something. A good example of the puzzles of such inscriptions is provided by two of the four small silver-gilt mounts from the Slemmedal hoard found in 1981 in Norway. The hoard, consisting of both gold and silver jewellery, was deposited at some time around 925. The mounts in the hoard were originally strap-ends of foreign manufacture, but they had been made into pendants for a necklace. One of the mounts has two names, one that was probably male (*Þórfreðr*, but it could also represent the female name *Þórfríðr*) and one certainly female (*Þóra*) scratched on its reverse, and these lead us to suspect that the necklace was a souvenir brought back by a viking for his wife or girlfriend. But then we have the difficulty of explaining why the other mount, seemingly from the same necklace, has another man's name (*Slóði*) scratched on its back. There is much material for the imagination here, but not many answers. Luckily we have a number of similar objects (such as the bronze mount from Vä in Skåne with the inscription 'Gautvid gave this scales-box to Gudfrid') which, all taken together, suggest that runes could be used to record a man's gift to a woman.

Of the several small Celtic house-shaped reliquaries that have been found in Scandinavia, one bears the inscription 'Rannveig owns this casket'. This could be another example of a gift brought back to Norway by a travelling viking for his woman. But, since no man's name is recorded, it is just as likely that Rannveig acquired the box while travelling herself. The runes of the inscription are of a type used in the Isle of Man as well as the southwest of Norway and Rannveig may have been visiting or even living in the Norwegian settlement in Man when she acquired the box.

Although negative evidence is never entirely trustworthy, it is interesting to note the absence of any female equivalents of inscriptions which give the name of maker of an object. While a comb-case found in Lincoln boastfully tells us that 'Thorfast made a good comb' we have no such runic evidence of Viking Age craftswomen. That these manual tasks were left to men is suggested by a knife-haft from Lindholm in Denmark (dated to about 800) with the legend 'Singasven polished for Thorfrid'. The elaborate carving of the runes making up the girl's name Thorfrid again suggests that this was a lover's gift.

However it seems that the course of love did not always run smooth in the Viking Age. A weaving tablet found in Lund bears (if it has been correctly interpreted) the curious inscription 'Sigvor's Ingemar shall have my weeping – aallatti!' This sounds like a curse on the errant Ingemar, who is now with another woman, Sigvor. Ingemar's rejected love took the nearest object to hand, one of her weaving tablets, and inscribed it with a curse, triggered by the final magic word.

The Slemmedal hoard with (bottom centre) rune-inscribed mounts.

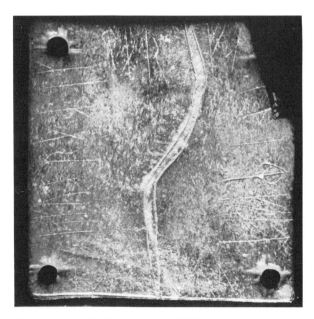

The rune-inscribed weaving tablet from Lund.

MEMORIAL STONES

Commemorating the dead

By far the most rewarding group of runic inscriptions are the thousands of memorial stones from Denmark, Norway and most of all from Sweden. As memorials to the dead, these stones give us the names of persons both living and dead, indicating the relationships between them and often providing additional information about their lives. In this way we get to know the names of several hundred women who lived in the Viking Age.

The custom of erecting stones to honour the dead goes back to at least the fourth or fifth century AD in Scandinavia. The Eddic poem *Hávamál* tells us that:

> memorial stones seldom
> stand near the road
> unless raised by kin after kin.

Many of these early stones have incomprehensible inscriptions, or a simple inscription consisting only of a name. There were also stones raised that had no inscription. Plain stones continued to be erected throughout the heathen period, but in the course of the Viking Age stones with detailed runic inscriptions and often elaborate ornament came into fashion.

Such memorial stones are not strictly comparable with our modern gravestones. They could be, but more often were not, directly associated with the place in which the dead person was buried. The inscriptions almost invariably begin with the name of the person or persons who commissioned the monument, rather than that of the dead person, the basic formula being 'A raised this stone in memory of X'. This standard sentence could be embroidered in several ways, by adding names of further commissioners (B,C, etc.) or commemorated (Y,Z, etc.), by stating the relationship between A(B,C) and X(Y,Z), or by noting any other interesting facts. Some of the stones mention an inheritance that has passed from the dead to one or more of the commissioners, or make other reference to the ownership of property. Even those inscriptions which make no direct reference to inheritance show such careful recording of family relationships that we can assume that the need to establish legal inheritance was one of the motivating factors behind the erection of these costly monuments.

The runic memorial stones vary in size and shape, but most of them are between one and two metres tall, not quite as broad and generally flattish in shape, with the inscription most often carved into the flat side, but sometimes up the edge, of the stone. Most are designed to be dug endwise into the earth so as to be free-standing in the landscape, but some inscriptions are cut into the flat surfaces of large earthbound rocks. Not all the stones are still in their original positions, but many are, especially in Sweden. They were clearly meant to be public monuments and can be found alongside roads, near bridges, or on parish or farm boundaries. Many are now in or near churches and at least some of them must have been intended to be seen in a Christian setting from the very start.

Denmark

The fashion for raising these inscribed memorial stones to honour the dead and glorify the living probably appeared first in Denmark – at least that is where we have the earliest stones. Numbers of Viking Age memorial stones are not as great as in Sweden but considerably more than in Norway. There are about 220 if we include the Swedish provinces that were a part of Denmark in the Viking Age (and later). Of these, approximately 45 mention women in one way or another (the number cannot be calculated exactly because some of the names could be either male or female and many of the inscriptions are fragmentary). On a surprisingly high proportion of the stones mentioning the names of women (about half of them), the woman is the sole commissioner of the monument. The next largest group consists of eleven stones commemorating a woman (including one which overlaps with the previous category, raised by a daughter to her mother), and then come a handful on which the women are joint commissioners with a man, or joint commemorated. These proportions are more like the Norwegian stones (admittedly too few in number to be statistically significant), but quite different from the Swedish stones. In the Swedish inscriptions, women are mentioned more frequently, but are much more rarely the most prominent person in the inscription, that of the commissioner whose name always comes first in the standard commemorative formula.

This pattern in the Danish runestones suggests what the inscriptions themselves often confirm: the stones were generally erected by rich and powerful families, and in such families women could play a prominent role. This impression of the high social standing of a very few women is strengthened by the fact that some women commissioned (either alone or jointly) more than one runestone.

One such woman was Ragnhild, the main commissioner, along with her sons, for the monument to her husband Ali at Glavendrup. This stone, as well as having the longest of all the Danish runic inscriptions, is part of an impressive monument to the dead man consisting of a stone ship setting and two small mounds, with the runestone on one of them. After telling us of Ali's deeds during his lifetime and mentioning the other persons who took part in raising the stone (Ali's sons are referred to but not named and a follower of Ali's called Soti is said to have carved the runes), the inscription closes with an invocation to the god Thor to 'hallow these runes' and a curse on anyone who moves the stone. Since one of Ali's positions in life had been that of a *goði*, or heathen priest, we get a fleeting picture of a family in about the year 900, actively involved in heathen religious practices and probably deriving their power and position from this.

Ragnhild was married at least twice, for both the style of the inscription and the use of the same carver tell us that she is the same Ragnhild who was responsible for the Tryggevælde stone. This tells us that 'Ragnhild, the sister of Ulf, placed this stone, and made this mound and this ship setting, in memory of her husband Gunnulf, a clamorous man, son of Nærfi. Few will be born who are better than him. May he be an outcast who tips this stone or drags it away from here.'

The most impressive runic monument from Viking Age Denmark is the complex centring on the village church at Jelling in Jutland. The church is situated between two enormous mounds and outside it stand two rune-inscribed stones, a small one set up by King Gorm in memory of his wife Thorvi (modern Danish Thyre), and a much larger and elaborately decorated one set up by their son, Harald (known as Blacktooth), in memory of both his parents. The monument is a complex one that tells us a lot about Danish history in the mid-tenth century. The inscription on Harald's stone, for instance, boasts that King Harald 'won the whole of Denmark for himself, and Norway, and made the Danes Christian'. But his parents had been heathens and King Gorm had made a worthy resting place for his queen, and for himself as well, when he should die. This first phase of the monument consisted of a double grave mound (now the northernmost of the two mounds) with two lines of standing stones flanking it and the smaller stone indicating whom it was all for: 'King Gorm made this monument in memory of Thorvi, his wife, Denmark's adornment'. Harald, on the other hand, was a Christian ruler, and felt the need to ease his parents' path to heaven by 'converting' their monument. He destroyed the stone setting and built an empty mound (the southern one) as a cenotaph for them, and may have been responsible for the first wooden church on the site. The last piece in the puzzle, the magnificently carved runestone, glorifies his own achievements more than it honours his parents. The monument was completed at some time between the conversion of Denmark in the 960s and Harald's death in 987, but cannot be dated any more precisely than that.

Queen Thorvi has only a walk-on part in this religious drama. We do not know what her husband had in mind when he prettily called her 'Denmark's adornment'. The grave chamber in which she was laid to rest was long ago plundered, so that we cannot even examine the objects she was given for her journey to the next world. Another runestone gives us an equally tantalising glimpse of her daughter-in-law, otherwise unknown from any other source. The Sønder Vissing stone (the only Danish runestone in which both the commissioner and the commemorated are women) records that 'Tofa, daughter of Mistivoj and wife of Harald the Good, son of Gorm, had this monument made in memory of her mother'. Mistivoj was a prince of the Obotrites, a Wendish tribe, although his daughter has a perfectly good Danish name. What her mother was called, and what her nationality might have been, we have no way of knowing.

Just as King Harald made a monument to honour his dead parents, so might a contemporary of his a bit lower down the social scale do the same. At Gunderup, a stone which was originally placed on top of a burial mound records that:

> Toki set up these stones and made this monument in memory of Abi, his stepfather, a noble warrior, and in memory of Tofa, his mother. They both lie in this mound. Abi granted Toki his property after him.

Clearly Tofa and Abi had no surviving children of their own, so her son by a previous marriage inherited from his stepfather and expressed his gratitude in an appropriate manner.

In some inscriptions we even detect expressions of family feeling such as we might expect to find on modern gravestones. An inscription on a stone from Rimsø, set up by a certain Thorir in memory of his mother, ends with 'death of a mother is the worst that can happen to a son'. But we may wonder if he was embarrassed at such a naked expression of feeling, for these last words of the inscription are written backwards.

Less embarrassed to let the world know of her tender feelings was a lady called Thorvi, 'wife of Vigot', who commissioned a stone (at Ålum in North Jutland) in memory of her nephew Thorbjørn 'towards whom she felt more kindly than towards a son of her own'. Nearby, her husband Vigot raised a stone in memory of his son Asger. Was Asger not Thorvi's son? Whether he was her son or stepson, had she quarrelled with him and transferred her affections to her nephew? Another Viking Age family drama must remain a mystery.

That runestones could be erected to honour people who were not family members is shown by some stones erected in memory of a 'lady'. Two of these (stones from Læborg and Bække in Jutland, only 6 km apart) were raised by the same man, Tufi, in memory of his 'lady' Thorvi (not the same as King Gorm's wife or Thorvi, wife of Vigot: it was a common name in Viking Age Denmark). Presumably this Thorvi had outlived her own relatives and it was left to a devoted employee to give her due honours in death.

Stones with runic inscriptions commissioned by women in memory of their male relatives often show a concern with the men's social and military status in life. Naturally, a widow would have a more secure status if her husband had been an important man in life, preferably one with some noble deeds under his belt, but mothers seem also to have basked in the reflected glory of their dead sons. Two stones that can be placed historically, from the important Viking Age trading centre of Hedeby, were commissioned by 'Asfrid, Odinkar's daughter' in memory of 'King Sigtryg, her son and Gnupa's'. Gnupa was a Swedish king who ruled in Hedeby in the 930s. He had married the daughter of Odinkar, a Danish magnate. Their son Sigtryg ruled briefly in Hedeby, but was soon killed in battle, survived only by his mother, who commissioned two stones in his memory. The stones themselves demonstrate the Swedish-Danish connections in Hedeby, as one is cut partly in Swedish runes.

Slightly lower down the social scale, status in Viking Age Denmark seems to have depended on being attached to the military or household retinue of a king or local magnate. Most of the stones raised by women in memory of their husbands find occasion to mention the men's roles in life, as we have already seen in the inscriptions commissioned by Ragnhild. The husband's status is more important in these inscriptions than whom he followed, as in the Bjerregrav inscription which simply says that 'Gyda erected this stone in memory of Thorbjørn, her husband, a very noble "thegn" '. Even when we are told who the husband's lord was, we cannot always identify him, as in the case of the Finnulf mentioned on the Sjørind stone: 'Asa placed this stone in memory of Amundi, her husband, who was Finnulf's retainer'.

These and other Danish stones show us the lives and deaths of the upper classes. Most of these runestones seem to have been raised by people at the centre of political and military events in the late Viking Age. The high proportion of stones commissioned by women acting on their own reflect not only the social status of the families involved, in which widows could be rich and powerful, but perhaps also mortality rates among the male aristocracy in a turbulent period.

Sweden

Inheritance and status

The people we meet in the runic inscriptions on Swedish stones cover a much broader range of society and come from a different historical period: while most Danish stones are from the tenth century, the Swedish ones are overwhelmingly from the eleventh. One group of related inscriptions will demonstrate the richness of the Swedish inscriptions. It includes the stones from Färentuna church (U 20–21), Hillersjö (U 29), Snottsta (U 329–31) and Vreta (U 332), all in Uppland. These inscriptions provide so much information about the persons mentioned in them that we can be sure they all refer to one family who lived in those parts some time in the eleventh century. Taken together, the inscriptions give us a detailed (although by no means complete) account of births, deaths and marriages in three generations of that family, particularly as they involved a woman called Geirlaug and her daughter Inga. Inga is the central character in this drama, in that all the other persons mentioned in it are related to her by blood or marriage, although it is her mother who turns out to be the most important person in the end.

The stones from Färentuna, Snottsta and Vreta all carry inscriptions of a fairly conventional type, in which the name of the commissioner comes first, followed by the name or names of the person or persons being commemorated, their relationship to the commissioner and any additional information about them. One of the stones from Snottsta also ends like many others with the conventional Christian formula, 'may

God help their souls'. The two fragments from Färentuna belong in fact to one stone, which commemorates someone's father and husband, although we cannot tell whose without comparing it with the Hillersjö stone.

The three stones from Snottsta and the one from Vreta were all erected by Inga in memory of her husband Ragnfast. Such duplication is not unique, as there are other instances of memorial stones with identical commissioners and commemorated, and sometimes even with identical inscriptions. However Inga's stones are unusual in their number (four) and in the fact that they seem to have been designed to supplement and complement one another. That they were erected at the same time is shown by the fact that three of the four stones (Snottsta 1 and 2, and Vreta) refer in the plural to 'stones' raised by Inga. Each stone notes a different aspect of Inga's memorial activities. Thus, Snottsta 1 refers only to the raising of the stones, but Snottsta 2 mentions that she also had a 'bridge' made, Snottsta 3 that she 'had runes carved' and Vreta that she 'raised a stave and stones'. Moreover, three of the four Inga-stones record different information about her husband, Ragnfast. Snottsta 1 notes that he had two sisters called Gyrid and Estrid, Snottsta 2 that he had a *huskarl* (a retainer) called Assur and Snottsta 3 that he was sole owner of 'this farm' (i.e. Snottsta) after his father Sigfast. The very elaborateness of Inga's monuments to her husband and the careful detailing of the information in the inscriptions suggest that their commissioner was motivated by something more than just affection for the dead. The family history behind these inscriptions is made clear when they are compared with the massive monument of Hillersjö with its lengthy inscription.

As well as being especially long, the Hillersjö inscription is unusual in that, unlike the vast majority of Swedish runestones, it does not begin by saying that 'X made this monument in memory of Y'. Rather, it tells us that:

> Geirmund married Geirlaug when she was a girl. Then they had a son, before he [i.e. Geirmund] drowned and the son died later. Then she married [Gu]drik, ... Then they had children, but only one girl survived. She was called [In]ga. She was married to Ragnfast of Snottsta, then he died and [their] son [died] later, and the mother [i.e. Inga] inherited from her son. Then she was married to Eirik. She died there, and there Geirlaug inherited from her daughter Inga.

Although some of the names cannot be deciphered, they are easily supplied: Inga from the end of the inscription and Gudrik from the Färentuna stone. The Färentuna inscription can thus be partially reconstructed as '. . . in memory of her husband Eirik and her father Gudrik. . .'.

Together these six stones tell a story in which two women become, in successive stages, wealthy property owners by the accidents of marriage and death. They erected the runestones to indicate to the world at large not only that they were the rightful inheritors of this property, but also to spell out exactly how this came about, in case anyone should doubt the facts of the case. The first stage in the history comes with the marriage of Inga, sole surviving child of her mother's two marriages and presumably her father's only child as well, and therefore with the prospect of a substantial inheritance to tempt her suitor. However her husband Ragnfast dies before her parents, leaving Inga with a son who then inherits his father's property (the farm at Snottsta). Although the stones at Snottsta and Vreta are all in memory of Inga's husband, it is likely that they were not put up until after the death of their son, since this was when Inga inherited the property, as it says on the Hillersjö stone ('the mother inherited from her son'). Thus Snottsta 3 first establishes Ragnfast's own title to the property: 'he owned this farm alone, after his father Sigfast'. Inga's and Ragnfast's son may not have lived much longer than his father, since he is scarcely mentioned except obliquely on the Vreta stone 'she inherited from her child'. The sisters of Ragnfast mentioned on Snottsta 1 and his retainer mentioned on Snottsta 2 may be seen as persons who might have had some expectations of inheritance from either Sigfast or Ragnfast, but who clearly got no part of the farm at Snottsta, at least.

Inga then married Eirik. Although spouses did not inherit directly from one another, each had a claim on their share of jointly owned property after the other's death. When Eirik died before Inga and her father Gudrik died at about the same time, she put up the Färentuna stone in memory of both of them. As the stone is fragmentary, we cannot be sure whether any other persons were involved in commissioning this monument. But from the point of view of title to property, it confirms Inga as the heir of her father and the rightful owner of her share of property in joint ownership with her husband, as they both died before her.

The importance of this becomes clear in the final stage of the story, which is when Inga dies. She is a wealthy woman, having acquired property from two marriages and inherited from her father, and has only one surviving relative with the right to inherit, her mother

Runestone from Hillersjö, Uppland, Sweden.

Geirlaug. Women could not inherit directly from their husbands if there were surviving children, but in the same way as Inga herself inherited her husband's property from their child who predeceased her, so Geirlaug also inherits Gudrik's property through their daughter Inga. As Inga's sole heir, moreover, she got quite a lot more wealth into the bargain and obviously used part of it to commission the Hillersjö monument, telling her life story and describing her path to riches.

That the information in the inscriptions was intended for public consumption is indicated by the exhortation 'interpret [i.e. the runes]!' incised in the eye of the serpent whose body contains the inscription of the Hillersjö stone. The most important information on the stone is found in the bands which make up the serpent's body, extraneous information such as that 'Thorbjørn skald carved these runes' is placed outside the body of the serpent.

The importance of women's inheritance as a means of transferring wealth from one family to another is demonstrated by a pair of memorial stones at Hansta (U 72–3). The first of these has a straightforward memorial inscription: 'Gærdar and Jorund had these stones raised in memory of their sister's sons Ernmund and Ingmund'. Stones erected by uncles in memory of their nephews are rare, but the reason for this unusual inscription is given on the other stone:

Runestone from Bro, Uppland, Sweden.

These memorials are made for the sons of Inga. She inherited from them, and the brothers, Gærdar and his brother, inherited from her. They [i.e. the sons of Inga] died in Byzantium.

Clearly where an inheritance had to be substantiated by the erection of costly runic monuments, the amount involved could not have been negligible. Nevertheless, the families just mentioned are likely, though wealthy, to have been of no more than local consequence. Although the sons of the Inga of the Hansta stone were in Byzantium, the inheritance which passed on to her brothers through her may only have concerned the farm at home, rather than any wealth her sons had amassed abroad, which may not have reached Sweden after their deaths in Byzantium. But other runic inscriptions are less narrowly concerned with wealth and inheritance, and show us families of a different kind of social and political importance.

An introduction to such a family is provided by the stones commissioned by two women, probably mother and daughter. One is the stone of Ramsundsberget (Sö 101), where the inscription is carved into a large earthbound rock near a river, along with scenes from the legend of Sigurd the Dragon-Slayer. The inscription tells us that:

> Sigrid, mother of Alrik, daughter of Orm, made this bridge for the soul of Holmgeir, her husband, father of Sigrød.

A companion stone at Kjula (Sö 106) was set up by Alrik, 'Sigrid's son', in memory of his father Spjut (presumably Sigrid's first husband). The Kjula stone continues with a short verse recording that Spjut had 'been in the west [i.e. on viking expeditions in Western Europe] and destroyed towns. . .'.

Sigrid's second son Sigrød is also mentioned on a stone now near Bro church (U 617) erected by his sister Ginnlaug in memory of her husband Assur. Again the importance of this family is emphasised by the description of Ginnlaug as 'Holmgeir's daughter and sister of Sigrød and Gaut. . .' The commemorated husband Assur was no insignificant farmer, either. He was 'the son of Hakon jarl, and was a 'viking-guard' [i.e. part of a defence force against pirates] with Gætir'. The name Hakon was not common in Sweden and it is just possible that Assur was the son of the Norwegian jarl, Hákon Sigurðsson, who died in 995, having practically ruled Norway during his lifetime. But even if Assur's father was only an obscure Swedish jarl about whom we know nothing, he clearly was a man with some power, for the name Hakon as recorded in Swedish runic inscriptions seems limited to royal and aristocratic circles. Assur himself had risen to an important position in Gætir's army (whatever the exact import of the term 'viking-guard').

The high social standing of the families commemorated in these three inscriptions is thus indicated by three things: (1) the fact that the women commissioning two of the inscriptions mention their own ancestry; (2) the references to military and political rank ('jarl', 'viking-guard') on the Bro stone; and (3) the artistic embellishment of the Ramsundsberget stone. Most Swedish runestones are decorated only with the elaborate serpent forms that contain the inscriptions themselves (and often also a cross). At Ramsundsberget this convention is wittily built on, with the serpent turned into the dragon of the legend, here pierced by the sword of the small figure of Sigurd below it and enclosing iconographical references to other episodes in the legend. This use of a heroic legend on a memorial stone was clearly meant to reflect on the heroism of the person being commemorated, but it also puts the commissioner (Sigrid) in the rank of a patron of the arts. That she was also a public benefactor is indicated by the statement in the inscription that she 'made a bridge'. Such constructions were doubtless expensive and, as they benefited the community as a whole rather than just individuals, were most likely to have been undertaken by persons of wealth and consequence, who were then able to boast of their beneficence by having the deed recorded in a runic inscription. Such a person was Sigrid, whose runestone is still near a river flowing into Mälaren, Sweden's large inland lake. Nor was her daughter Ginnlaug to be outdone: her bridge-building activities are recorded in the Bro inscription.

Foreign adventures

We have already seen how several of the stones refer to the fact that men travelled, fought and occasionally died abroad, whether in the east or the west. Such runestones both confirm and complement the picture of viking expansion that we get from other sources. The runestones themselves display the consequences of such foreign travel: the wealth of a society in which so many people could afford to commission elaborate memorials must at least to some extent have come from abroad. The Christianity so evident in the crosses or prayers carved on the stones again demonstrates influence from abroad at a time when Sweden was not yet officially or wholly converted and when the only church organisation was a few itinerant missionaries.

The impact of this foreign travel on the lives of Swedish women is more difficult to assess on the basis of the runestones alone. First of all, we cannot tell whether women ever went on such expeditions. With only one exception, all references to travel or death abroad in runic inscriptions apply to men. Such negative evidence does not preclude the possibility that women accompanied men on viking expeditions, but we must say that there is no positive evidence that they did so. However it is likely that, with such a large number of men abroad, women were occasionally left alone in charge of the farm and household at home. Whether the viking adventures of Swedish men gave women greater influence and status than in times when the men stayed at home is difficult to determine. The vast majority of runic inscriptions do not give the cause or place of death of the commemorated, so it is impossible to judge whether the female relatives of foreign vikings commissioned more stones than those of stay-at-homes.

The possible attrition rate in one family can be demonstrated by the (doubtless extreme) example of the stone at Högby (Ög 81). The inscription is a long one and not fully interpreted, but it is clear from it that the stone was raised by a certain Thorgerd, in memory of 'her mother's brother Assur, who died east in Greece'. The inscription then goes on to relate, in verse, how the five sons of Gulli (Thorgerd's maternal grandfather) died. Depending on the interpretation of the inscription, at least two and possibly all of these sons died or were killed abroad, including Assur. As it is not usual for nieces to commission stones in memory of their uncles (this is in fact the only example), it seems a reasonable assumption that Thorgerd's five uncles all died as young men, or at least without leaving any heirs, so that Thorgerd (whose mother had presumably also died by this time) inherited from them all, on the death of the last of her uncles. It is likely that Thorgerd was the last survivor of her mother's side of the family, i.e. that she had no brothers or sisters alive, otherwise they would have been co-inheritors and participated in the commissioning of the monument.

Runic verses

Like Thorgerd's stone at Högby, many of the monuments to men who had died abroad contain a short verse, including several where women were the sole commissioners of the monument. We do not know how far a commissioner was responsible for the content of the inscription on a monument. Many of these inscriptions are couched in stock formulas into which the runemaster must simply have inserted the appropriate names, based on information given to him by the commissioner. Where an inscription contains a verse, we cannot know whether this had also been entrusted to the runemaster, or whether any commissioners may have composed the verses themselves. The verses in runic inscriptions are all unique, so they cannot have been part of the runemaster's formulaic stock-in-trade and are therefore not comparable to conventional verses found on modern gravestones. Each seems to have been composed especially for the occasion and we are entitled to wonder whether some of the female commissioners of monuments composed them themselves.

Apart from Högby, examples of runestones with poetic inscriptions commemorating the death of men abroad and commissioned solely by a woman or women all come from the province of Södermanland.

A stone at Gripsholm (Sö 179), raised by a woman called Tola in memory of her son Harald, brother of Ingvar (the leader of a famous expedition to the East), cites the following verse which seems to express perfectly the ethos of eleventh-century viking adventurers:

þaiʀ furu trikila	They went gallantly
fiari at kuli	far for gold
auk austarla	and in the east
[a]rni kafu.	fed the eagle.
Tuu sunarla	They died in the south
a sirklanti.	in Saracenland.

The metre of this verse is *fornyrðislag*, familiar from Eddic poetry, with regular alliteration and an irregular number of syllables per line. The common heroic trope ('feeding the eagle' = 'killing') is more familiar from skaldic poetry and the total effect is similar to the conventional poems of heroic praise composed by the skalds.

The same metre is found in a verse on a stone at Fagerlöt (Sö 126) erected by two women, Holmfrid and Hedinfrid, in memory of their father Eskil:

Han traui orustu	He offered battle
i austruihi	on the eastern route
aþan fulks krimʀ	before the war-fierce one
fala orþi.	had to fall.

Also in *fornyrðislag*, but with hints of a more skaldic style is the verse on the Djulefors stone (Sö 65), raised by Inga in memory of Oleif (his exact relationship to her is not clear from this fragmentary inscription):

Han austarla	He ploughed
arþi barþi	in the east with his prow
auk o lakbarþa	and in Langobard-
lanti antaþis.	land died.

Here we find the internal rhyme (*arþi/barþi, lant-/ant-*) and the compressed metaphor ('ploughed with his prow') so characteristic of skaldic poetry, even if the Djulefors verse is not in fullblown skaldic metre.

Women commissioners did not have a monopoly on runic verses as dead men were commemorated in verse on stones erected by other men, or by mixed groups of men and women. A man called Thorstein received a particularly stately memorial from his sons Ketil and Bjørn, his brother Anund, his wife Ketiløy and his *huskarlar* or retainers in the stone at Turinge (Sö 338) which cites the following verse:

Bruþr uaru þaR	The brothers were
bistra mana	the best of men
a lanti	on land
auk i liþi uti.	and out in the levy.
Hiltu sin[a]	They maintained their
huskarla uil.	men well.
Han fial i urustu	He fell in battle
austr i karþum	east in Russian forts,
lis furugi	levy-leader,
lanmana bestr.	best of landmen.

Like other runic inscriptions with memorial verses, this one gives no indication of who composed the verse.

It has been suggested that women had a special responsibility to commemorate the dead in a poetic lament. This argument is based on the evidence of a double monument at Bällsta (U 225–6), raised by the sons of Ulf in memory of their father, which cites the following verse:

[M]unu iki mirki	There will not be
maiRi uirþa	a bigger memorial
þan Ulfs suniR	than the sons of Ulf
iftiR kir[þu	made,
snial]iR suinaR	stout fellows,
at sin faþur.	for their father.
Ristu stina	They raised stones
uk staf [unnu]	and made staves,
uk in mikla	the high one too,
at iartiknum.	as tokens.
Uk Kuriþi	And Gyrid
kas at uiri.	was gratified with her husband.
Þu mon i krati	This will in a lament
kiatit lata.	be proclaimed.

The problem is how to interpret *i krati* (standard ON *í gráti*), whether it simply means 'in tears', or whether it means 'in a lament', with connotations of poetry. Although the evidence is limited, it is certainly possible that women composed poetry in praise of their dead husbands or other male relatives. An even more obscure inscription which points in the same direction is a stone from Norra Härrene (Vg 59), erected by three sons in memory of their father, 'a very good warrior'. These poetic lines then refer to the dead man's wife:

Sua hifiR Osa	Asa has also [done]
as igi mun	that which never will,
sum kuin ift uir	as wife after husband,
siþon kaurua.	again be done.

What was it that Asa did in memory of her husband? On the surface of it, it seems to be that she participated in the raising of the memorial stone, but the inscription does not actually say this, it refers to the four sons who 'placed' the stone and, at the end, to the two men who 'carved the runes'. It is possible that Asa did something else, like composing a lament, either the simple one quoted on the stone or, just possibly, one that is not recorded.

Like the last example, many poetic inscriptions in memory of dead husbands and fathers do not say that the man in question died in battle, or abroad, although it is often implied. The heroic mode of runic poetry was obviously most suited to commemorating those who had in fact died in battle (an event most likely to have taken place abroad). But we also find poetic traces in inscriptions commemorating men who must have died more prosaic deaths. Thus one of the stones at Skånela church (U 300, now lost but recorded in older descriptions) had a simple inscription, 'Thyrvi had this stone raised in memory of Halfdan', and the line:

merki mukit	a great memorial
eftiR man kuþan.	to a good man.

This poetic line can scarcely be called a verse, yet the inverted word order of the adjective after the noun (*man kuþan*) can only be explained by the need to have the alliterating word (*man*) in the metrically correct place.

Public and private

The Swedish runestones are public memorials. Prominent in the landscape, the standing stones rise out of fields and by the roadside, the earthbound ones are large, natural features. Most of them are in public places, beside roads and bridges, or at parish or farm boundaries. Thus they present the public face of the family members who appear on them. The ones that have been discussed here suggest reasons for these public statements about family life: to confirm relationships and inheritance, or to proclaim the heroic deeds of a family member. It is possible that some of the vast majority of inscriptions which merely contain the formula 'A(B,C . . .) had this stone raised/these runes carved in memory of X(Y,Z . . .), his/her/their . . .' also had some such public purpose. In the small, isolated communities of central Sweden, it could be expected that passersby would know the persons involved and the facts of their lives, and that the runestone would merely be there to jog their memory. But it would be reading too much into these inscriptions to claim that most of them were anything but memorials to the dead, intended to assist their passage to the next (usually Christian) world and to comfort the living.

What emotional response these memorials might have evoked we cannot tell. The inscriptions themselves are severely laconic and even the prayers which round many of them off are strictly formulaic, 'may God (and God's mother) help his/her soul' being the most common. Nor do the inscriptions give much indication of how the survivors felt about their commemorated relatives, either before or after their death. Inscriptions that do indicate some kind of emotional response stand out by their very rarity. One such is a stone from Sund (Sö 318) commissioned by two brothers to commemorate their dead father and sister. Of the father it is said that he drowned in a nearby lake, 'his death much lamented', but nothing is said of the manner of death of their sister or of any feelings it aroused in them. The stone from Eggeby (U 69), raised (along with a bridge) by a certain Ragnelf in memory of her son Anund, asks God to 'help his soul better than he deserved' and adds the poetic note:

Munu iki mirki	There will not be
miRi uirþa	a greater memorial,
muþir karþi iftir	mother made after
sun sin ainika.	her only son.

Here we are in a world which has accepted Christian concepts of sin and the sensibility we feel we detect in the lament of a mother for her only son may come from the same source.

Since the stones give us so little private information about either the commissioners or the commemorated, they are not good sources of information about the everyday lives of women in Viking Age Sweden, although just enough glimpses are provided to make us wish we had more. Thus a couple of stones, both erected by widowers, praise their dead wives. The stone at Saleby (Vg 67) merely says that Thora was 'best among people'. The inscription on the stone from Hassmyra (Vs 24), however, contains a verse in praise of Odindis (the only verse on a

Swedish stone commemorating a woman). The whole inscription may be translated as follows:

> The good farmer Holmgaut had this raised in memory of his wife Odindis.
>
>> A better housewife
>> will never come
>> to Hassmyra
>> to run the farm.
>> Red Balli carved
>> these runes.
>> She was a good sister
>> to Sigmund.

A Viking Age 'housewife' had of course a wider range of responsibilities than her modern counterpart, for she was in charge of all the work that went on indoors (and certain types of outdoor work near the main buildings as well), which included the production of food and textiles from raw materials. But women's as well as men's work was presumably so taken for granted that it was not thought necessary to mention it in memorial inscriptions. We rarely catch a glimpse of Viking Age men's work in the runic inscriptions either. The expression *boandi góðr* ('a good farmer') used of many a commemorated man is no more than a conventional formula of introduction and not necessarily a judgement on his farming practices. When we do meet men engaged in activities, it is in activities which are out of the ordinary, they are steering ships, feeding eagles and amassing gold abroad.

Women's role in producing the next generation is of course implicit in all the inscriptions. Not all inscriptions are necessarily commissioned by one family member in memory of another, there are for example some commissioned by men in memory of their 'fellows', i.e. trading partners or companions on viking expeditions. But where women are concerned, runic inscriptions are strictly a family affair. It is not surprising to find more mothers and wives in runic inscriptions than sisters and daughters, for a woman's reproductive role could only be fulfilled in her husband's family and not in her own. But beyond this basic fact, only a very few runic inscriptions give us clues as to how childbirth and child-rearing impinged on the lives of women. The inscription at Hillersjö and related ones have suggested the possibility of high infant and child mortality. Of the four or more children whose birth is mentioned in this one inscription only one, Inga, survived to adulthood and even she was

Runestone from Gripsholm, Södermanland, Sweden.

outlived by her mother. That such high mortality rates need not always be the case is demonstrated by the many inscriptions in which four or more children (with or without another relative) commission a monument in memory of a parent or sibling. The fact that nowhere near as many daughters are mentioned in these inscriptions as sons suggests

Runestone from Hassmyra, Västmanland, Sweden.

that families were often even larger, not counting those children who did not survive at least to early adulthood.

The inscriptions never mention the age of the person being commemorated, nor do any specify that a woman died in childbirth, but it is certain that some women at least died in this way. The problems caused when a woman died before her children were grown are suggested by the rather plaintive inscription commissioned by a husband in memory of his wife on a stone at Ardre in Gotland (G 111), 'she died young from the helpless'. Other fatal dangers occasionally crop up in the inscriptions. Thus a stone from Näsby (U 455) tells us that it was erected by a certain Ingifast in memory of his father and mother, both of whom drowned. Unfortunately it does not tell us where they drowned, so we cannot tell whether Gunnhild was on a longer journey with her husband, or whether they drowned in some local lake on their way to church.

Christianity

The examples of runic inscriptions given above are already enough to suggest the close links between eleventh-century Swedish runestones and Christianity. The vast majority of the stones contain either a prayer formula in the inscription or a cross incorporated into the design of the stone, and very often both. The sheer number of these stones suggests an obvious link between the fashion for erecting them and the introduction of Christianity to Sweden. We have already seen that neither the heroic ethos nor the links the runic script had with the (pagan) past inhibited its use on these Christian monuments. Of course we have monuments that predate Christianity, or are unaffected by it, or even ones that are clearly pagan, both in Sweden and elsewhere, but they are not comparable in number or distribution with the Christian monuments of eleventh-century Sweden.

The introduction of Christianity had great consequences for Scandinavian society. As one of the factors which contributed to the transition to the medieval period, it opens up an enormous set of problems relating to the history of the Viking Age. But here we must first ask the more restricted question of the nature of Christianity in eleventh-century Sweden, especially as it related to women. Are the Christian aspects of the runestones purely superficial, or do they reflect strongly held religious convictions? If the latter, did these convictions affect society in any way that altered the lives of women, compared with the heathen period? And are these changes actually reflected in the runic inscriptions themselves, or can they merely be guessed at?

Runic inscriptions that give us clear answers to these questions are very rare. One that does is on a stone, now unfortunately lost, from Stäket (U 605). The inscription is of the slightly unusual, although not unique, type in which the commissioner has the monument made to her- or himself. This commissioner is a woman, described as 'Ingirun (?), daughter of Hord' and the inscription states that she 'intends to travel east, and to Jerusalem'. Clearly the woman who commissioned this stone was going on a pilgrimage and not sure that she would return. Although she may have commissioned the monument herself because she had no living relatives to erect one in her memory in case she did not return, the actual purpose of this inscription may have been different from that of most runestones. Ingirun wished to proclaim her personal piety as much as to be remembered after her death. This inscription shows new opportunities available to women with the introduction of Christianity. Although we cannot know from runestones alone to what extent women were able to make long journeys, especially abroad, before the conversion, we can say for certain that the new Christianity did offer women the chance to go on pilgrimages, even abroad. It was, at the very least, a broadening of their opportunities.

Ingirun could proclaim her piety by going on pilgrimage, and there were other ways of letting the world know that you were a good Christian. The making of 'bridges' (often causeways or fords, rather than bridges in the usual sense) as a public service has already been mentioned. This activity could however also be a symbolic, Christian, act. Thus while many inscriptions state that the commissioners raised a stone and made a bridge in memory of whoever was to be commemorated, a few are more explicit. A stone from Morby (U 489) proclaims that 'Gullaug had a bridge made for the soul of her daughter Gillaug, whom Ulf had to wife' and the design incorporates a cross. In the same way as a bridge aided travel in this world, so making one for the deceased could symbolically help their soul into the next world. In building a bridge, therefore, a social and a spiritual act went hand in hand. Whether all the 'bridges' recorded in runic inscriptions were actually built, or whether the runestone itself was considered a kind of symbolic bridge, cannot be determined in every case. But it is likely that many new bridges were built, or old ones repaired, in eleventh-century Sweden.

As most of the Swedish runestones come from a relatively short period in the eleventh century, we do not normally have a time span long enough in which to observe any changes in religious beliefs, even where we have a group of runestones covering several generations of a family. Thus the 'Jarlabanki' stones, a group of 16 stones erected by various members of Jarlabanki's family in memory of their relatives

(including six commissioned by Jarlabanki to commemorate himself)
are Christian right through four generations of the family. But the stones
of this group are relatively late and we are justified in looking at some
earlier stones to see whether there is any sign of religious change.

Two stones from Råsta (U 77–8) commemorate two generations of one
family. The first one was raised by Holmstein and his brother (or sister?)
Hosvi along with their mother Gyrid in memory of their father Jobjørn.
On this stone the band containing the inscription dissolves into a complex interlace serpent. There is no cross anywhere nor is there any religious reference in the inscription. The second stone was erected by Hosvi
and his (or her) two sisters in memory of their brother Holmstein. It also
has an interlace serpent design, but this one does contain a cross. Although the absence of any overt signs of Christianity is not proof that
the commissioners or the commemorated of the first stone were not
Christian, it is nevertheless possible that this family's religious preferen-
ces changed between the deaths of the father Jobjørn and the son
Holmstein.

Norway

Although Norway has runic inscriptions from the whole period of runic
writing, from some of the earliest right through to the medieval ones
recently discovered in Bergen and Trondheim, it does not have anything
like the number of Viking Age stones raised in memory of the dead as
are found in Sweden, where it was clearly a temporary and local
fashion. Many of the Norwegian runestones are not even memorials to
the dead but inscriptions recording boundaries or other legal matters.
Of the thirty-eight raised stones with the standard formula of 'A erected
this stone in memory of X', six are so worn or fragmentary that we
cannot any longer decipher the names or sex or family relationships of
the commissioners and the commemorated. Of the remaining thirty-
two, however, seven inscriptions mention women and in six of these the
women are either the sole commissioners of the monument or the person being commemorated. What they lack in numbers, these stones
make up for in interest, particularly the four which were commissioned
by women, both for their inscriptions and their decoration.

The stones from Alstad (no. 61) and Dynna (no. 68) are two of the
most important runic monuments from late Viking Age Norway. Both
stood until at least the end of the last century on the spot where they

were first erected at some time in the eleventh century, on the farms of Alstad (on the shores of Lake Mjøsa, near the modern town of Gjøvik) and Dynna (near Gran, about 50 km south-south-west of Alstad).

The stone at Alstad is the older one and has two inscriptions, one clearly contemporary with the raising and decorating of the stone, the other added later. The first inscription records that:

Jorunn raised this stone after . . ., who had her to wife and [she] brought [it, i.e. the stone] from Ringerike, out of Ulvøya

and the stone will honour
them both.

The stone is covered in both abstract and figurative ornament, the figures being horses, with and without riders, dogs (or wolves?) and birds. Although difficult to interpret exactly, the iconography does suggest praise of the dead, as a huntsman, perhaps as a warrior. Neither the inscription nor the decoration has any Christian characteristics. The most interesting thing about the inscription is the information it gives about the provenance of the stone. The place has been identified as the small island of Ulvøya in the Tyrifjord, near the modern town of Høne-foss, in other words a good 100 km south-west of Alstad itself, across some quite difficult, mountainous terrain. Clearly a woman who could organise and pay for the transport across this distance and carving of a stone nearly three metres long was a rich and powerful widow.

The stone from Dynna has many similarities with Alstad, and yet it is a thoroughly Christian monument. This is only one of several reasons why it has been dated to a generation or so later than the Alstad stone. It is made from the same red sandstone, probably also from Ringerike (although the inscription gives no clues to its provenance), it is also tall, narrow and flat, and carved with figures on one of its broad faces, with the runic inscription along the narrow edge. It was also raised by a woman, this time in memory of her daughter:

Gunnvor Thidrik's daughter made a bridge in memory of her daughter Astrid,

she was the handiest maiden
in Hadeland.

Both inscriptions give the information about commissioner and commemorated in normal prose, but conclude with a metrical tag. But there

71

the similarities end. With Gunnvor's bridge-building we are in the realm of Christian acts and this is reinforced by the iconography of the stone which depicts the birth of Christ and the adoration of the Magi. We do not know what particular skills Astrid had to make her the 'handiest maiden in Hadeland', or why this particular scene should be chosen for her memorial. A possible explanation is that Astrid was particularly good at weaving or embroidery and that the figures were copied from a tapestry that she made in her lifetime.

Other eleventh-century Norwegian stones that mention women follow the pattern with which we are familiar, without adding much of especial interest. A stone from Gran church (no. 66), very near Dynna, was raised by a woman called Steinvor in memory of her husband Onund. It is remarkable that these three monuments commissioned by women (of four in the whole of Norway) come from such a small area in eastern Norway, where it may have been a local fashion. Two stones from the west of Norway, Klepp (no. 225) and Stavanger (no. 251) were both raised by men in memory of their wives, and one from the south coast, Skollevoll (213) was raised by a wife in memory of her husband.

The Isle of Man

The twenty-six or so Viking Age runic memorials from the Isle of Man are unusual in several respects. The first is their sheer number for such a small island, compared to less than forty in Norway, the country whose stones they most nearly resemble. Secondly, their Christianity is even more pronounced than on mainland Scandinavian stones. Most are either cross-shaped or are a slab with an incised cross and the inscriptions refer to raising 'a cross' and not 'a stone'. Finally, the names and occasionally the language of the inscriptions show Celtic influence. On the whole, the Manx stones are also earlier than the Swedish and Norwegian ones, being roughly contemporary with many Danish runestones. It is clear that the runic crosses of Man are not a purely Norse phenomenon but a result of the Celtic-Norse cultural mix that took place on the island following Norse settlement there.

The inscriptions, too, differ when we look at them more closely. Although most of them follow the familiar formula 'A raised this cross in memory of X . . .' (as Ray Page put it, 'they apply a common Norse formula of commemoration, with a common Celtic variation of wording'), we find a different selection of commissioners and commemorated.

Rune-inscribed cross-slab from Kirk
Michael, Isle of Man. erected by Joalf in
memory of his mother Friða.

Runestone from
Alstad, Oppland,
Norway.

Of the twenty-six Manx runestones that have an inscription long and clear enough to be interpreted, eight indubitably mention women. This is a fairly high proportion, considering that three others are so fragmentary that none of the names can be deciphered and yet three more, while preserving one male name, are also only fragments with the other names lost. Any of these could also have contained women's names in the inscription. However, unlike inscriptions from Denmark, Sweden and Norway, none of these women are described as commissioners of the stone, or are mentioned in passing as relatives of the commemorated. Instead, all eight stones that mention women are in fact memorials to dead women: one mother, one fostermother, one daughter and five wives. Most of the inscriptions are laconic and give only the barest information about the commissioner and the commemorated. Only a stone from Kirk Michael is more expansive and has the inscription:

> Mallymkun raised this cross in memory of his foster[mother] Malmury, the daughter of Tufkal, the wife of Adils. It is better to leave a good foster son than a bad son.

This inscription demonstrates the Celtic influence on Man very clearly, since all of the persons mentioned have Celtic names except for Adils, the husband of the commemorated woman. Yet apart from the names, the inscription is entirely in Norse, although it is in such grammatically poor Norse that the exact interpretation of the inscription is precarious and the one given above is only one possibility.

It would be invidious to draw any conclusions about the position of women in Viking Age Manx society on the basis of a mere eight runic inscriptions. Yet it is worth noting the lack of female commissioners and therefore the lack of any positive evidence that women were able to control finances and act publicly by ordering memorial stones. And although the proportion of stones commemorating women is high enough to suggest a society which accorded a certain respect to women, there is no evidence that it accorded them any power to go with that respect.

CHAPTER III

Female Colonists

THE EVIDENCE OF NAMES

Scandinavian women in England

Memorial stones with runic inscriptions are important documents that record the names and some of the details of the lives of women in the Viking Age. Although the stones are geographically unevenly spread and are overwhelmingly from the late Viking Age, and although only a minority of them mention women, they remain by far the most important quasi-documentary sources for the history of women in the Viking Age. There is nothing quite like them outside Scandinavia. The annals and chronicles that are our main contemporary sources for the activities of vikings outside Scandinavia have little to say about women. But a careful study of other types of documents from countries affected by vikings can tell us something. In practice, this means England, where we have a variety of sources, both from the Anglo-Saxon period and later.

To identify Scandinavian women in documents from other countries we would expect to rely on finding references to women with obviously Scandinavian names. This, however, is an unreliable procedure. Names are vulnerable to fashion and a Scandinavian name does not necessarily indicate that a particular person is Scandinavian or even has some Scandinavian ancestry. But when we do find a large number of Scandinavian names in a particular area where we have other evidence of Scandinavian influence, we can at least assume that such names are the result of immigration. Usually, the documents containing such names are from a later period and therefore do not represent the original immigrants. Instead, what we have is evidence of the mixed population descended from both the native English and the incoming Scandinavians.

Domesday book, compiled for William after his conquest of England, records for much of the country the ownership of land as it was in the time of his predecessor, Edward, providing invaluable material for the study of both personal and place names in eleventh-century England. In it we find female landowners bearing names of Scandinavian origin. These names are most numerous in the eastern half of the country, particularly Yorkshire and Lincolnshire. This is precisely where, as we know from other evidence, there was a substantial settlement of Scandinavian immigrants.

Where we find Scandinavian names in other parts of the country such as the south and west, this reflects the settlement of a few people of high social status during the reign of the Danish king Cnut (1016–35). These are likely to have come over in his train and their relative frequency simply reflects the fact that high ranking people are more likely to show up in documents. Where Scandinavian name giving is an effect of large scale immigration in an earlier period, it is noticeable that there is a much wider range of such names.

For instance, the very common Scandinavian name of *Gunnhild(r)* was borne by several of King Cnut's female relatives, including his sister and daughter, and was therefore fashionable in eleventh-century England. We find it recorded seven times (although some of these references may be to the same person) in *Domesday book*, for the counties of Sussex, Essex and Somerset. These represent either English women given a fashionable name, or else women who were members of a few landowning families established by Cnut in areas where there was previously no Scandinavian element in the population. The popularity of this name persisted after the Conquest and there are quite a few examples from twelfth- and thirteenth-century sources in the south-west.

In contrast, while those areas of the country where there was a sizeable Scandinavian element in the population do not provide any examples of *Gunnhildr* from *Domesday book*, they give us most of the available evidence for female Scandinavian names. In his study of the personal names of *Domesday book*, von Feilitzen recorded 21 female Scandinavian names – of these, 16 occur only in Yorkshire, Lincolnshire or East Anglia, while the other 5, which are more widespread, include popular aristocratic names such as *Gunnhildr*, *Gunnvǫr* and *Gyða*. The relative scarcity of female names in *Domesday book* is explained by the fact that women were less likely to be landowners: von Feilitzen found well over 400 male names of Scandinavian origin in *Domesday book*.

Although the Domesday material is limited, it can be supplemented with evidence from a later period. Documents from the twelfth and thirteenth centuries show that a range of Scandinavian names, both male and female, were still in use in Yorkshire and Lincolnshire, in most social groups (this material shows that *Gunnhildr* was in fact the most popular Scandinavian name in Lincolnshire and Yorkshire, followed by *Sigríðr, Ragnhildr* and *Gunnvǫr*). By this time, we are dealing with a thoroughly Anglicised population, but the persistence of Scandinavian names shows how deep the Scandinavian influence went.

The *Liber vitae* of Thorney Abbey (Cambs.), a list of people in confraternity with the monks, compiled in the eleventh to thirteenth centuries, contains around 660 different names, 123 of them Scandinavian in origin. At least 20 of these are women's names, the most popular is again *Gunnhildr*, but there are multiple examples of *Ása, Bóthildr, Gunnvǫr* and *Ragnhildr*. These names are most likely to be the names of persons resident in the region.

Personal names in place names

The exact history of the Scandinavian immigration to eastern England which gave rise to this influence has been hotly disputed by scholars of the Viking Age and has not been resolved yet. The unanswered question is the scale on which this immigration took place, with the most important evidence being the distribution, density and type of place names with Scandinavian elements thought to have been given as a result of this immigration. The answer has consequences for the history of women. If the Scandinavian immigration to England was on a small scale, a matter of members of the viking armies of the ninth century staying behind and controlling areas with a largely native population, it is not likely that many (if any) Scandinavian women were included in this immigration. If, on the other hand, there was large scale secondary migration in the wake of the initial settlement by members of the armies, then this must have included women. Although viking immigrants may have taken English women as wives, demographic pressures would mean that a large influx of males would have to be accompanied by at least some female immigration.

There are no sources which can definitively solve the question of female immigration from Scandinavia, particularly in the earliest period, but a study of place names gives some clues. Many of the Scandinavian place names of eastern England contain a personal name as the first element, combined with a typically Scandinavian second element such as -by or -thorpe. In most cases, the personal name is a male one, but occasionally we find such place names compounded with female personal names. This suggests that the place at one time had a female owner or tenant with that name (although the exact reasons why places came to be named after people are not always certain). Thus, both Yorkshire and Lincolnshire have places now called Raventhorpe. Early spellings of these (*Rag[h]eneltorp*, *Ragnildtorp*) indicate that the first element was originally the woman's name *Ragnhildr*. We cannot know when these place names were first given, it could have been at any time between the late ninth and the late eleventh century. There are very few place names with female personal name elements recorded as early as *Domesday book*, often the first notation of such names is in documents from a much later period, so that the original form of the name has to be reconstructed.

Given that Scandinavian personal names continued to be popular throughout and after the viking period, the possibility cannot be excluded that some of these names are later creations and do not reflect actual female immigrants from Scandinavia. Nevertheless, in her study of Lincolnshire and Yorkshire, Gillian Fellows Jensen identified 57 place names containing 28 different Scandinavian female personal names. Only nine of these place names are recorded in *Domesday book* and only one any earlier. Seventeen of the personal names are recorded only in place names, suggesting that these are mainly early place names, given before the personal names went out of fashion. Most of the sites seem to have been marginal and many became depopulated, so that the names were often preserved only in field names or other minor names. This suggests that there were other such names that have disappeared from the historical record. In the ninth to eleventh centuries, women are likely to have become tenants or landlords only in unusual circumstances and even then this may not necessarily have been reflected in the place name. Given this, both the place name evidence and the wide range of Scandinavian female names preserved in all sources (Fellows Jensen counts 57 different names in Lincolnshire and Yorkshire) are perfectly compatible with the suggestion that there was female immigration from Scandinavia to England. Some of these women may have come with the invading viking armies in the ninth century. But it is more likely that they formed a part of the peaceful migration that took place in the wake of these armies, both in the tenth century and in the reign of Cnut.

THE SETTLEMENT OF ICELAND

England was a highly developed and densely populated country at the time of the Scandinavian settlements. Iceland, on the other hand, was completely empty, except for a few Irish hermits who, their main aim being to get away from it all, promptly took flight when the first Norse colonists arrived in the ninth century. Along with the Faroes, Iceland was the only uninhabited country settled by Scandinavians in the Viking Age. The colonists must have included women, if the colony was to survive into the next generation.

As there was no one in Iceland to observe the arrival of the Scandinavians, we have no contemporary accounts to describe how they did it. But the settlement of Iceland was one of the great adventures of the Viking Age and, later on, the Icelanders romanticised their ancestors' discovery and settlement of the country. This is a recurrent theme in their literature of the thirteenth century, particularly the Sagas of Icelanders, which give a heavily mythologised view of the settlement. Many of the settlers are said to have left Norway to escape the tyranny of the Norwegian king, Haraldr Finehair. They are almost always shown as highborn Norwegians, full of bravery and a sense of adventure. For these reasons the sagas cannot be considered reliable sources for the earliest history of Iceland and the process of settlement in an uninhabited land. Yet the fact that, in the thirteenth century, the Icelanders were still writing about what had happened nearly three centuries earlier shows that the sagas were based on historical traditions that sprang from those events. Although we do not have any Icelandic writings from the period of the settlement, we do have later recordings of those traditions which preserve some relevant facts. The Icelanders were the great historians of Scandinavia and some of their earliest historical writings, beginning in the early twelfth century, were about their own history.

For the history of the settlement, the two most important texts to come out of this Icelandic historical school were *Íslendingabók* ('The book of the Icelanders') and *Landnámabók* ('The book of the settlements').

Íslendingabók was probably the most influential work written in medieval Iceland, for it was the first example of historical writing in the vernacular at which the Icelanders were later to excel. Unlike most other Icelandic works, for this we know the name of the author (Ari Þorgilsson) and the approximate date at which it was written (in the 1120s). The work gives a reliable picture of the settlement of Iceland and its early history, and was widely used by later writers, both medieval and modern. Its main drawback is its brevity: the settlement of Iceland is described in just a few hundred words. Nevertheless, Ari lists the four most important settlers of Iceland, one for each of the four quarters of the country. One of these is a woman, Auðr, the daughter of Ketill Flatnose, a Norwegian chieftain, who settled in Breiðafjörður in the west of Iceland. *Íslendingabók* tells us no more about her than these facts (although we can deduce from some genealogies at the end of the work that she was an ancestor of the author).

Luckily, we have *Landnámabók* to help fill out our picture of the female settlers of Iceland. *Landnámabók* is a catalogue of all the first settlers of Iceland. These settlers are arranged in clockwise fashion around the island, according to the location of their settlement, which is usually described in some detail, along with information about the origins of the settler and his or her genealogy, both backwards and forwards. Occasionally we are given little anecdotes about events in which the settlers or members of their family were involved.

The earliest version of *Landnámabók* was based on the same sort of historical and genealogical information as that available to Ari Þorgilsson and it is likely that he was involved in the historical researches that led to its being written, if not in writing it himself. Unfortunately we no longer have this earliest version of *Landnámabók* from the twelfth century, we have instead five later redactions of the text, from the thirteenth and later centuries, all much expanded and revised in different ways. The complicated textual history of *Landnámabók* makes it very difficult to use as a historical source, although the temptation is great, since it purports to name a large proportion of the earliest inhabitants of Iceland and where they lived. Thus many of the anecdotes are taken from thirteenth-century literary works or local folklore and most scholars dismiss these as later accretions to the text, with no independent historical value. Even in the core material, some of the names of people and places were probably invented or creatively deduced by the zealous historians of the twelfth and thirteenth centuries. For instance, when *Landnámabók* tells us that a woman called Arnbjǫrg lived at a place called Arnbjargarlœkr, we are faced with deciding whether the compilers of *Landnámabók* had reliable information about this woman who really existed and after whom the place was named, or whether they simply had the place name and deduced her existence from that. Like modern scholars, the Icelandic historians reasoned that a place name containing a personal name element must have been named after a person with that name, but that does not mean they knew anything about that person.

Despite such difficulties, the overall picture we get from *Landnámabók* must be correct, even if it is possible to discount some of the details. This shows us not only that large numbers of women were among the settlers of Iceland, but also that in certain circumstances they too could be primary settlers and not just a part of a man's bag and baggage, along with the children, slaves and cattle.

Landnámabók lists well over four hundred such primary settlers: heads of households who are described as the person who 'took land' at such and such a place. The vast majority of these are male. A typical chapter describing a settler will tell us that:

> Geirmundr, the son of Gunnbjǫrn gandr, took the peninsula between Norðrá and Sandá, and lived at Tunga; his son was Brúni, the father of Þorbjǫrn at Steinar, who fell in the Heiðarvíg battle.

In this, and in many similar chapters, we simply do not know how Geirmundr came over to Iceland, whether it was on his own or with a ready made household. That he had a wife at some stage is implied by the fact that he had a son, but we cannot know whether she came with him, or whether he married her after his arrival. Since there are plenty of women mentioned elsewhere in *Landnámabók*, we have to assume it was not lack of interest but lack of information that led the early compilers to leave out the names of the wives of so many of the first settlers.

But often they had this information, so that in under a quarter of cases (around ninety settlers), we are told the name of the wife of a first settler. Sometimes it is made clear that the wife accompanied her husband from his former homeland, sometimes that they married in Iceland, in many cases there is no information. But we do often get an idea of husband and wife emigrating to Iceland in partnership:

> Eyvindr kné and his wife Þuríðr rumgylta went from Agder [in Norway] to Iceland; they claimed Álptafjörður and Seyðisfjörður and lived there.

In a few cases we find sisters settling in Iceland in company with their brothers, or mothers with their sons. Usually, the sisters are young and later marry, while the mothers are old and widowed.

In thirteen instances we are told of a first settler who was a woman. Some of these are women who came over with a brother or brothers, but unlike other examples of sibling settlers, they are listed separately as the first settler in a particular place, which often bears their name:

> Hildir and Hallgeirr and their sister Ljót came from the British Isles; they went to Iceland and claimed land between Fljótr and Rangá. . . Hildir lived in Hildisey. . . Hallgeirr lived in Hallgeirsey . . . and Ljót lived at Ljótarstaðir.

Other women became settlers by default, such as Þorgerðr, whose husband died at sea. She arrived in Iceland with her sons and claimed land in southern Iceland.

But women could also take the initiative in emigrating to Iceland, as Ásgerðr Asksdóttir seems to have done. Her husband Ófeigr had an altercation with King Haraldr Finehair of Norway and was killed by the king's henchmen. Ásgerðr took their children and her half-brother off to Iceland and settled there. That it was her brother who was under her protection rather than the other way around is shown by the next chapter which says that he claimed land 'with her consent'. She later married another settler.

None of the women listed above is mentioned anywhere besides *Landnámabók*. But the most famous female settler of Iceland is known from a variety of literary texts, many of which are highly fictional. Auðr, daughter of Ketill Flatnose, is mentioned in *Íslendingabók*. She is best known from the opening chapters of *Laxdœla saga*, which describe her adventures in the British Isles, and her settlement and early years in Iceland. Many of these sources differ in detail, yet we are left with a fairly clear picture of her achievement. Auðr became a legendary figure in thirteenth-century Iceland and she is accorded a corresponding amount of space in *Landnámabók*, as well as being included in the list there of the 'noblest' settlers of western Iceland.

According to *Landnámabók*, Auðr was the daughter of the Norwegian chieftain Ketill flatnose who went to the Hebrides as an agent for King Haraldr Finehair. She married a Norse king of Dublin, who was killed in battle in Ireland. Her son Þorsteinn was killed fighting in Scotland. Auðr's two main projects were then to leave for Iceland and to marry off Þorsteinn's many daughters. She prepared a ship in secret and twenty free men accompanied her. She married off a granddaughter each in Orkney and the Faroes, and arrived in Iceland where two of her brothers were already living. Her retinue was so large that the first brother only felt able to invite half of it to stay. Offended, Auðr went to stay with her other brother. The following spring she went to look for a place to settle in Breiðafjörður and a number of the place names of that area are explained by little anecdotes to do with her, such as that Kambsnes ('Comb headland') is so called because she lost her comb there. Auðr chose to live at Hvammur, where she raised a cross, because she was a good Christian, although her descendants later relapsed. In this district, she distributed land to her shipmates and freed slaves, and the remaining granddaughters were married. Finally, we are given a detailed description of her death. She invited all her relatives to a magnificent feast. After three nights, she gave everyone gifts and good advice, saying the feast should continue another three nights, so that it could be her funeral feast. She then died and was buried on the seashore, as she had not wanted to be buried in unconsecrated earth.

However much of this we choose to believe, it is clear that Auðr was an exceptional woman. Although there were probably few, if any, other female settlers quite like her, she shows the maximum a woman could achieve in the socially turbulent times of the Viking Age. Deprived of the support of both husband and son, she had to take initiatives and undertake a male role if she was to get her family to Iceland. Having done so, she clearly commanded respect. In the more settled societies of the Norway they came from and Iceland as it became, women probably had fewer opportunities to play any role other than those of wife, mother and housekeeper. But in the brief interval between leaving Norway and arriving in Iceland, some women clearly had to be more. There is no doubt that Auðr took advantage of the greater opportunities and fewer social constraints in the Norse colonies of the British Isles and that the later stories and legends about her, however romanticised, preserve a true picture of the possibilities opened up for women in the upheaval of the viking movements.

CHAPTER IV

Foreign Views

INTERNATIONAL CONTACT IN THE VIKING AGE

Viking expansion

International contact is the key to the Viking Age. In Scandinavian history this period is distinct because large numbers of Scandinavian people left their homelands and voyaged abroad. Some of these voyages were temporary expeditions to amass wealth which was brought back to Scandinavia, others led to permanent settlements abroad, whether as immigrants in countries with a substantial native population, such as England, or as pioneer settlers in hitherto uninhabited or sparsely inhabited lands, such as Iceland. The period is thus defined by the impact the Scandinavians had on the world around them, an impact that was greater than at any time before or since. Some of the impressions the expansionist vikings made can be found in the writings of the people they came into contact with.

This cosmopolitan contact worked both ways. As the Scandinavians found their way out into the world, so the world found out about Scandinavia and some of it even found its way there. References to Scandinavia in sources written before the Viking Age are few and often reveal more ignorance than knowledge. But in the Viking Age, Europe woke up to its northern neighbours and even people further away, such as the Arabs, established contact. Once the Scandinavians were better known, the Church would want to convert them, rulers would want to establish diplomatic contact and merchants would want to trade with them. Such churchmen, rulers and merchants provide us with rare but valuable glimpses of early Scandinavian life.

Most of the foreign sources refer to women at some point in their accounts of vikings, although these references are most often fleeting. There is no source that is both detailed and reliable in its description of women. And since the foreign sources are of widely differing type, function, date, place of origin and general reliability, they cannot simply be pieced together to provide a composite picture of women's roles in the activities which characterised the Viking Age. A brief survey of these sources will not only indicate the differences between them, but also emphasise the wide variety of peoples and places in contact with the vikings and of the nature of those contacts. It should also make clear the special problems these sources pose for understanding the history of women in the Viking Age.

The sources

The sources available for the study of the interactions between vikings and other peoples range from nearly contemporary and more or less reliable annals recording viking attacks, to fanciful accounts which may or may not be describing Scandinavians or vikings, written up to four centuries later for the purposes of political or religious propaganda, or even just entertainment. It is important to remember that, because of these differences, the type of information about women that can be extracted from these sources varies enormously. Indeed, the only thing that all the sources to be considered in this chapter have in common is that they record a non-Scandinavian view of the Viking Age.

The earliest foreign sources we have, such as the annals, have nothing exactly comparable in the Scandinavian material, since there was no tradition of chronicles of contemporary events in Scandinavia during the Viking Age. Only some skaldic poetry can be compared with them, in being contemporary and in dealing with public events, and the same might be said of many runic inscriptions, although there the emphasis is much more personal. At the other extreme, some of our foreign accounts are most like the later Scandinavian sources, particularly the sagas produced in Iceland in the thirteenth century and later. These, although dealing with the Viking Age and ultimately based on events that took place then, present a romanticised view of the past that tells us perhaps more about the time in which they were written than about the time about which they purport to write.

Thus, at one extreme we have Frankish annals from the ninth century which have been called 'the fullest and most varied contemporary written evidence' for viking history. At the other extreme, also purporting to be about ninth-century events, we have the twelfth/thirteenth century Spaniard Ibn Diḥya's account of al-Ghazāl's embassy to a viking court, which has been dismissed by many scholars as a romantic fabrication.

Even within this range, sources that seem to be equivalent may have a variable usefulness. We have annals describing viking attacks from England and Ireland as well as Frankia. Many of these, although ultimately deriving from contemporary records, are in fact much later compilations. Thus, one of the most important of the Irish texts, the *Annals of Ulster*, exists in a fifteenth-century version. The painstaking source criticism which must decide how such texts can be used for historical study is not always completed, nor do scholars always agree on its conclusions. Even where years of study have produced some agreement on which parts of a composite text are contemporary, or if not contemporary, then how soon after the events they were written, we have to allow for other shortcomings in the historical value of the source. Although there is a fair amount of consensus about the development of the *Anglo-Saxon chronicle*, for instance, its account of the viking impact on two and a half centuries of English life is partial at best. Its view of the viking attacks of the ninth and tenth centuries is not only biased against the invading Scandinavians (like most other such annals), but also presented almost exclusively from the West Saxon point of view, so that there is a regional bias within the English bias of the text. The selection of events recorded is also a kind of bias, in that the *Chronicle* is concerned mainly with military and political matters. Settlement and trade are scarcely mentioned, if at all. Thus we have the paradox that the *Chronicle* tells us hardly anything about the area later known as Lincolnshire although this is the part of England that has by far the heaviest concentration of place-names of Scandinavian origin in the country, suggesting large-scale viking settlement. Such biases of course make the *Chronicle*, along with most of the other annals, a particularly thin source for women's history as women apparently played little or no part in the political and military events described.

Other works which at first glance resemble the annalistic sources may not be what they seem. The *Russian primary chronicle*, although it is arranged chronologically like the *Anglo-Saxon chronicle*, is a twelfth-century compilation that cannot depend on contemporary written sources for its account of the Viking Age for the simple reason that they were unknown then among the illiterate Slavs and semi-literate Rūs.

Apart from such historiographical considerations, we must remember other ways in which our sources could fail to provide the information we are looking for. There is, for instance, the question of language. How did our foreign authorities communicate with the vikings they met, how did they know who they were, what they were, where they came from? Presumably the vikings themselves were adaptable and soon learned the language or languages of the areas they visited or settled in. In places like England, where there was contact with a relatively large number of vikings over a long period of time, continually refreshed by new arrivals, the inhabitants may have learned some of the language of the incomers. Where neither the vikings nor the people they came in contact with knew each others' language, they must have made use of interpreters. But communication through an interpreter can be a tricky business. This is particularly important in reading the sources in Arabic, which more than once make mention of interpreters. We have to be particularly wary of information that was transmitted first through an interpreter, then subjected to the vagaries of revision and adaptation of the text. Much of Ibn Faḍlān's eyewitness account of the Rūs he met on the Volga is dependent on the understanding granted him by an interpreter. Some of the things he describes he could not have seen, he must have been told about them, either by his interpreter, or by someone else talking through an interpreter. Even those scenes which he witnessed could not always have made sense to him unless they were explained by someone who knew what was happening.

Unfortunately we know nothing about these interpreters. Was Ibn Faḍlān's interpreter a Rūs of Scandinavian origin? If so, was his Arabic (or indeed, whatever third language they might have communicated in) good enough to explain ideas and concepts so foreign to the culture of his interlocutor? Or was the interpreter an Arab (or Khazar, or whatever)? In which case, did he really understand the ceremonies he was explaining and the system of belief which lay behind them? Such questions will never be answered, but the doubts they raise must be borne in mind as we read these fascinating texts.

Such considerations apply to all uses of these sources, but there are additional ones which come into play when we examine the sources in order to write a history of women. Thus the high frequency of references to sex and divorce in Arabic sources may tell us as much about the position of women in Islamic societies as it does about the seemingly macho world of vikings.

A problem in writing the history of 'viking women' is to know whether they were Scandinavians or not. The sources rarely if ever tell us the nationality of the 'viking' women they are describing. Was the average viking's companion a Scandinavian woman brought from home, or was she picked up somewhere en route? If the latter, was she a local woman, or was she a slave from a far-off land? It is likely that all of these were possibilities, but it is frustrating not to know in individual cases.

There is in principle no reason why Scandinavian women could not accompany their men on journeys abroad, they certainly did on journeys of emigration, such as to Iceland. On the other hand, it is unlikely that bands of warriors would actually set out with women on their first annual expeditions of raiding and plunder. Later on, when viking armies became more settled and established bases abroad, they would have a place where they could keep their women and children in safety, as we find in several of our sources. Those vikings who were primarily traders and who dealt in slaves would normally travel with a large company of women. Presumably, while most of these slaves would be sold, some became the companions of their captors, either temporarily or sometimes permanently, perhaps even going back home to Scandinavia with them. The story of the Irish princess Melkorka in *Laxdœla saga*, although a romantic fiction, is what may very well have happened to many young women of all nationalities captured by vikings (or indeed by other slave traders active at that time). Some well-born girls were luckier, like two Moroccan sisters who were captured by and then ransomed from vikings in 858/9.

It would be unwise to draw too many firm conclusions from the foreign sources for viking activities abroad, because of their selective bias. The European annalists are mainly concerned with military activities, the Arab geographers with describing slave traders. But it can be said that these foreign sources do not provide any clearcut evidence that Scandinavian women participated in the great viking adventures overseas. We must look to other types of evidence, such as archaeology and place-names, for that. On the other hand, the accounts of those foreign travellers who visited Scandinavia are oddly enough full of women. The problems of interpreting these accounts should not obscure the fact that Scandinavian women could make a strong impression on men from other cultures.

VISITORS TO SCANDINAVIA

St Ansgar

The earliest viking raids on western Europe brought the heathen Scandinavians into contact with the Christian religion from the late eighth century onwards. The Scandinavians who settled in Christian countries were soon converted, while the full conversion of their homelands, Denmark, Norway and Sweden, took considerably longer, and was not complete until well into the eleventh century. Ultimately, it was English influence which played the greatest role in converting the Scandinavians, but some of the earliest missionary activity which attempted to convert the Scandinavians came from the continent.

Ansgar, a monk of Corvey in Saxony, later archbishop of Hamburg, and known as the 'Apostle of the North', first went as a missionary to Denmark in about 826. He had been chosen to go home with the petty king, Harald klak, who had been baptised along with his wife at Mainz as a condition of the Emperor Louis the Pious's support for his claim to rule Denmark. But Ansgar's main sphere of activity turned out to be in Sweden, at the trading town of Birka, where he went first in 829 at the request of King Björn, staying for a year and a half, and again in 852. His followers carried on the missionary work in the intervening period.

Ansgar's work is described at length in the *Vita Anskarii* by his associate and successor Rimbert, written in about 875 and clearly based on first-hand information from Ansgar himself and on Rimbert's own observations (for he had also visited Birka). As such, the *Vita* is an invaluable source, not only for early missionary activity in Scandinavia, but also because it provides much important information about daily life in one of the great emporia of the Viking Age. At the same time, it has to be remembered that the function of the text was primarily to glorify the life of St Ansgar and to illustrate certain religious principles.

Chapter 20 of the *Vita* relates how one of the Christian inhabitants of Birka, a woman by the name of Frideburg, refused to sacrifice to the heathen gods. The author quotes the speech with which she supposedly answered those wicked persons who urged her to sacrifice. In it she remembers the promise she made to Christ at her baptism to renounce other gods (indicating that she was an adult convert) and declares that Christ will reward her loyalty with good health and property. And indeed, she lives to a ripe old age. The *Vita* describes how she keeps a small container of wine in preparation for her last rites, which she instructs her daughter Catla to give her, as there was no priest in Birka at the time. But the priest Ardgar arrives, just in time to minister to Frideburg before she dies.

After Frideburg's death, her daughter Catla follows her mother's instructions to give away her accumulated wealth in alms in the Frisian trading town of Dorestad. In Dorestad, Catla distributes alms as advised by some pious women there, visits holy places and finds that her empty bag of money is one day miraculously replaced (minus four pennies which she had spent on wine to refresh herself and her companions!).

The chapter ends by mentioning Ardgar's departure from Sweden and the author's comment that his visit had been for the purpose of strengthening Frideburg's faith, recommending her to God's mercy at her death and allowing her to receive the last rites as she fervently desired.

The *Vita* does not normally concentrate on individual Christians in Birka, presumably because there were not that many – the mission had no real lasting effect. Frideburg and Catla were two of its real successes and that is why they are accorded such prominence in the account of Ansgar's missions. Otherwise, apart from mentioning that there were Christian slaves in Birka, the only other Christian discussed at length is the town's *praefectus* Herigarius (chs. 11 and 19). On Ansgar's second visit, at a meeting to decide whether to allow Christian practices, an old man makes a speech in which he notes that people used to go to Dorestad to learn the Christian religion and that they should therefore accept it when it came to them (ch. 27). The assembly agrees to allow Christian priests to practise. There is thus no overt suggestion in the *Vita* that Christianity had a greater appeal to women than to men, as we might suppose from the fact that two of the most prominent Christians in Birka were women. Christ is on the contrary presented as a very practical helper to all. In a stylised contest in which the heathens appeal to their gods and Herigarius appeals to Christ, a heavy rainfall avoids him but not the others, and the old man's speech at the assembly emphasises Christ's power to help those who pray to him. It has been argued that the individuals described were chosen by Rimbert primarily to illustrate 'the centrality of constancy in faith, which inspired Anskar'.

Although the themes of the *Vita* may be tendentious, we can trust many of the details used to expound them. What the Frideburg episode suggests to us, for instance, is that women could control considerable property in the trading town of Birka. The *Vita* mentions no husband (but Frideburg is called a *matrona*) and, although God is ultimately responsible for her accumulation of wealth, it is likely that his blessing merely ensured the prosperity of whatever trading activity she was already engaged in. What this could have been, we unfortunately cannot know.

While we may feel there are no more grounds for disbelieving in the existence of Frideburg and Catla than of any of the other Swedes mentioned in Rimbert's *Vita*, Adam of Bremen, writing his *History of the archbishops of Hamburg-Bremen* in the eleventh century, clearly did not share this view. Writing of Ansgar's mission in Book I, ch. 21, and citing the *Vita* as his authority, he states that Herigarius maintained Christianity *alone* during the years when Sweden was without a priest. But then Adam was prone to exaggeration, for he also claims that Herigarius saved 'many thousands' of pagans!

Ibrāhīm b. Ya'qūb al-Ṭurṭūshī

Viking Age trading towns were clearly meeting places for many different types of people and we owe another of our brief glimpses of viking women to a traveller called Ibrāhīm b. Ya'qūb. He was a native of Tortosa in Andalusia (Muslim Spain), probably a Jew, and travelled extensively in Europe in the tenth century. He may have been a merchant, or some kind of diplomat. His account of his travels unfortunately does not survive and, for information about the places he visited, we are dependent entirely on snippets used by later writers in Arabic. His brief encounter with vikings is preserved in a geographical work by al-Qazwīnī, who was based in Damascus in the thirteenth century, at we do not know how many removes from the original.

Ibrāhīm b. Ya'qūb visited 'a very large town on the coast of the Ocean', thought to have been Haithabu (the forerunner of modern Schleswig), one of the most important trading ports of the Viking Age and well known from many sources as well as from detailed archaeological excavation. The account as it is preserved is hardly a description of the town, no more than a brief notation of certain facts and observations that might strike a visitor from Muslim Spain as strange. Thus, he describes a feast held in honour of one of their gods, and he notes that the town is poor in goods but rich in fish and that unwanted children are thrown into the sea to save the costs of bringing them up. He notes that 'their women have the right to divorce; a wife gets divorced when she wishes.' More improbably, he says that the inhabitants of Schleswig have 'an artificially produced eye-makeup' which he claims is used by both men and women to improve their beauty. He concludes with some scathing remarks about the quality of the singing there.

Although perhaps not too much weight should be placed on this information, the claim that women could sue for divorce does reinforce the impression we get from later Scandinavian law codes that they 'preserve some evidence of an older, native system under which it was only necessary for a formal declaration to be made before witnesses by either husband or wife for divorce to be legally effective'.

Travellers coming from the Arab world were particularly struck by the relative freedom accorded to women in Scandinavian society. Thus, we find Ibrāhīm b. Ya'qūb's brief comments echoed in another account attributed to an Andalusian visitor to Northern Europe.

Al-Ghazāl

Al-Ghazāl was a poet, philosopher and diplomat in ninth-century Andalusia, and so handsome that he was called 'the gazelle'. He was a confidant of the Umayyad emir of Muslim Spain, 'Abd al-Raḥman II, who sent him on important missions abroad, particularly to the Byzantine emperor. He also acted as envoy to a viking ruler, 'the king of al-Majūs'.

Many scholars have doubted the truth of the account of al-Ghazāl's embassy, dismissing it as a romantic fabrication of its twelfth-century author. This was Ibn Diḥya, also an Andalusian, born in 1149. Unlike al-Qazwīnī and the other works in Arabic which give us information about vikings, his work is not historical or geographical. It is called 'An amusing selection of poetry by Westerners' and is part anthology and part literary criticism. Ibn Diḥya includes the account of al-Ghazāl's embassy (which is preserved nowhere else) to illustrate the poet's character and because three of his verses are cited in it. Although Ibn Diḥya claimed to be copying from a source who had the story from al-Ghazāl himself, it is not a text that can be used uncritically for viking history. Nevertheless, it is worth quoting for the portrait it gives us of a viking queen.

Al-Ghazāl's diplomatic mission has plausibly been connected with the viking attack on Andalusia in 844, after which 'envoys of the king of al-Majūs' came to see 'Abd al-Raḥman to persuade him to send a delegation to visit their king. But even scholars who agree that such a mission must have taken place, and that Ibn Diḥya's tale is a more or less faithful account of that mission, cannot agree on the destination of the mission. The most common suggestions have been Ireland, at the court of the Norwegian king Turgeis, or Denmark, at the royal seat in Lejre, which seems more likely. This uncertainty leaves us with a fundamental problem in interpreting the text: if it represents a viking court at all, does it give us a picture of life in the Scandinavian homeland or of an upstart court among a conquered people?

Ibn Diḥya describes the difficult voyage to 'the lands of *al-Majūs*', with a storm in the Bay of Biscay which inspires al-Ghazāl to poetry. The country they arrive at is described as being

> a large island in the ocean, with flowing streams and gardens. . . . Many islands are situated near that one, both large and small, all populated by *al-Majūs*.

The people are described as being Christians

> with the exception of the people of some islands in the sea, who persist in fire-worship, their original faith, in marrying their mothers, sisters and other kinds of abomination.

The envoys cause quite a stir among these people by their appearance and their dress.

Al-Ghazāl is received by the king of this land and, by a polite trick, avoids prostrating himself before him and thus implying the inferiority of his own ruler. Gifts and messages are exchanged and we are laconically told of al-Ghazāl's besting of the locals:

> on occasion he disputed with their learned men and defeated them, and on occasion struggled with their champions and overcame them.

The rest of the account (about half of the text) is entirely devoted to al-Ghazāl's relations with 'the wife of the king of *al-Majūs*'. It is mostly in dialogue form, either witty repartee between the exotic ambassador and the flirtatious queen, and including two poems composed by him, or al-Ghazāl's boasting about his success to his friend Tammām:

> When the wife of the king of *al-Majūs* heard of al-Ghazāl, she sent for him so that she might see him. When he entered her presence, he greeted her and then stared at her for a long time, looking at her like one amazed. She said to the interpreter, 'Ask him why he stares at me, whether because he

finds me exceedingly beautiful or the opposite?' He said, 'For no other reason than this, that I never imagined to see such a sight in this world. I have seen women of our king who were chosen for him from all nations, but I never saw among them a beauty similar to this'. She said to her interpreter, 'Ask him whether he is serious or jesting'. He said, 'I am in earnest'. She said, 'Then there is no beauty in their land'. Al-Ghazāl said, 'Show me some of your women so that I may compare them'. The queen sent for women well-known for their beauty. They came, and he looked them carefully up and down, and then said, 'There is beauty among them, but not like the beauty of the queen, for her beauty and fine attributes cannot be perceived by everyone, and can only be expressed by poets. If the queen wishes me to describe her beauty, her lineage and her intelligence in a poem to be recited throughout our land, then I shall do so.' She was greatly pleased and elated, and ordered him a gift, but al-Ghazāl refused to accept it, saying, 'I will not.' She said to the interpreter, 'Ask him why he does not accept my gift. Is it because he despises it or he despises me?' He asked him, and al-Ghazāl replied, 'Her present is indeed magnificent, and to accept it would be an honour, for she is a queen and the daughter of a king, but to look at her and to be received by her is an adequate gift for me. I am content with that gift. I wish her to make me the gift of constantly receiving me.'

The queen (whose name is given as 'Nūd') is 'even more pleased and astonished' at this request and so begin regular meetings between the two:

> the wife of the king of *al-Majūs* was infatuated with al-Ghazāl, and could not pass a single day without sending for him. He used to stay with her, talking of the lives of the Muslims, their histories and their lands, and of the neighbouring peoples. Never did he leave without her sending a gift after him as a sign of good-will, either a garment, some food or some perfume, until her relationship with him became notorious. His companions disapproved of it, and he was warned of it, and visited her only every other day. She enquired of him the reason for this, and he told her of the warning he had received. She laughed, and told him, 'We have no such thing in our religion and we have no jealousy. Our women stay with our husbands according to their choice. The woman stays with him as long as she wishes, and parts from him if she no longer desires him.' The custom of *al-Majūs* before the religion of Rome was attained by them was this, that none of their women would refuse herself to a man, unless a low-born man accompanied a nobly-born woman, on account of which she would be disgraced, and her family would keep them apart.

So al-Ghazāl continues his visits and conversations. He was so good-looking that he did not look his fifty years, leading Queen Nūd to ask him why his hair was grey. This gives al-Ghazāl the chance to declaim a couple of jokey poems and leads eventually to his agreeing to dye his hair black. The poems give the author (Ibn Diḥya) cause to venture into a literary criticism intended to boost the reputation of Western Arabic poetry against the dominance of the Eastern, classical poets:

> the poem is forgotten, because the poet was an Andalucian. Otherwise it would not have been left in obscurity, for such a fine poem does not deserve to be neglected. . . . And are we not wronged and treated un-justly?

Eventually, al-Ghazāl returns to Toledo, having been away for a total of twenty months.

It is easy to see the rather thick romantic gloss over this story and to suspect al-Ghazāl of wishful thinking in the matter of the freedom and availability of northern women. Moreover, the primary purpose of the tale is clearly to glorify a great Andalusian poet. Just as al-Ghazāl refuses to prostrate himself before the king, and gets the better of his 'learned men and champions', so he, more subtly perhaps, gets the upper hand with the queen. Al-Ghazāl's comment that 'her beauty and fine attributes cannot be perceived by everyone, and can only be expressed by poets' is revealing, along with the conversation reported by his friend Tammām:

> I heard al-Ghazāl telling this story. I said to him, 'Did she in fact possess beauty to the degree you have indicated?' He said, 'By your father, she had charm, but by saying this I attracted her affection, and gained from her more than I wanted.'

Yet in spite of the literary tricks, there is nothing that is totally in-credible in this account and some of it fits with what we already know of Scandinavian society in the Viking Age. The legal freedom women had to leave an unsatisfactory marriage has already been noted. If the court of the king and queen of al-Majūs was indeed in Denmark, then the obvious independence and status of Queen Nūd fits in neatly with the picture we get of high-born Danish women from the runic inscrip-tions 50–100 years later. The custom of royal patronage of the arts, particularly the giving of gifts to a poet in exchange for a poem of praise, is of course known from many cultures, but played an especially prominent part in the Viking Age. If Arabists reject the story of al-Ghazāl's embassy as a fiction, this cannot be because of its inherent improbability as a reflection of royal viking life in the ninth century.

VIKING WOMEN OUTSIDE SCANDINAVIA

England

Before 925

The most important sources for the earliest history of viking women in England (and in the British Isles generally) are the archaeological evidence and place-names. Apart from two brief entries in the *Anglo-Saxon chronicle*, there is little that traditional written sources can tell us.

Although the related sets of annals known collectively as the *Anglo-Saxon chronicle* are an invaluable source for our knowledge of the viking campaigns in England in the ninth and early tenth centuries, and for the English, or rather West Saxon, resistance to them, they remain no more than a sketchy record for the history of the period as a whole. Thus, there are gaps in the coverage of certain periods (e.g. from the beginnings of Norse activity to about 850) and of certain areas (e.g. northern England in general and particularly the northwest). Moreover the obsessive concern with the viking campaigns means that the *Chronicle* is of very little use for the study of any aspect of viking history other than the military and political. Not surprisingly, then, references to women in the period of Scandinavian invasion and settlement are minimal.

Nevertheless, an interesting glimpse of women in the mobile viking army is provided by the entries for the years 892–5. At this time we are in the final phase of the first great period of viking activity, in which an equilibrium was reached before the 'reconquest' by Edward the Elder of territories in the north and east ruled by the Danes. In the period from the 870s to the 890s, the original viking army had been divided into separate forces, many of the men had settled down to a life of farming in Yorkshire, Lincolnshire and East Anglia, and those that carried on raiding had suffered a number of defeats, both in England and on the continent.

In 892, eighty ships under the leadership of a man called Hæsten entered the mouth of the Thames. The raiders built several fortifications and engaged in skirmishes with the English levies, who were distracted by the arrival in Exeter of a fleet of raiders based in Northumbria and East Anglia. One of Hæsten's fortifications was at Benfleet in Essex. With the help of reinforcements from London, those English who had not gone west stormed this fort and

> captured all that was within, both goods, and women and also children, and brought all to London; and they either broke up or burnt all the ships, or brought them to London or to Rochester. And Hæsten's wife and two sons were brought to the king; and he gave them back to him, because one of them was his godson, and the other the godson of Ealdorman Ethelred. They had stood sponsor to them before Hæsten came to Benfleet, and he had given the king oaths and hostages, and the king had also made him generous gifts of money, and so he did also when he gave back the boy and the woman.

Although not very informative in itself, this account does allow some deductions. We know that Hæsten was the leader of a section of the viking army which had been raiding on the continent for many years and we have to assume that his wife and sons had been with him there, since he had hardly had time to acquire a wife and two sons in the short time he had been in England. The Old English word *wif*, translated variously as 'woman' and 'wife' in the above extract, is ambiguous and could mean either, but whether the mother of Hæsten's sons was his legally-wedded wife or no, we are entitled to assume that it was a stable relationship. The fact that the English felt it worth their while to take her hostage suggests that she had high status and a certain value to Hæsten, that she was not just a slave-girl who could be replaced. But how long she had been with Hæsten and whether she was a Scandinavian or not are impossible to guess. That not only the leader of the army was allowed to take a female companion (and thereby risk having children to look after) is indicated not only by this entry but by one a couple of years later, where we are told that the Danes, still hotly pursued by the English, 'had placed their women in safety in East Anglia before they left that fortress'.

The information provided in this part of the *Chronicle* must be thought to be reliable, as the entries were originally written at the time of the events they describe. But because of the chequered history of the versions of the *Chronicle*, we can make no deductions from the fact that female companions of the viking invaders are not mentioned elsewhere in it. These two references might be the result of the chronicler's astonishment at something that had not been heard of before, or they might simply be a consequence of the fact that these entries are among the fullest and most detailed in the *Chronicle*.

After 925

With people of Scandinavian origin settled throughout eastern England and the West Saxon kings in control of much of the country, viking attacks in the tenth century took on a different character. The attacks on the kingdom of York by Hiberno-Norse vikings from the west, or on the whole of England by mercenary bands of Danes and Norwegians later in the tenth century, were campaigns aimed at political conquest, led by high-ranking rulers. In such campaigns, political as well as military strategies were called for. Such political strategies could involve the use of women who, as daughters and sisters on one side, would cement an alliance by becoming a wife on the other. Again, our main source for the history of the period is the *Anglo-Saxon chronicle*.

The nearly contemporary entries of the late ninth and early tenth centuries did not lead to an unbroken stream of annal writing. The *Chronicle* remains at best a patchy document, with large gaps for certain periods and for certain areas of the country. Northern England remains largely unnoticed in most of our surviving chronicles and the period of Danish rule under King Cnut is also sketchily covered, so that viking history in particular suffers from a paucity of sources.

Women do not fare much better in this period than in the earlier one, but we begin to get a clearer idea of the possible fates for a viking woman, at least for one attached to a high-ranking military or political leader. The exigencies of politics in this period meant that the wife of a viking leader need not have been a Scandinavian at all, but was quite likely to be an English princess. In 926:

> King Athelstan and Sihtric, king of the Northumbrians, met together at Tamworth on 30 January and Athelstan gave him his sister in marriage.

Sihtric was a Hiberno-Norse viking who ruled briefly in York. Luckily for Athelstan, his brother-in-law died the next year and he could conveniently step into his shoes and take over Northumbria. What his sister thought of being taken up to Tamworth in winter to be given over to Sihtric, we cannot know. The *Chronicle* does not even tell us her name (but see below).

In 978 King Ethelred succeeded to the English throne. Soon afterwards, large shipborne forces of Scandinavian mercenaries began attacking the south and east of England in a series of campaigns which eventually led to the accession to the English throne of the Danish king Cnut in the winter of 1016–17. Although Danish imperialism may not have been the original intention, Danish rulers such as Cnut's father Swein Forkbeard soon realised the potential of attacking a weakened England and assumed leadership of the attacking armies. The wars acquired the character of a contest between two nations, England and Denmark. In such a situation, the many Scandinavians and people of Scandinavian or mixed origin living in eastern England had, or could be perceived to have, divided loyalties. Ethelred, at any rate, was suspicious of them, and in 1002 he

> ordered to be slain all the Danish men who were in England – this was done on St Brice's day – because the king had been informed that they would treacherously deprive him, and then all his councillors, of life, and possess this kingdom afterwards.

In Old English the word *menn* could, and often did, mean 'people' rather than just 'people of the male sex' and the above translation should probably read 'Danish people'. We might not have suspected Ethelred of murdering Anglo-Scandinavian women as well as men were it not for the evidence of later historical works, which make it clear that he did and which also saw dire consequences arising from this massacre (see below).

Cnut, once established on the throne, did as many another viking leader had done before him and immediately made a political marriage, in this case to the widow of his predecessor, as the *Chronicle* tells us in the entry for 1017:

> the king ordered the widow of King Ethelred, Richard's daughter, to be fetched as his wife.

It does not sound as if she had much choice in the matter.

Emma of Normandy, known in English as Ælfgifu, was the wife or mother of four kings of England. A brief account of her origins and her marriages provides a neat example of the intertwining of national strands that was so characteristic of the late Viking Age. Her own life brings together the three elements that contributed to English society in the eleventh century: the Scandinavian, the Norman and the English. On her father's side (he was Duke Richard I of Normandy), Emma was great-granddaughter of Rollo, the viking founder of the Duchy of Normandy. Emma's mother was Richard's concubine Gunnor, described in later sources as 'Danish'. This need not be taken too literally, but she was certainly of Scandinavian origin and her name (ON *Gunnvǫr*) is one of only three Scandinavian women's names attested in Normandy. Emma thus had an important Scandinavian strand in her background when she went to England to become Ethelred's queen. This may have made her more predisposed to marry Cnut when he became king. In any case, Emma was perhaps luckier than many of her lowlier predecessors who were forced into marriage with a viking leader. Cnut, once he was king of England, became more English than the English themselves and a model Christian husband.

Not all the female members of Cnut's family were so lucky. In 1044, one of the *Chronicle* versions tells us,

> Gunnild, that noble lady, King Cnut's kinswoman, was banished, and she then stayed at Bruges for a long time, and then went to Denmark.

Who this rather obscure 'kinswoman' of the king, with the good Scandinavian name of *Gunnhildr*, was has to be deduced from other sources. She was at any rate not his daughter (by Emma) of the same name. It is possible that she was his sister and almost certain that she had been married to Hákon Eiríksson, a Norwegian jarl who was one of Cnut's subordinates until the king, fearing treachery, sent him into exile, where he soon died. His widow clearly posed no threat to her brother Cnut, but why Edward the Confessor felt the need to banish her in 1044 is not clear.

The Anglo-Norman historians

Although the *Chronicle* remains our main source for the history of the Anglo-Saxon period, it is possible to supplement it with information drawn from Anglo-Norman historians writing in Latin in the twelfth and thirteenth centuries. The great flowering of historical writing in this period is important mainly for the history of England after the Norman conquest but there are occasional fringe benefits for anyone seeking to understand the pre-conquest period. Chroniclers such as Roger of Wendover, William of Malmesbury and 'Florence' of Worcester based their history of the Anglo-Saxon period on sources very like those still available to us and primarily on the *Anglo-Saxon chronicle*. But often they used versions of the *Chronicle* that are no longer extant, or they had access to traditions that are now lost, and have therefore preserved information which we would otherwise not have.

The later historians must be used with great care for much of what they say is sheer invention, or commonplace historical fiction. Historians are still busy determining their sources and establishing the reliability of their information for the Anglo-Saxon period. Individual statements in these later histories cannot be given immediate credence without further investigation. The following notes on women in viking England are offered without great claims for their literal truth. But they do show us what Englishmen living only a century or two later thought the role of such women could be, based on some core of tradition available to them.

It is perhaps useful to distinguish the additional information from lost sources which the Anglo-Norman historians passed on to us from their rhetorical embellishment of that information. An example is provided by Roger of Wendover's *Flores historiarum*. Like the *Anglo-Saxon chronicle*, Roger tells us that Athelstan married his sister to Sihtric of York, but he also tells us her name, Eadgyth (Edith). Roger probably used some lost northern annals as a source and it is very likely that her name comes from them. He goes on to tell us that Sihtric

> gave up the heathen religion for the love of the maiden and received the faith of Christ. But not long afterwards he cast off the blessed maiden and, deserting his Christianity, restored the worship of idols, and after a short while ended his life miserably as an apostate. Accordingly the holy maiden, having preserved her chastity, remained strong in good works to the end of her life, at Polesworth, in fasts and in vigils, in prayers and in zeal for almsgiving. She departed after the passage of a praiseworthy life from this world on 15 July, at this same place, where to this day divine miracles do not cease to be performed.

Roger's source may very well have contained a notice of Sihtric's conversion upon his marriage, but the rest of the passage sounds very much like a product of Roger's hagiographical interests and anti-Norse bias.

Other additions in the later historians are more difficult to evaluate. In relating the St Brice's Day massacre of 1002, Florence of Worcester follows very closely the account from the *Chronicle* quoted above, but adds that 'old and young, regardless of sex' were to be killed (thus confirming that the *Chronicle* entry should be translated using 'Danish people', rather than 'Danish men'). This may just have been rhetorical exaggeration, although it is not clear why the author would want to emphasise the brutality of an English king. But then we read in William of Malmesbury's *Gesta regum Anglorum* that in Swein Forkbeard's invasion of England in 1013 he was 'intending primarily to avenge his sister Gunnhild'. William goes on to explain that Gunnhild, who had come to England with her husband Palling and become a Christian, was murdered along with her husband and her son. William's chronology is a bit confused at this point, but it is likely that he was referring to the St Brice's Day massacre.

The story of Gunnhild's murder probably cannot be given credence as literal fact, but unless William made it up entirely, it does provide some interesting insights. Whether the story arose among the English to explain the otherwise inexplicable attacks of the Danes, or was put about by the Danes to justify their invasions, it indicates that people thought it understandable that a foreign king should invade a country to avenge the death of his sister. Most churchmen of the early eleventh century (such as Archbishop Wulfstan in his sermons) explained the Danish attacks as divine punishment for the moral failings of the English people. The compiler of one of the versions of the *Chronicle* on the other hand ascribed them to the political failure of King Ethelred. The story of Swein's revenge may have been a third, popular explanation of the causes of the war.

As well as an aunt called Gunnhild, Cnut had, if we are to believe the sources, both a sister and a daughter of the same name. The daughter is well documented in English, Scandinavian and continental sources, the latter because she married the German emperor-to-be Henry III. The sister may have been the 'kinswoman of Cnut' who was exiled by King Edward in 1044. Certainly even one member of Cnut's family with the name of Gunnhild would be enough to explain the popularity of the name in England in the eleventh century and even later.

Continental vikings

Frankish annals

Unlike the *Anglo-Saxon chronicle*, Frankish annals were written in Latin and are more obviously monastic products. They were also produced at several centres throughout the Frankish empire, at different times and are therefore frequently (although not always) independent of each other. They also cover a wider range of affairs than the *Anglo-Saxon chronicle*, being less single-mindedly concerned with the viking raids, at least in the period in question. For the eighth and early ninth centuries we have the *Royal Frankish annals* (*Annales regni Francorum*) and their continuations (named after the monasteries in which the manuscripts were found in modern times), the annals of St Bertin (*Annales Bertiniani*) and Fulda (*Annales Fuldenses*). For the ninth and tenth centuries we have monastic chronicles such as the Xanten annals (*Annales Xantenses*) and those of St Vaast (*Annales Vedastini*). Together these annals provide us with a detailed account of viking movements on the European continent in the ninth century, with their information often confirmed or supplemented by various other chronicles and royal biographies and, on occasion, even by poems.

Where the Frankish annals do resemble their Anglo-Saxon counterparts is in having few references to women. Again, it is not always possible to tell whether this is a result of the military and political bias of such chronicles, or whether there were simply no women whose presence could be reported. The few references that do exist suggest the former is more likely.

Several entries in the Frankish annals confirm what we know from other sources (although not from the *Anglo-Saxon chronicle*), that one of the purposes of some of the viking raids was to replenish the supply of captives for their trade in slaves. Thus, several of the annals mention a raid in 837 on the Frisian island of Walcheren by the *Nordmanni* or *pagani*, during which they took captives. The *Annales Xantenses* specify that these captives were *multas feminas* ('many women'). What the ultimate fate of such women was can only be guessed. Some of them may have ended up as the 'wives' of their captors.

As in the case of Hæsten in England, we occasionally catch a glimpse of the wives of the viking leaders. One very early reference is in the *Annales regni Francorum*, where we are told that a certain Dane called 'Heriold' (the petty king Harald klak), probably in an attempt to get the support of the Carolingian Emperor Louis the Pious for his political ambitions at home, was baptised at Mainz in the year 826. This event, which is remembered in a number of texts, was clearly a great occasion: Heriold was baptised *cum uxore et magna Danorum multitudine* ('with his wife and a large number of Danes'). A contemporary biography of Louis adds that the Emperor and his Empress Judith themselves acted as baptismal sponsors to the Danish couple. This conversion of a Danish king was the occasion for St Ansgar's first visit to Scandinavia (as noted above), although Denmark was not to be fully Christianised for another century or more.

The *Annales Bertiniani* tell us of another viking leader, Weland, who was baptised in 862 after a defeat by Charles the Bald, son of the Emperor Louis: 'Weland came with his wife and children to Charles and was made a Christian with them.' Baptism was a tool of power politics: the emperor symbolically asserted his overlordship by sponsoring the new convert. Both Louis and Charles probably thought, moreover, that by baptising the whole family, they could encourage other Danes to follow suit and thus be remembered in history as baptising the whole Danish nation, although they may have underestimated the power of example of these petty rulers. That both Heriold's and Weland's wives were Danish we can surmise from the fact that they needed to be baptised: a captured slave-girl is more likely to have already been a Christian.

Other viking leaders however got themselves wives in the course of their campaigns, as very often a bride was part of the price of ridding your land of invaders. The *Annales Vedastini* tell us that in 882, the Emperor Charles the Fat gave his cousin Lothar II's daughter Gisla in marriage to the viking king Godfred, along with the rule of Frisia, 'and got the Norsemen to leave his kingdom'. Regino of Prüm, a nearly contemporary chronicler who wrote a world history in 908, says that Godfred had agreed to become a Christian on condition that he got both Frisia and Gisla, and that the rest of the vikings were bought off with 'a vast amount of gold and silver'. Godfred entered into a political alliance with Lothar's (illegitimate) son Hugh, who was attempting to regain his father's kingdom, but was soon removed from the scene by the emperor's men.

Normally, however, vikings were engaged in less peaceful activities among the Franks than being baptised and getting married. By the second half of the ninth century, long campaigns were the usual mode of operation. The Danish Great Army which had been harassing the continent was drawn off to England in the 860s, after which there was a period of relative peace in Frankia, apart from a band of Norsemen active in the Loire valley. Regino tells us that this band found the city of Angers deserted by its inhabitants and established themselves in it, 'with women and children', in 873. The city was well fortified and impregnable because of its situation and the vikings found it a useful base for their sorties into the surrounding countryside. Charles the Bald found the city unassailable and only got the vikings out by dint of a long siege. Thus we see that, as in England a decade later, the viking armies liked to have a fortified place of safety for their women and children which also served as a base for their military activities. The army's concern shows that these women are not likely to have been a mere handful of camp-followers, but a sizable contingent of established female companions.

Abbo of St Germain

Another notorious viking attack on a Frankish city in the late ninth century was the siege of Paris in 885–6. This siege is described in detail in the *Annales Vedastini*, but it was also the subject of a poem in Latin by Abbo, a monk of St-Germain-des-Prés in Paris, the *Bella Parisiacae urbis*. Abbo was himself present during the siege and the poem is thought to be a fairly accurate eyewitness account, allowing perhaps for some literary exaggeration.

A number of details in Abbo's poem but not in the annalistic accounts of the siege confirm the evidence from other sources that the viking armies of the late ninth century had women with them on their campaigns. We meet the *Danae*, 'Danish women', as Abbo designates them, twice in the course of the poem. The first time is on the second day of the attack (27 November 885), during a lull in the fighting. A number of fatally wounded vikings return to their boats where they expire. At this the *Danae*, tearing their hair and weeping, turn to their 'husbands' (the word used is *maritus*) and urge them back to the battle, accusing them of 'fleeing the furnace', calling them 'son of the devil' and suggesting that they are hanging around for a second helping of the bread, wild boar and wine which the women have just served them. The men take the hint and rush off to resume the attack on the tower.

The second time Abbo mentions 'Danish women' is when the vikings return to attack Paris in May 887 after an unsuccessful five-month siege of Sens. The vikings had gone off to Sens after having been bought off with 700 pounds of silver by the Emperor Charles the Fat and, when they returned, clearly nothing less than divine intervention would protect the inhabitants of Paris. Abbo describes a series of miracles in which St Germain fights back at the invaders. One of these involves a well by the saint's relics, the water from which has curative properties and is sold by the priest at a high price. A Danish woman caused some of this water 'to be brought to her by force', as she needed it for making bread!

But when she put the bread on the fire, it went red, like blood. Another woman attempting to steal the water could draw only blood.

Whatever we may think of these 'miracles' and the powers of St Germain, behind them lie the harsh realities of being a viking wife. An army with women would expect those women to do the cooking, but getting the essentials for that cooking, or the water for the washing up, cannot always have been easy for the female companion of a viking warrior.

Ireland

Annals of Ulster

As in England and Frankia, the monastic centres of Ireland produced annals recording contemporary events. Elucidating the history of this annal writing is perhaps even more complicated than in the case of the English and Frankish annals, mainly because the Irish annals are almost universally preserved in late and often interpolated manuscripts. Nevertheless, it is agreed that the *Annals of Ulster*, although preserved in a manuscript from the fifteenth century, represent fairly accurately the contemporary accounts of the viking raids in Ireland. The *Annals of Ulster* are, of all our sources for viking raids, the one in which it is possible to follow most closely the annual progress of the 'heathens' in one country, beginning in 795 with 'the burning of Rechru [Lambey] by the heathens' and continuing right through to well into the eleventh century, by which time the Norse of Dublin were a fixture in Irish politics, although they are still called 'foreigners'. Vikings appear frequently in the annals throughout this period, but in the periods 821–51 and 914–53, references to them (often multiple) appear in almost every annal. It is thus all the more unfortunate that almost none of this detailed information concerns women. This cannot be because of a lack of interest in women by the monkish chroniclers, for the names of women appear quite frequently in the entries dealing with purely Irish affairs, especially in the death notices of which the *Annals* are so full. But the Irish, like the Frankish and the English, annals have a strong bias towards military and political events, so that it would be over-hasty to conclude that the lack of mention of any viking women meant that there were none in Ireland.

As we have already seen from the Frankish annals, the earliest viking raids seem to have had the capture of slaves as their objective. In 821, the *Annals of Ulster* tell us,

Etar [Howth] was plundered by the heathens, [and] they carried off a great number of women into captivity.

There are several other references to the capture of slaves, but this is the only specific reference to women, although it must be admitted that references to the capture of men are also rare. But given the vikings' predilection for attacking religious centres, they must have captured a lot of male slaves, as in 840, when they plundered Lugbad [Louth] and 'led away captive bishops and priests and scholars'. References to Irish captives in later Norse literature suggest that many Irish women were abducted in this way.

As early as 850 we find the 'foreigners' making common cause with some of the Irish, who were in any case much given to fighting among themselves. Such alliances would be natural among those vikings permanently based in the country and may have arisen from intermarriage with the local population. Evidence for this is scant, but the annals do tell us of an attack in 933 made jointly by 'Fergal son of Domnall son of Aed and Sicfrith son of Uathmarán, i.e. the son of Domnall's daughter'. The viking Uathmarán married into an Irish family, and he and his son with the good Norse name of *Sigfreðr* both benefited from this alliance.

Vita Findani

The abduction of Irish women to be sold as slaves is confirmed by a contemporary source of a somewhat different type. This is the *Life* of St Findan, a Leinster monk who, like so many other Irishmen, spent most of his adult life on the continent, at the monastery of Rheinau (in present-day Switzerland), where he died in about 878. His biography was written soon after. It concentrates on his youth and the dramatic events that led to his life of religious exile on the continent. This involved capture by Norsemen but, before Findan himself is captured, his sister suffers the same fate:

Foreigners called Norsemen had captured Findan's sister, along with other women during raids on that Scottish island called Ireland. His father then gave his son Findan some money and ordered him to buy his sister back and return her to her father.

Findan is not successful, as he is very soon captured by 'pagans' himself and from then on the narrative follows his trials and tribulations. We have to assume that he never found his sister. But her fate may have been very similar to that which befell Findan later on:

> Then, according to custom, his Norse master, not wishing to return to his homeland, sold him to another, who sold him to a third, who in turn sold him to a fourth. This last master, longing to see his native land again, gathered his companions together and took Findan and others with him into captivity.

From the account of Findan's sister and some others (such as the ransoming of two Moroccan girls referred to above), we might conclude that vikings practised kidnapping rather than slave trading. A captive ransomed could be as lucrative as and much less trouble than one that had to be fed and clothed.

Later histories

As in England, the twelfth century in Ireland saw the production of histories which present a romanticised view of the viking past, such as the *Cogadh Gaedhel re Gallaibh*, ('The war of the Irish with the foreigners'). This text has long been used as a primary source for the viking wars in Ireland as it provides much fuller information than the brief notices of the annals, including a couple of brief mentions of women. However these references give as clear an indication as any of the essentially legendary character of this work: although it is based on information of the kind we find in the annals, much of it is romantic fiction, written as historical propaganda to glorify the Irish king Brian Boru.

In its description of the viking leader Turgeis, who is said to have assumed the overlordship of all the vikings in Ireland, the *Cogadh* mentions that his wife Ota used to give 'answers' on the altar of the church at Clonmacnoise, implying that she was some kind of pagan priestess. From this briefest of references, some have concluded that she was in fact the Queen Nūd encountered by the poet al-Ghazāl on his embassy to a viking court (see above), but there is no evidence for this surmise.

The other legendary female in the *Cogadh* is the *Inghen Ruaidh*, or 'Red Maiden'. In ch. 36, we are given a long list of the viking fleets that attacked Munster in the tenth century and their leaders. The last of these is the fleet of the Red Maiden and we are told that 'the evil which Erinn had hitherto suffered was as nothing compared to the evil inflicted by these parties'. The legend of the warrior maiden who invaded Ireland was to be a pervasive one in later Irish lore of all kinds. But the reference in the *Cogadh* is so brief that we have no way of judging whether it can have any historical basis. Women warriors were certainly part of the mental universe of the early Scandinavians, for we find them both in literature and in art, but it is more difficult to argue that they existed in fact. The Red Maiden, if she ever existed, is too elusive to be pinned down.

Russia

The Rūs

Archaeological evidence, particularly of burials, shows that Scandinavians (mostly from Sweden) penetrated far into what we today call Russia, establishing centres of trade and government at Novgorod and Kiev. The artefacts show also that there must have been women among these Scandinavians. However, expanding on the archaeological evidence to provide some kind of narrative history of viking women in Russia is more difficult, mainly because of the nature of our sources. In Russia itself, the earliest historical sources are much later than the heyday of the Rūs, who did not know writing except possibly for runes. The main source is the *Russian primary chronicle*, which exists in a number of versions. As this is roughly contemporaneous with the Icelandic sagas which also contain references to viking activity in Russia and Byzantium, it is not necessarily of any greater historical value than them. There are also sources which may be closer in time, written by people who came across the Rūs in their transcontinental wanderings. These are mostly the works of various Arab geographers and historians, and these sources present their own special problems. Of all the viking colonies abroad, the Rūs are perhaps the most difficult to grasp and their women probably even more so. Again we meet the problem we have met before: did viking merchants and colonists take Scandinavian women with them on their journeys or was their relatively quick assimilation into local culture due to intermarriage with native populations? Was a 'viking woman' any woman attached (by marriage or otherwise) to a viking, or was she a travelling and trading woman of Scandinavian origin? However, it is probably unfair to ask this question of the written sources, since in their pages we meet only a very few and probably unusual individuals.

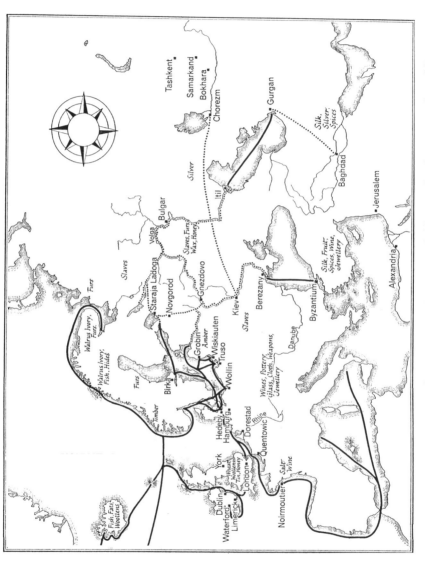

Viking Age trade routes. Sea routes are shown as solid lines, inland routes as dotted lines.

Olga, viking princess and Russian saint

In spite of the archaeological evidence that women from Scandinavia accompanied the men who went trading and adventuring in the east, we are never told this explicitly in the written sources. Personal names are an unreliable guide to ethnic origin. The few women with Norse names that we do meet in the sources are just as likely to have been the children of Scandinavian men and local women as they are to have been the offspring of a viking couple. But whatever the precise mixture of blood in its individual members, it is clear that at least the ruling dynasty of Kiev, if not its population, had a very strong Scandinavian element throughout the ninth and tenth centuries. One of the most colourful members of this dynasty was a lady with the good Scandinavian name of Helga (she gave the name Olga to the Russian language) who ruled Kiev for over a decade in the mid-tenth century.

Historians dispute whether Olga was of Scandinavian or of Slavic origin. There is little hard evidence either way, except her name, which could have been given to her later, and a much later *Life* (in a manuscript from the sixteenth century), which says that her parents were 'of the Varangian tongue'. The main source for the life of Olga is the *Russian primary chronicle*. We first meet her there in the entry for 903, when she is brought from the city of Pskov as a wife for Igor', the son of Rurik and future Great Prince of Kiev. She is mentioned again in the entry for 945, when Igor' renews a treaty his predecessor Oleg had made with the Emperors of Byzantium, giving the Rūs trading and other rights in Constantinople. The *Russian primary chronicle* copies out the whole treaty, including the list of fifty envoys sent by the Prince, nearly every one of them with a Scandinavian name. Some of these envoys are merchants, but the first group are there as representatives for individual members of the ruling dynasty. Along with representatives for Igor' and his son Svyatoslav, we find a certain Isgaut representing the Princess Olga and two further representatives of women: 'Kanitzar for Predslava [a Slavic name]; Sigbjorn for Svanhild, wife of Oleif'. The text of the treaty gives no clue as to whether these envoys had anything particular to negotiate for these women, or whether they were just part of the stately band. But it is worth remembering the Princess' interest in diplomacy in view of her visit to Constantinople a few years later.

It is when Prince Igor', in search of greater tribute from his subject peoples, is killed by the neighbouring Derevlians in 945 that we are treated to a lengthy account of the deeds of the Princess Olga. Igor' and

Olga's son, Svyatoslav, is still a boy when his father is killed. The Derevlians hope to forestall future attacks from him by persuading Olga to marry their Prince Mal and thereby gaining control over the boy. The *Chronicle* gives an elaborate account of how Olga not only foils this plan but avenges the death of her husband by a threefold tricking of the Derevlian envoys sent to carry out the plan.

The first group of Derevlians arrive to the city by boat. Although the royal palace is at the top of a hill, far above the river, Olga summons them to come and see her, and stipulates that they should be carried in their boat. When they arrive, the boat is dropped into a deep ditch dug especially in the castle and the envoys are buried alive. Olga then summons further 'distinguished men' from Dereva, who are invited to bathe on arrival before appearing in her presence. They are locked into the bathhouse and burned to death there. Finally, Olga invites the Derevlians to 'prepare great quantities of mead' and to meet her for a funeral feast at her husband's grave. When they are drunk, she orders her followers to kill them and they 'cut down five thousand of them; but Olga returned to Kiev and prepared an army to attack the survivors'.

Olga leads the attacks against Derevlian cities in the ensuing war, with her small son as a figurehead. We do not know how old he is supposed to be, but he is so young that when he throws a spear at the enemy, it 'barely cleared the horse's ears, and struck against his leg'. Olga does not engage in actual combat herself, but she is clearly the commander-in-chief of the campaign. When only the city of Iskorosten' still holds out against the Russians, Olga demands their submission. With clear insight into her character, 'the Derevlians replied that they would be glad to submit to tribute, but that she was still bent on avenging her husband'. Yet they still fall for her trick, which is to ask for a tribute of three pigeons and three sparrows from each house. Having gathered these birds

> Olga gave to each soldier in her army a pigeon or a sparrow, and ordered them to attach by a thread to each pigeon and sparrow a piece of sulphur bound with small pieces of cloth. When night fell, Olga bade her soldiers release the pigeons and the sparrows. So the birds flew to their nests, the pigeons to the cotes, and the sparrows under the eaves. Thus the dovecotes, the coops, the porches and the haymows were set on fire. There was not a house that was not consumed, and it was impossible to extinguish the flames, because all the houses caught fire at once.

Olga's triumph over Dereva is complete and she proceeds to bring administrative order to it. As the chronicler tells us, 'her trading posts and hunting-preserves are there still'.

Revenge taken, Olga brings order to the rest of the Kievan dominions:

> Olga went to Novgorod, and along the Msta she established trading-posts and collected tribute. She also collected imposts and tribute along the Luga. Her hunting-grounds, boundary posts, towns, and trading-posts still exist throughout the whole region, while her sleighs stand in Pskov to this day. Her fowling preserves still remain on the Dnieper and the Desna, while her village of Ol'zhichi is in existence even now. After making these dispositions, she returned to her city of Kiev, and dwelt at peace with it.

The third stage in Olga's career is her conversion to Christianity. The *Russian primary chronicle* presents this as taking place in Constantinople, when Olga meets the Emperor Constantine (II Porphyrogenitus) in 955:

> when he saw that she was very fair of countenance and wise as well, the Emperor wondered at her intellect. He conversed with her and remarked that she was worthy to reign with him in his city. When Olga heard his words, she replied that she was still a pagan, and that if he desired to baptize her, he should perform this function himself; otherwise she was unwilling to accept baptism.

When Olga has been baptised by the Emperor, and instructed and blessed by the Patriarch, Constantine reminds her of his proposal of marriage. The reply is characteristic of Olga:

> 'How can you marry me, after yourself baptizing me and calling me your daughter? For among Christians that is unlawful, as you yourself must know.' Then the Emperor said, 'Olga, you have outwitted me.' He gave her many gifts of gold, silver, silks, and various vases, and dismissed her, still calling her his daughter.

Back in Kiev, Olga rebuffs a message from the Greek Emperor, asking for 'presents of slaves, wax, and furs, and . . . soldiery to aid me' in exchange for what he has given her, replying that

> if the Emperor would spend as long a time with her in the Pochayna as she had remained on the Bosporus, then she would grant his request. With these words, she dismissed the envoys.

Olga's son Svyatoslav did not accept Christianity and the first Christian ruler of Kiev was her grandson Vladimir I who ruled from 978 to 1015. Both Olga and Vladimir later came to be venerated as saints.

Our final glimpse of Olga's tempestuous life is in the entry for 968 in the *Russian primary chronicle*, which describes her escape with her three grandsons from the city of Kiev when it is under siege by a new enemy, the Pechenegs. In the following year Olga dies, having given a command 'not to hold a funeral feast for her, for she had a priest who performed the last rites over the sainted Princess'. The chronicler ends with a eulogy over Olga, 'the first from Rus' to enter the kingdom of God'.

Clearly there is much that is legendary and apocryphal in the *Russian primary chronicle*'s account of the rule of Princess Olga. The chronicle was written long after the events described and presumably based at least partly on oral traditions. We may detect the influence of oral tradition, particularly in the account of Olga's threefold revenge and in the ruse of the 'incendiary birds', which is a common motif in literature elsewhere and particularly in Scandinavia. We also detect the chronicler's interpretation of the events controlling his presentation of them. If the inhabitants of Iskorosten' had really realised that Olga 'was still bent on avenging her husband', as the chronicler has them say, they would hardly have fallen for her incendiary bird trick.

The Scandinavian parallels that can be found for many of Olga's adventures suggest she is a literary sister of the strong and vengeful women we find in saga literature. Nora Chadwick wrote that the 'entire story of Olga's relations with the Drevlians reads exactly like a Norse saga'. But if we are suspicious of her early adventures, there can be no doubt that she ruled the Principality of Kiev for many years. The rather fanciful account in the *Russian primary chronicle* must be based on memories of that rule and indeed on its visible results, as the chronicler points out.

Moreover, the *Russian primary chronicle* is not the only source which tells of Olga's visit to the Greek Emperor around the time of her baptism. We have a description of her visit from the pen of the Emperor himself. Constantine Porphyrogenitus was a prolific writer and historian, and one of the several prodigious works he wrote was *De ceremoniis aulae Byzantinae*, describing the elaborate and lavish ceremonies practised at his court. A chapter on the reception of foreign visitors describes the ceremonies attending the visit of the 'Great Princess Elga of Russia'. We are able to correct the Russian *Chronicle*'s account in some particulars from this source. Thus, Olga's visit must have taken place in 957 rather than 955, and there is no mention of her baptism. It is assumed that this in fact took place before her visit. Otherwise, Constantine's account has a very different emphasis. He mentions no proposal of marriage, for instance. If indeed this ever did take place (and it seems more likely to have been invented by the Russian chronicler to glorify Olga), it is hardly surprising that Constantine would not mention such a humiliation. In keeping with the purpose of his book, Constantine instead concentrates on describing in great detail the official receptions and banquets given for Olga.

The size and composition of Olga's retinue in Constantinople give some hint as to the type of court she held back at home. She meets the Emperor followed by her female relatives by both blood and marriage, and the noblest of her ladies-in-waiting. Her male diplomats and advisors bring up the rear. After being received by the Emperor, Olga and her ladies are received by the Empress and her daughter-in-law, with a large following of aristocratic ladies and wives of the Emperor's dignitaries. In a third reception, Olga is received by the Emperor and Empress and their children, and is allowed to speak to the Emperor for as long as she likes.

At the banquet following these receptions, Olga is honoured by being fed in the same room as the Imperial family, if not at the same table. Having been put in her place in this way, she is then allowed to sit with the Imperial family for dessert in a small dining room. Her followers are fed and all of the Russian delegation receive the customary after-dinner gifts of money from the Emperor. Olga's male followers are enumerated: they consisted of nine kinsmen of hers, twenty diplomats, forty-three commercial counsellors, a priest, three interpreters (including Olga's personal one) and six servants. Another banquet was held at the end of the Russian visit. At this one, Olga and her ladies dined with the Empress and her children, and the male delegates with the Emperor.

Rogned and Ingigerðr

Other than Olga, women are most conspicuous by their absence in the *Russian primary chronicle*, with the brief exception of Rogned (ON *Ragnheiðr*), a wife of Vladimir I, who, like Olga, has much in common with her sisters in the sagas. Rogned is the daughter of Rogvolod (ON *Rǫgnvaldr*), of whom it is said that he 'had come from overseas, and exercised the authority in Polotsk'. Vladimir

> sent word to Rogvolod in Polotsk that he desired his daughter to wife. Rogvolod inquired of his daughter whether she wished to marry

> Vladimir. 'I will not', she replied, 'draw off the boots of a slave's son, but I want Yaropolk instead.'

Although her father accedes to this request, Vladimir's response is to kill Rogvolod and his two sons, marry Rogned and, eventually, kill his own brother Yaropolk.

Rogned bore Vladimir four sons and two daughters, according to the *Chronicle*, including Yaroslav I, the Wise, who ruled Kiev 1019–45. Vladimir seems to have been quite a ladies' man, and the *Chronicle* describes his many liaisons with gusto, presumably to emphasise by contrast the effect on his lifestyle of his eventual conversion to Christianity. When this happened in 988, Vladimir had to have a proper Christian wife and married Anna, sister of the Greek Emperor. Rogned is not mentioned again, except for a brief notice of her death in 1000.

Rogned's father must have been a Scandinavian, both his name and the fact that he is said to have come from 'overseas' point to this. Rogned's mother may or may not have come with him, but Rogned herself was at least half, if not wholly, Scandinavian and the scene in which she is consulted about her marriage is one that could have come from any saga. Although a father had the right to marry off his daughter to whomever he liked, she could be consulted and her wishes taken into account. Like Rogned, many a saga heroine rejected a potential suitor because of his supposed low birth. Thus, in *Laxdœla saga*, Þorgerðr, the daughter of the poet Egill Skallagrímsson, refuses at first to marry Óláfr Peacock because he was the 'son of a serving-woman', although she changes her mind when she finds out that his mother was in fact an Irish princess.

It may have been his mother's influence that encouraged Yaroslav I to foster Scandinavian connections. As a young man, before becoming Prince of Kiev, he ruled the city of Novgorod and relied on Scandinavians and Varangians for support. Yaroslav was the first of the Russian rulers with a truly international position and he is cited in many Norse sources. It is from these Norse sources that we know that his wife was Ingigerðr, the daughter of King Óláfr of Sweden. She is not mentioned by name in the *Russian primary chronicle*, but her existence is implied by the notices of the births of a succession of sons to Yaroslav and the entry for 1050 which records the death of 'the Princess, wife of Yaroslav'. It is also to the Norse sources that we must turn for the information that Yaroslav had a daughter called Elisabeth (ON *Ellisif*), whom he married to the future king Haraldr (the Hard-ruler) of Norway.

Vikings and the Arab world

If the historical accounts of the Rūs are too late to be entirely reliable and the archaeological evidence for Scandinavian traders and colonists in Russia is relatively sparse, we do have a further source of information about Russian vikings. The Viking Age coincided roughly with the Islamic empire at the height of its power. This was in the period of the Abbasid Caliphate, based in Baghdad, which was established in 750 and lasted in various forms until the conquest of that city by the Turks in 1055. It was inevitable that two such expansionist peoples as Arabs and vikings should come across one another in their travels. It is to the Arabs that we owe contemporary accounts of the people they called *ar-Rūs*.

The Arab world at its height was renowned for its learning. In sciences such as medicine, physics, music and mathematics, it was far in advance of contemporary European civilisation, because of the Arabs' knowledge of and further development of Greek traditions. Hand in hand with these studies went the development of all kinds of prose writings, making these three centuries the Golden Age of Arabic literature. The branch of this vast literature most relevant here is that of the geographical works which arose out of the needs of administering a large empire. The Abbasids had a well-developed postal system and the first geographical literature was a practical list of post roads. Soon, these geographical works included maps and charts, descriptions of marvels and travellers' tales, and ethnographic accounts of the peoples who lived along the routes. It is in such works that we find descriptions of the Rūs.

The textual history of the geographical works produced in the cities of the Islamic empire is a complicated one. Most texts were endlessly revised, changed and added to: Arabic scholars had as much respect for written authority as their Western counterparts and took much of their information from works already published. Thus we find many of the stories about the Rūs repeated in several works, but the sheer number of such repetitions is not in itself a guarantee of the truth of the tale. Nor have all the texts yet been subjected to modern source criticism to establish how much of what the writers tell us is based on personal experience and how much on more or less fictional sources. The definitive history of Arab-viking contacts has yet to be told. But the Arabic sources cannot be ignored: they provide very valuable evidence for a period for which we have very few narrative sources.

Ibn Rusta

One of the earliest and most important sources in Arabic for the Rūs was written in the early years of the tenth century by Ibn Rusta in Isfahan, Iran. It is the seventh (and only remaining) volume of a work entitled 'The book of precious finery'. After a cosmological and geographical introduction, the book describes Iran and its neighbouring lands, including a description of the land of the Rūs. This description is not likely to have been from Ibn Rusta's personal experience, since it seems to describe an earlier period of Rūs history, before they were settled in Kiev.

Ibn Rusta says the Rūs live on an island or a peninsula (the Arabic word is ambiguous) in a large lake. It is thought that this refers to the city of Novgorod, known to the Scandinavians as *Hólmgarðr* (which can be translated as 'island city'). The inhabitants' way of life is described in detail. Ibn Rusta emphasises that they own no farms or agricultural land, but that they live entirely by trading and have many cities. They use ships to raid the Slavs, capturing the people and selling them to the Bulgars. As well as slaves, they deal in furs, especially sable and squirrel, for which they receive money in exchange. After describing their polite and protective behaviour towards strangers, their fighting methods and their ways of resolving disputes, Ibn Rusta goes on to describe their religious practices. These seem to be under the guidance of a magician or medicine man, who decrees when they must sacrifice 'women, men and cattle' to their creator. The sacrificial victims, both human and animal, are hanged by a rope from a wooden pole. Finally, we are given a brief account of their funeral customs. When one of their chief men dies, says Ibn Rusta, they dig him a grave like a big house and place him in it, together with his clothes, his gold arm-rings and much food, many drinking vessels and coins. His favourite wife is put alive into the grave with him, the entrance is blocked up and she dies there.

Slavery and suttee

Most of the elements of Ibn Rusta's account are repeated in other Arab sources. The glimpses these sources give us of women's lot in the harsh world of the marauding Rūs traders may occasionally be exaggerated, but there seems no doubt that the essentials are true. We rarely meet women in these Arab accounts and, when we do, it is as captured slave girls or as the sacrificial victims of suttee. A more detailed, indeed lurid, eyewitness account of the sacrifice of a woman to accompany a dead man on his journey into the next world is given by Ibn Faḍlān, but most of the Arab writers mention the practice, whether in connection with inhumation (as in Ibn Rusta) or cremation. Al-Iṣṭakhrī, writing in Iran around 951, notes that the Rūs burn their dead and that together with the rich ones, their slave girls are cremated of their own free will. Al-Mas'ūdī, born in Baghdad and writing between 947 and 956, gives us a more complete account of Rūs funerary customs. They burn their dead, he says, together with their horses, tools and jewellery. When a man dies, his wife is burnt with him, even though she is alive. But, al-Mas'ūdī notes with a hint of irony, when a woman dies her husband is not cremated. If a man dies unmarried, then he is 'married after death' (which may be the ceremony Ibn Faḍlān is describing). According to al-Mas'ūdī, women desire greatly to be cremated, so that they can enter paradise together with their masters. Finally, he notes the similarity with the Indian custom of suttee, except that Indian women are cremated without their consent.

Clearly these sources (and others like them) are describing essentially the same practice. Although some writers refer to inhumation and some to cremation, we know that both these methods of disposal of a corpse were practised in Viking Age Scandinavia. There is also an apparent contradiction in that some of the accounts state that the woman sacrificed was the dead man's wife, others say she was a slave girl, but not too much should be read into this. It is likely that the Arab writers (many of whom had not travelled themselves, but were copying out accounts of earlier travellers) had no clear idea of exactly what types of marital and sexual relationships were current among the Rūs. Slave girls would have been in abundant supply as the Rūs traded in them and the itinerant warrior-merchants of the Rūs may not have been settled enough for many regular marriages to have taken place. Indeed, the person sacrificed did not even necessarily have to be female, according to Ibn Miskawayh, who wrote a general history in 982. Describing Rūs funeral customs, he notes that a man would be buried with his weapons, clothes, equipment and 'his wife or another woman, and his (male) slave, if he was fond of him'.

Ibn Faḍlān

One of the best-known, most important and certainly most dramatic descriptions of the Rūs way of life and death is a detailed eyewitness account by Ibn Faḍlān. He was a member of a diplomatic mission sent by the Caliph of Baghdad to the Bulgars, a Turkic people on the Volga, in the years 921–2. On his return he wrote an account of his journey and his experiences. Since the Bulgars were important trading partners of the Rūs (as we know from Ibn Rusta's account), it is not surprising that Ibn Faḍlān came across a party of Rūs traders during his stay on the Volga. About one-seventh of his book is devoted to the Rūs: first a description of their appearance and dress, their hygiene and sexual habits, their religious practices, and their treatment of the sick and of thieves. About half of the section on the Rūs is then devoted to a detailed description (one of the longest parts of his whole account) of the funeral of one of their chieftains which took place while Ibn Faḍlān was there.

The Rūs, according to Ibn Faḍlān, are 'perfect physical specimens, tall as date palms, blond and ruddy'. The men wear a kind of cloak that leaves one of their arms free and always carry axe, sword and knife. The women's adornment is described in detail:

> Each woman wears on either breast a box of iron, silver, copper, or gold; the value of the box indicates the wealth of the husband. Each box has a ring from which depends a knife. The women wear neck rings of gold and silver, one for each 10,000 dirhems which her husband is worth; some women have many. Their most prized ornaments are green glass beads of clay, which are found on the ships. They trade beads among themselves and pay a dirhem for a bead. They string them as necklaces for their women.

We recognise these ornaments as typical of those found in women's graves throughout the viking world (the 'breast boxes' probably referring to the pairs of brooches worn by Scandinavian women).

Ibn Faḍlān has a close interest in both the hygiene and the sexual practices of the people he met on his journey and these are described in most detail in the case of the Rūs. They do not wash after urinating, defecating, ejaculating or eating and when they do wash (once a day) they all do it out of the same bowl of water, into which they also blow their noses and spit. The merchants have sex with their slave girls in public, often in the presence of a prospective purchaser. These slave girls appear several times in Ibn Faḍlān's account. They are not only the wares in which the merchants deal, but also their personal property, providing both sexual and other intimate services:

> It is a custom of the king of the Rus to have with him in his palace four hundred men, the bravest of his companions and those on whom he can

rely. These are the men who die with him and let themselves be killed for him. Each has a female slave who serves him, washes his head, and prepares all that he eats and drinks, and he also has another female slave with whom he sleeps. These four hundred men sit about the king's throne, which is immense and encrusted with fine precious stones. With him on the throne sit forty female slaves destined for his bed. Occasionally he has intercourse with one of them in the presence of the companions of whom we have spoken, without coming down from the throne.

Presumably the Rūs dealt in all kinds of slaves, male as well as female, and simply chose certain of the female ones to be their personal attendants and bed companions. Whether this status was accorded permanently to a female slave, or whether she would eventually be discarded and replaced by another, Ibn Faḍlān does not tell us.

One way of reducing the numbers of slave girls was the custom of suttee, the ritual sacrifice of a woman at a man's funeral. Ibn Faḍlān witnessed such a funeral and describes it in great detail. He had a special interest in religious rites in general and funerals in particular: he tells us that 'I had heard that at the deaths of their chief personages they did many things, of which the least was cremation, and I was interested to learn more'.

A great man has died and he is placed in a temporary grave while the preparations for the funeral take place. One of the first things is the selection of a volunteer for the suttee:

> When a chief has died his family asks his slave women and slaves, 'Who will die with him?' Then one of them says, 'I will'. When she has said this there is no backing out . . . most of those who agree are women slaves . . . [When, in this case, a girl had volunteered] two female slaves were appointed to guard her wherever she went so that they even washed her feet with their own hands. Then they began to get things ready for the dead man; to cut out his clothes and do all that should be done, but the slave drank and sang every day happily and joyfully.

The dead man and his slave girl are to be cremated in a ship which has been drawn up onto a pile of wood on the shore. It has a richly furnished bier on which the dead man is placed, elaborately dressed and surrounded by his grave-goods of food and animals killed and cut into pieces for the purpose. Meanwhile the woman is performing her last duties:

> The slave woman who wished to be killed went to and fro from one tent to another, and the man of each tent had intercourse with her and said, 'Tell your master that I have done this out of love for him.'

She then takes part in a curious ritual in which she sees into the next world which she is about to enter:

> . . .they took the slave away to something which looked like the frame of a door. Then she put her legs on the hands of the men and was thus lifted, so that she was above the top of the door-frame, and she said something . . . [this was done three times]. Then they gave her a chicken and she cut off its head and threw it away. Then they took the hen and threw it into the ship. Then I asked what she had done and my interpreter answered, 'The first time they lifted her up she said, "Look, I see my mother and father"; the second time she said, "Look, I see all my dead relations sitting together"; the third time she said, "Look, I see my master sitting in paradise and paradise is beautiful and green, and together with him are men and young boys. He called to me, so let me go to him." '

She is taken to the ship, where she is met by an old woman 'whom they call the Angel of Death', who had been responsible for preparing the corpse and whose two daughters had been looking after the slave. She gives the old woman two arm-bands and her daughters two ankle-rings that she had been wearing, before going onto the ship for the final act of the drama:

> Then came men who had shields and staves, and gave her a beaker of *nabidh* [some kind of alcoholic drink]. She sang over it and drained it. The interpreter said to me, 'She now takes farewell of her friends.' Then she was given another beaker. She took this and sang for a long time, but the old woman warned her that she should drink quickly and go into the tent where her master lay. When I looked at her, she seemed bemused, she wanted to go into the tent and put her head between it and the ship, then the old woman took her hand and made her enter the tent and went in with her. The men began to beat with their staves on the shields so that her shrieks should not be heard and the other girls should not be frightened and thus not seek death with their masters. Then six men went into the tent and all had intercourse with the girl; then they laid her by the side of her dead master, then two took her legs, two took her hands, and the old woman who is called the Angel of Death put a rope round her neck, with the ends in opposite directions, and gave it to two men to pull; then she came with a dagger with a broad blade and began to thrust it time and again between the girl's ribs, while the two men choked her with the rope so that she died.

The slave girl having been killed, it is time for the cremation. The ship is set on fire and the fire took hold of the pyre, then of the ship, then of the tent and of the man and of the girl and of all that was in the ship.

The importance of Ibn Faḍlān's account is that he was an eyewitness both to these momentous events and to the daily life of the Rūs, unlike most Arab writers who were simply revising earlier ethnographic descriptions. We are reminded of this frequently in his account, where he emphasises his interest in particular customs and shows how he groped for an understanding of them. True, he must have had some disadvantages in understanding exactly what he was witnessing. For instance, he needed an interpreter to tell him what was going on and, even with an interpreter, communication may not have been perfect. He also seems to have been particularly interested in the sexual habits of the peoples he came across. Frequently in his book, not only in the account of the Rūs, he describes the dress and behaviour of the women he meets and is usually careful to note whether these conform to Muslim standards of decency and decorum. Thus his rather shocked description of the sexual activities of the Rūs is not unique, there are others like it in the rest of his book, although not always so detailed. And if he was shocked at the funeral customs of the Rūs, it may have been for slightly different reasons than our modern revulsion at human sacrifice.

Although Ibn Faḍlān's account is an invaluable and fascinating source, it would be dangerous to generalise from it about practices elsewhere in the viking world. Everywhere vikings went, they developed new ways of living which owed something both to the culture of the immigrant vikings and to that of the country in which they found themselves, so that no two areas colonised by Scandinavians were alike. Not only would the nation of the Rūs be such a cultural mixture of Slav and Scandinavian, but the Rūs that Ibn Faḍlān met were, of course, not on their home territory, but a long way away on the lower Volga. They are likely to have been a select band of merchant-warriors who, like other touring professionals, may not have behaved the same way when abroad as they did at home.

CHAPTER V

Art, Myth and Poetry

FEMALE FIGURES IN THE ART OF THE VIKING AGE

The Oseberg tapestry

We see a stately procession, with two rows of horses prancing from right to left. The horses have knotted tails and three of them are pulling carts. There are two figures sitting in one of the carts, apparently female. Between the horses, also processing from right to left, is a large number of figures, both male and female. The males wear long, wide trousers and a short tunic. The females wear a long dress with a train and an outer cloak, a round shape indicating the brooch on their breast. Many of the figures, both male and female, carry spears, and some of the males have a shield or sword as well. Scattered among the figures there are more spears, swastika symbols and other geometric shapes, and birds.

This scene is a rare example of figurative art from the Viking Age and is totally mysterious. Who are the figures and where are they all going so purposefully? Why are some of the females carrying spears? What is in the wagons? Who are the two people riding in the cart and are they somehow different from the other figures?

This processional scene is from one of the fragments of tapestry found in the Oseberg ship burial. The fragments are very poorly preserved, but enough remains to indicate that they come from a long and narrow strip (20–23 cm wide) which was carefully woven in different coloured wools (mainly red, yellow and black) with a geometric border. The quality of the design indicates a long tradition of weaving such tapestries. Originally the fragments belonged to a wall-hanging that could be used to decorate a room, like a frieze. We have later literary descriptions of such

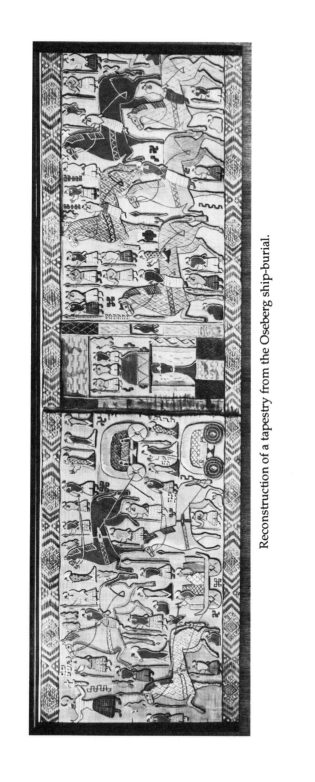

Reconstruction of a tapestry from the Oseberg ship-burial.

tapestries, but very few of them survive from the Viking Age and the Oseberg fragments, despite their sorry state, are the best preserved.

The context in which the Oseberg tapestry was found, a burial mound, suggests one explanation for the scene depicted. It is likely that it represents a procession in connection with a religious ritual, possibly even a funeral procession. The women buried at Oseberg were well supplied with horses, sledges and a cart for their journey into the next world. Could it be them that are pictured sitting in the cart at the bottom left of the picture? Other fragments of the tapestry also suggest the iconography of death. Massed ranks of warriors with their shields represent a battle scene, human figures hanging from a tree suggest the cult of Odin, god of the hanged. The motifs of the tapestry appear to have been chosen to suit an existence in the next world.

The welcome to Valhall

Most art of the Viking Age is applied art and imaginative art for its own sake is rare. Thus 'Viking art' usually means the decoration (mostly abstract or zoomorphic) of otherwise functional objects of wood, metal or stone. Narrative art, showing recognisable figures in identifiable situations, is rare until the very end of the Viking Age, and before then is found mainly in the tapestries of Oseberg and on the picture stones of Gotland. As an island in the Baltic that was a meeting point for travellers from all over the region, Gotland had its own culture that was not always the same as elsewhere in Viking Age Scandinavia. Yet the picture stones of Gotland, a remarkable series of carved memorial stones from throughout the period, have close parallels in both content and style with Viking Age art and mythology elsewhere in Scandinavia. They can provide a context which makes the mysterious narratives of Oseberg somewhat clearer.

Picture stones were carved in Gotland before the Viking Age, but the earliest ones are not relevant here as they consist of abstract and geometric designs. The Viking Age picture stones are fairly consistent in their design and iconography. They are flat stones with a keyhole-shaped outline and have scenes carved on one side in relief. A recurring scene is of a ship in full sail, loaded with armed warriors. On some of the stones, we see a rider on an eight-legged horse, being welcomed in front of a building by a female figure holding a drinking horn. Often there are armed men on the stones, either fighting or stretched out as if dead. The mythical world represented on the picture stones of Gotland is that of Valhall, a special heaven for warriors who are killed in battle. The ships represent the journey to the next world, reminding us of the many ship burials of the Viking Age. The eight-legged horse is Sleipnir, the horse of the god Odin who presides over Valhall. The warrior inhabitants of Valhall had endless food and drink, served to them by valkyries. These valkyries were, quite literally, 'corpse-choosers', female mythological figures who, on the battlefield, selected the warriors who would be admitted to Valhall. When not eating or drinking, the denizens of Valhall passed the time in fighting battles. The picture of Valhall painted for us by the later, literary sources corresponds so closely to the iconographic world of the Gotland stones that there can be no doubt what the stones show. Erected as memorials to warriors, the Gotland picture stones show the journey to the other world and the afterlife of those warriors.

The valkyries welcoming the warriors to Valhall wear an outfit very like that of the female figures of the Oseberg tapestry, a long trailing dress with a pointed cloak over it, and they have their hair knotted in the same way as the horses on the tapestry. Both the spears (a weapon particularly associated with Odin) and the birds (possibly Odin's ravens) on the Oseberg tapestry reinforce its connections with beliefs about death and the afterlife. It may not even be too fanciful to see the female figures on the Oseberg tapestry as valkyries, choosing the slain for the honour of Valhall.

These very masculine motifs seem an odd choice for a tapestry that was to accompany two women into the next life. One thing the Oseberg burial did not contain was any sort of weapon, its grave goods are purely domestic. But while the valkyries' military functions may not have reflected anything in the lives of human women, there is no doubt that their role as servers of food and drink show exactly what their human counterparts had to do. The whole concept of Valhall with its endless food and drink served by willing valkyries shows that some warriors in the Viking Age expected to be waited on hand and foot in the next world, just as in this one! However, the presence of cooking equipment in some male burials of the Viking Age shows that this expectation could not realistically be relied on.

Mythological scenes

In addition to the representations of the death and afterlife of warriors, a number of Gotland picture stones also show scenes which we can recognise as mythological narratives. The richest of these is a stone from Ardre, which contains references to at least three recognisable stories from Norse myth and legend, as well as others which cannot be identified since we lack the literary parallels which would explain them.

In the bottom right of the Ardre stone is a representation of Loki bound. Loki was the trickster of the gods who, as a punishment for killing Baldr, was bound to a rock with snakes dripping their poison into his face. His wife Sigyn held a vessel to catch the drips, and we can just make her out on the Ardre stone, with what looks like a drinking horn in each hand, beside the figure of Loki encircled by snakes.

In the centre of the Ardre stone are scenes from the legend of Vǫlundr the smith. We see quite clearly his smithy with its tools and to its right the headless bodies of the young sons of his enemy, King Níðuðr. To the left, a winged creature and a woman with her back turned to it represent Vǫlundr's rape of Níðuðr's daughter Bǫðvildr, and his escape using a set of wings he had made himself.

At the bottom left of the Ardre stone, we see scenes from the myth of the god Thor fishing for the world serpent, a popular story that is known from a variety of literary and iconographic sources. The figures to the right of the ship on the Ardre stone, including a woman wielding two swords, have not been identified with any known myths or legends.

The pictures on the Ardre stone demonstrate that the art of the Viking Age is not a substitute for narrative. The series of pictures shows individual dramatic scenes from a narrative which must be known to the viewer for them to have any meaning. The elements chosen make the story instantly recognisable to those who know it. Thus we are certain we can recognise Vǫlundr's suit of wings, his smith's tools and the boys he beheaded, and we can associate these unmistakeable images with the narrative we know from other sources. The female figure with the two swords from the same stone may have been just as unmistakeable if only we knew the story behind the image.

A more complete representation of a well-known narrative is found on a series of stones from the parish of Lärbro. Two stones in particular, Lärbro Stora Hammars I and Lärbro Tängelgårda I, although originally part of two separate multiple monuments, show a sequence of scenes

Picture-stone from Lärbro Stora Hammars, Gotland.

from one narrative, the legend of Hildr and the Everlasting Battle. The scenes are laid out in strips which we can read from top to bottom, first on the Stora Hammars stone and then on the one from Tängelgårda. We see a female figure between two men with swords, being taken captive. In the next scene, two men seem to be preparing for battle. The third strip shows a scene of sacrifice, with a figure about to be hanged in a tree, and an army ready for battle. The next scene shows the meeting of the two sides, one arriving by ship, the other meeting them on the shore. A female figure with a raised arm stands between them. The final scene on the Stora Hammars stone shows the battle scene, with one warrior dead, having fallen off his horse. A very similar battle scene is the first strip of the Tängelgårda stone. Then follows a funeral procession with the dead man being carried on horseback. The final scene shows the hero's triumphant procession into Valhall.

The role of the female figure in this martial narrative enables us to identify the story as that of Hildr. Later, literary, versions of this legend tell us that Hildr was the daughter of a king called Hǫgni. She was abducted by another king called Heðinn. When her father came to rescue her, she went between the two sides with false messages and egged them on to fight, discouraging attempts at a settlement. The battle continued all day and at night Hildr woke all the slain to life so that the battle could continue the next day, and the next day. And it is said that this battle will continue until the end of the world. The literary sources present Hildr in an unflattering light, but she has to be seen, not as a human woman, but as the personification of battle, which must have seemed neverending in the Viking Age. Her name is a valkyrie-name, and is also used as the word for 'battle' in skaldic verse.

Thus, the Lärbro stones belong to the same iconographical range as the other Gotland picture stones, also representing the harsh lot of the warrior. In the legend of Hildr the unpleasant aspects of battle and death are projected on to female figures. The ruthlessness of Hildr in opposing a settlement is like that of the female figures of the Icelandic sagas, urging their men on to vengeance. It is characteristic of military societies to personify the martial spirit as a female, removing the responsibility for war from the warriors themselves. Such projection is needed to persuade warriors to carry on fighting. Women have been blamed for war at least since Helen's face launched a thousand ships. The Viking Age was no exception to this rule, as becomes clear from a study of its art and mythology.

The art of the Gotland picture stones is thus a projection of the male warrior society of the Viking Age and cannot tell us much about the role of real women in that society, in spite of its use of female figures. Indirectly, it tells us that women impinged on that warrior society mainly in mythologised and symbolic form. Since most Viking Age narrative art is closely connected with the rites of death, and since these narratives of death are largely mythological or legendary, it is all far removed from the realities of everyday life. Yet such mythological projections do give us an insight into the thought structures of the society that created them. We have to go right to the end of the Viking Age to find art forms that reflect what we would recognise as the experience of women.

Picture-stone from Ardre, Gotland.

Dynna

The Dynna stone, an eleventh-century memorial from eastern Norway, has already been mentioned as one of the few examples of a runestone erected by a woman in memory of another woman, in this case a mother to her daughter. As well as the runic inscription, the Dynna stone has what is the earliest representation of the Epiphany in Scandinavian art.

Like the picture stones of Gotland, the Dynna stone has, not a coherent sequence of pictorial events, but a number of motifs signifying the narrative to which it refers. Thus, towards the top we see the Christ

131

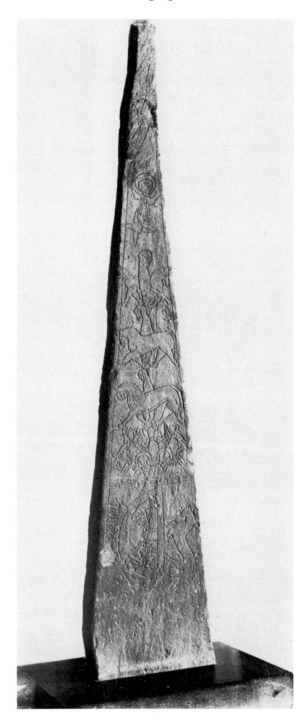

Runestone from
Dynna, Oppland,
Norway.

child with a halo, identified by the Star of Bethlehem. Below him are the three kings riding to visit him. The bottom scene (turned at a 90° angle) shows a structure (possibly a grotto) in which Mary, to the left, receives two of the kings, with the infant's crib visible in the centre. Outside, one of the horses waits.

As a work of art, the Dynna stone does not reach the same heights of draughtsmanship and design as the Gotland stones. Yet there are significant parallels. Like the Gotland picture stones, Dynna is a memorial to the dead. For this memorial, mythological scenes have been chosen and are represented in the same way, using recognisable motifs. But the differences are perhaps even more significant. The scenes chosen come from a new mythology, that of Christianity. References to the afterlife are oblique, if present at all. An artist who wished to indicate the significance of Christ as the path to heaven would surely have chosen the Crucifixion rather than the birth of Christ as a subject. The subject chosen may, however, have appealed particularly to the female patron commemorating her daughter, for it is at the birth of Christ that his mother Mary is given prominence in the story. Female converts to Christianity at the end of the Viking Age had a particular fondness for Mary. Thus, the runic inscriptions of late Viking Age Sweden, many of them erected by women, often contain invocations to 'God and God's mother'.

SEXUALITY, WISDOM AND HEROISM: FEMALE FIGURES IN NORSE MYTH AND LEGEND

The sources

The Christian scenes on the Dynna stone can be identified because we are familiar with the narratives on which they are based. The fact that we can identify some of the pre-Christian mythological figures in other Viking Age art is due to the antiquarian interests of the Christian medieval Icelanders who wrote down the myths in which they figure. Most of what we know about the Norse mythology of the pre-Christian era comes from two Icelandic collections of the thirteenth century, both called *Edda*.

The Poetic Edda

The *Poetic Edda* is a manuscript anthology of 29 poems, written down in about 1270. A third of the poems are on mythological subjects, the rest deal with characters from heroic legend. The mythological poems divide further into poems of wisdom and poems which tell stories, often amusing, about the gods. Many of the poems in the *Poetic Edda* are very old, even as old as the Viking Age, and were preserved in oral tradition until they came to be written down in medieval Iceland, probably in the twelfth century. Other poems in the *Edda* were first composed not long before the collection was made, but may have been based on much older material. Since there is disagreement among specialists about the relative dating of the Eddic poems, and about their provenance (some of the older ones could have been composed in Norway, or elsewhere, before the settlement of Iceland), the safest thing to say about the collection is that it is heterogeneous, containing poems of a wide variety of date and provenance, in a variety of styles, at least some of which originated in the Viking Age and therefore reflect the culture of that period.

The Prose Edda

The *Prose Edda* is also a thirteenth-century product, but here we know the author's name and the reason why it was written. It is a guide to poetry and mythology put together by the Icelandic author, antiquarian and politician, Snorri Sturluson, who died in 1241. The Prologue and the first section (called *Gylfaginning*) of the work present a systematic account of Norse mythology. There are also some stories involving mythological and legendary figures in the second part of the book (called *Skáldskaparmál*), where they explain the Norse system of poetic diction.

The *Prose Edda* is the only comprehensive account of Norse mythology that we have and without it our knowledge of that mythology would be patchy indeed. But it is primarily a guide to poetry and the mythological elements included are ultimately subordinated to this aim. Snorri was a Christian, writing for other Christians. He was certainly sympathetic to the old heathen myths and took an antiquarian interest in them, but he was both consciously and unconsciously influenced by Christian culture. Recent studies have tended to emphasise the Christian, medieval framework within which the book was written, but there is no doubt that it is based on a thorough knowledge of the beliefs of the pagan past. Snorri knew some of the mythological poems of the *Poetic Edda* and he also made use of other similar poems now lost. Even if we strip away Snorri's Christian interpretation, we are left with a substantial body of information about the heathen myths of Snorri's viking ancestors.

Snorri's Edda

Goddesses in the Norse pantheon

We get a glimpse of the Norse gods (called the Æsir) at home in Ásgarðr, entertaining a person called Ægir:

> And in the evening, when it was time to drink, Óðinn had swords brought into the hall which were so bright that they gave off light, and there was no other light while they sat drinking. Then the Æsir began their drinking party and the twelve Æsir who were to be judges sat on their thrones, and they were called Þórr, Njǫrðr, Freyr, Týr, Heimdallr, Bragi, Víðarr, Vali, Ullr, Hænir, Forseti and Loki; likewise the Ásynjur, Frigg, Freyja, Gefjun, Iðunn, Gerðr, Sigyn, Fulla, Nanna. Looking around, Ægir thought it magnificent; the wall panels were all covered with beautiful shields. There was intoxicating mead and a lot was drunk.

This description of the feast presents the main gods and goddesses (the latter known collectively as the Ásynjur).

Frigg is the foremost of the goddesses, for she is the wife of Óðinn and mother of Baldr. Her role in the mythological narratives is that of a tragic mother. When her son dreams that he will die, she travels the earth getting promises that Baldr will not be harmed by 'fire and water, iron and all kinds of metal, stones, the earth, trees, diseases, animals, birds, poison, snakes'. However, she omits the mistletoe, thinking it too young to make such a promise. Thus, when the gods amuse themselves by throwing things at the invincible Baldr, the evil Loki, trickster of the gods, persuades Baldr's brother to throw some mistletoe at him and he dies instantly. Baldr's death is the beginning of the end of the world, the doom of the gods or Ragnarǫk.

The most colourful goddess is Freyja, whom Snorri calls 'the most glorious of the Ásynjur'. She lives in a large and beautiful hall, and drives around in a chariot drawn by two cats. She is the goddess of love, the equivalent of Venus or Aphrodite. Freyja is the goddess who figures most frequently in the stories of Snorri's *Edda* and it is usually her beauty and desirability which are the cause of trouble for the gods.

Gefjun is the first of the Æsir we meet in *Gylfaginning*. As a reward for 'entertaining' the Swedish king Gylfi, she is given as much land as four oxen can plough up in a day and a night. Gylfi had not reckoned with the fact that Gefjun had four oxen which were the sons of her and a giant, and therefore had supernatural powers. They plough so much land that Zealand (the largest island of modern Denmark) is created out of land that had originally been in Sweden, thus depriving Gylfi of much of his kingdom. Gylfi is so intrigued by these extraordinary powers of the Æsir that he journeys to their country to find out more about them and the first section of the *Edda* relates what he found out. *Gylfaginning* means the 'Tricking of Gylfi' and Gefjun is emblematic of the way the Æsir trick human beings. The motif of deceit is emphasised by Snorri in a number of ways that add up to a Christian message: the Æsir were not real gods, only the Christian god is a real one. As Snorri put it:

> Christians should not believe in heathen gods or in the truth of this narrative other than the way it is presented at the beginning of this book, where it is told . . . how people from Asia called Æsir falsified accounts of the events which happened in Troy so that the inhabitants would think they were gods.

Objects of desire

The gods were engaged in constant battle with the giants, who were always threatening to take over Ásgarðr and had a taste for the Ásynjur. The Æsir relied on Þórr and his giant-killing hammer to keep them at bay. A giant called Hrungnir once burst into the sanctuary of the gods, saying he was going to

> sink Ásgarðr and kill all the gods, except Freyja and Sif whom he wanted to take home with him

Freyja behaves with commendable cool and continues serving him ale, until Þórr arrives home to deal with the situation.

The gods' deceitful behaviour goes right back to the beginning of time, when they arrived in Ásgarðr and needed a fortification built. A giant offered to do it for them if they would pay him by giving him Freyja as his wife, as well as the sun and the moon. The gods make the

Gold foil from Klepp, Rogaland, Norway, possibly showing
Freyr and Gerðr.

bargain with him, but never intend to pay such an outrageous price, and
they get Loki to trick him out of completing the building work on time,
so that they can annul the agreement.

Although the Æsir were not at all keen to let giants marry the goddess
of love and beauty, the dividing line between gods and giants was not
always so clearcut. Gerðr, wife of Freyr and sister-in-law of Freyja, was
originally a giantess, 'the most beautiful of all women'. Both Snorri and
the Eddic poem *Skírnismál* tell how Freyr fell in love with her at first
sight and 'he did not sleep, he did not drink, and no one dared to try to
speak with him.' Freyr even gives his precious sword to his servant
Skírnir, to get him to woo the fair Gerðr for him. As is pointed out in
Snorri's *Edda*, this was to be of great disadvantage to Freyr at the end of
the world, when he was unable to defend himself against the forces of
evil, leading to his death.

The most decorative goddess must have been Sif, the wife of Þórr. In the section on poetic language, Snorri's *Edda* tells why gold is called 'Sif's hair'. The mischievous Loki had once cut off all Sif's hair and Þórr threatened to break every bone in his body unless he got the dwarves to make Sif some hair out of gold that would grow like any other hair. Another mythological explanation of the origin of gold relates it to Freyja. When her husband Óðr went away, she wept tears of real gold, so that in poetic language, gold can be called the 'tears of Freyja'.

Warrior women

While most of the goddesses exemplify desirable female characteristics such as beauty, or demonstrate female emotions such as maternal grief, some female figures in Norse mythology illustrate another concept of womanhood. Such figures interact with the male world of the warring gods and giants, rather than just being the passive causes or victims of the endless conflict.

The giant Þjazi, in eagle form, had abducted the goddess Iðunn, keeper of the magic apples which kept the gods eternally young. The gods, in their desperation to get her and her apples back, killed Þjazi:

> But Skaði, the daughter of the giant Þjazi, took helmet and mail-coat and all weapons of war, and went to Ásgarðr to avenge her father. The Æsir offered her a settlement and, in compensation, first that she should choose herself a husband from among the Æsir, and that she should choose him by his feet, without seeing any more of him. When she saw one man's amazingly beautiful feet, she said, 'I choose this one, there can be little that is ugly on Baldr'. But it was Njǫrðr of Nóatún.

As a god of the sea, Njǫrðr presumably had very clean feet!

The marriage between Njǫrðr and Skaði was not a success, for he wanted to live near the sea and she was most at home in the mountains. They made an agreement to spend alternately nine nights at each place:

> But when Njǫrðr came back to Nóatún from the mountains, he spoke this verse:
>
> > I'm tired of mountains, I wasn't there long,
> > only nine nights;
> > the howling of wolves seemed ugly to me
> > compared to the song of swans.
>
> Then Skaði spoke this verse:

> I could not sleep on the bed of the sea
> because of the racket of birds;
> he wakes me, coming from the wide sea
> each morning: the mew.

> Then Skaði went up into the mountains and settled in Þrymheimr. She
> goes about a lot on skis, with a bow, and shoots animals.

Skaði is hardly a paragon of soft femininity, either in her warlike
mission of vengeance for the death of her father, or in her retirement in
the mountains, hunting and skiing. Her role is somewhere between that
of the male giants, who invariably get bested by the gods, and the
female giants who, if they are beautiful like Gerðr, simply get assimi-
lated into the world of the Æsir. The attempt to assimilate Skaði was not
successful. Although a minor character in Snorri's *Edda*, she is one of the
most interesting, an odd-woman out among the goddesses.

There is one group of female figures with an allotted place in the
warrior society of Valhall, Óðinn's hall of the slain:

> whose job is to serve in Valhall, bringing drink and looking after the
> tableware and the drinking vessels . . . These are called valkyries. Óðinn
> sends them to every battle, they choose who is to die and allot victory.

The word *valkyrja* means, literally, 'chooser of the slain'. These hand-
maidens of Óðinn, welcoming the dead hero with a drinking-horn, are
represented in Viking Age art, often associated with memorials to the
dead, such as the Gotland picture stones. Their otherworldly function
mirrors that of ordinary human women, who (at least in heroic literature) were expected to give returning, victorious warriors a warm
and boozy welcome at home.

Eddic poetry

Ægir's banquet

Snorri tells us that Ægir returned the hospitality the gods had offered
him by inviting them back to his place for a banquet:

> On this journey went first Óðinn and Njǫrðr, Freyr, Týr, Bragi, Víðarr,
> Loki, and then the Ásynjur Frigg, Freyja, Gefjun, Skaði, Iðunn, Sif. Þórr
> was not there, he had gone to the east to kill trolls. And when the gods
> had sat in their seats, then Ægir had shining gold brought into the middle

of the hall, which brightened and lit the hall like fire. This was used as light at his feast just as there had been swords instead of fire in Valhall. Then Loki had words with all the gods there, and killed Ægir's slave. . .

Snorri tells this story as an explanation of why gold is called 'Ægir's fire', and he must have known a poem very like one preserved in the *Poetic Edda* called *Lokasenna*. The title of this poem means 'Loki's invective' and it gives, in dialogue form, details of how 'Loki had words with all the gods'. Loki's invective consists of insults hurled at the other guests at the feast, both gods and goddesses, in which the gods are generally accused of injustice, cowardice and effeminacy, and the goddesses of promiscuity and incest.

When Loki initiates an unseemly wrangle with the god Bragi, Bragi's wife, Iðunn, attempts to intervene by restraining him. Her only thanks is when Loki turns on her:

> Shut up, Iðunn! I say you are of all women
> the most eager for men,
> since you laid your clean-washed arms
> around your brother's slayer.

Iðunn rather feebly retorts that she had only been attempting to keep Bragi quiet, and Gefjun takes up the challenge:

> Why should you two gods attack each other
> in here with hateful words?

Loki then accuses Gefjun of having 'laid her thigh over' a certain boy. Óðinn intervenes and also becomes the butt of abuse from Loki. When Frigg intervenes on behalf of her husband, Loki says to her:

> Shut up Frigg! You are the daughter of Fjǫrgyn
> and have always been mad for men,
> when you, wife of Viðrir, took both [Óðinn]
> Vé and Vili to your bosom. [Óðinn's brothers]

When Frigg says that if only Baldr were present, he would deal with Loki, Loki cruelly reminds her that he was responsible for Baldr's death. Freyja springs to Frigg's defence and is of course reminded that

> every god and every elf in here
> has been your lover.

Unlike the other goddesses who all try to defuse the situation, Skaði intervenes in characteristically aggressive mode, by telling Loki of the punishment that awaits him for the murder of Baldr

> the gods will bind you on the sword with the guts
> of your rime-cold son

Loki reminds her that he was the primary killer of her father Þjazi, but Skaði is equal to this. She reminds him of her giant origin and the continual threat from that quarter:

> from my groves and meadows shall ever come
> cold counsels to you

When Loki accuses her of having invited him into her bed, Sif intervenes by offering Loki a cup of mead. The poem ends with Þórr's arrival, and a great exchange of insults between him and Loki.

In *Lokasenna* the Ásynjur are gentle souls who attempt to make peace when an unseemly brawl breaks out between Loki and their husbands. His accusations about their sexual lives call attention to their attractiveness, the characteristic prerequisite for a goddess. Only Skaði breaks the pattern, not only standing up to Loki, but turning the tables on him and reminding him of his fate. Loki attempts to insult her sexuality in the same way as he has done with the other goddesses, but is less successful. His reference to her father gives her the chance to remind him that the gods gave her compensation for that – and she is now a god, too. Yet she is a giant in origin and thus much more dangerous to Loki than the other goddesses.

There has been much debate about whether *Lokasenna*, with its unflattering view of the gods, could ever have been a heathen poem, or reflect the attitudes of the Viking Age. A polytheistic religion would allow more scope for making fun of a deity, so this need not be an argument against its age. In any case, the myths on which *Lokasenna* is based certainly had their origin in the Viking Age.

Þórr recovers his hammer

Another Eddic poem of disputed date is *Þrymskviða*, the story of how Þórr's hammer was stolen by a giant and how he got it back. Although it may very well be post-Viking Age, this poem illustrates the attraction of Freyja for the giants and shows how the gods turned this to their advantage to recover Þórr's all-important hammer.

A giant, Þrymr, had stolen Þórr's hammer, but said he would give it back if he could have Freyja as his wife. The gods are in a quandary – Þórr must have his hammer back to protect them from the giants, but they do not want to give up Freyja. She herself is hopping mad at the idea. So the gods persuade Þórr, much against his will, to dress up as Freyja. He and Loki (disguised as her maid) go to Giantland, where Þrymr is taken in by the disguise, but a little surprised that the bride can put away one ox, eight salmon, all the dainties intended for the ladies, and three barrels of mead! As the giant brings up the hammer to claim his bride, (s)he grabs it and kills him. And that is how Þórr got his hammer back.

Along the way, the poem makes much fun of sexual roles in early Norse society. Effeminacy was the greatest insult to a man and Þórr is not at all happy at having to dress up as a woman (although the highly ambiguous Loki seems to have no problems with this); yet the picture of Þórr, with his bridal headdress, his jewellery and his keys dangling from his belt, is a supremely comic one.

Eddic wisdom

Not all the poems in the *Poetic Edda* tell stories about the gods. About half the poems belong to the cycle of legends surrounding the hero Sigurðr the Dragon-slayer. Yet other poems of the *Edda* are compendia of wisdom and knowledge. There are disputes about the dating of these gnomic poems, and we can never be guaranteed that they represent a Viking Age view of life, since all we can say for certain is that the poems must have been composed some time before they were written down in about 1270.

A poem that has attached itself to the Sigurðr cycle, but was originally unrelated, is *Sigrdrífumál*. In it a female figure (possibly a valkyrie) offers advice to a warrior. This advice consists mainly in listing the runic formulas that a man must know in order to avoid or deal with difficult situations. Thus, he must know 'victory runes' if he wishes to have victory, he must know 'sea runes' to avoid getting shipwrecked, he must know 'healing runes' to be able to treat wounds, he must know 'speech runes' to avoid others causing him harm, and he must know 'thought runes' to be wiser than others.

Two of the kinds of runes the warrior must know also involve women in this otherwise rather masculine world. Thus

> You must know ale-runes, if you wish the wife of another
> not to deceive you in your trust, when you feel secure

It is an inverted view of the woman as hostess, offering a poisoned drinking horn rather than the more normal welcome to a guest, the instrument of her husband's treachery.

While the warrior's 'healing runes' make him useful for dressing wounds on the battlefield, he was obviously expected to have more peaceful medical knowledge as well:

> You must know saving runes, if you wish to save
> and loosen children from women

Even warriors had to act as midwives, it appears!

The advice given in *Sigrdrífumál* covers a range of human activity, giving a broad education to the young warrior, with a female figure as the repository of this useful wisdom. The wise woman who, as well as having practical knowledge, could see into the past and future, is common in Old Norse literature. The very first poem in the *Poetic Edda* is *Vǫluspá*, the 'Prophecy of the wise woman', composed in Iceland towards the end of the Viking Age. The poem outlines the history of the world from its beginning to its end in Ragnarǫk and the only one who knows this whole history is the female narrator, who can remember the beginning and foresee the end.

Vǫluspá is a complex and obscure poem, on which much scholarly ink has been spent, but its basic narrative structure is clear. Óðinn, the god of wisdom, who knows a thing or two himself, has asked the sibyl to expound her knowledge. The poem is partly addressed to Óðinn, partly to the assembled company of gods and men, it is partly in direct speech, partly an indirect account of what the sibyl said. The emphasis is very much on her experience, she tells what she remembers, what she knows and what she sees. This happens to encompass the whole history of the world, from its creation through to its destruction in Ragnarǫk, with a glimpse of the birth of a new world after the end of the old one. At the end of the poem, the sibyl 'sinks'. The wise woman who knows more than the god of wisdom has no place in the post-Ragnarǫk world, but then neither does Óðinn.

Suffering women in heroic poetry

Women's foreknowledge is often in contrast to their inability to act on that knowledge and thereby avert fate or change men's course of action. In the heroic poetry of the *Edda*, tragic heroes and villains clash, and women are caught in the middle.

The heroic poems of the *Edda* are based on a common Germanic inheritance of heroic legend whose origins and early development are obscure. The scene of the action is usually the continent in the Migration period, when Europe was peopled by tribes of Huns, Burgundians and Franks. Originally separate traditions became associated into longer cycles of tales. Half of the *Poetic Edda* is thus a cycle centring on the life of the hero Sigurðr and on the tragic fate of his widow Guðrún. The later Eddic poems dealing with the life of Guðrún show a very medieval concern with romantic love and were almost certainly composed in the twelfth century. They cannot tell us much about how such a tragic heroine might have been viewed in the Viking Age, but they are useful in showing the development of romantic literature about women in the medieval period.

However, one of the Eddic poems dealing with Guðrún seems genuinely old, even ancient. This is *Atlakviða*, or the 'Lay of Atli'. Atli is the Hun Attila, whom Guðrún has married after the murder of her husband Sigurðr. Atli wishes to get hold of the Niflung treasure, the whereabouts of which are known only to Guðrún's brothers, and entices them to his court to kill them. Guðrún exacts a terrible revenge for the deaths of her brothers, not only killing her husband, but first killing her two sons by him and feeding him their corpses. It is not a pretty tale, although expressed in some of the most powerful of Old Norse poetry. Nor is there anything especially Scandinavian about it, as the action mostly takes place at the court of the Huns. Nevertheless, it provides a Viking Age interpretation of a long-popular story (known also from the *Nibelungenlied*, for instance).

Guðrún is first mentioned in st. 8 of *Atlakviða* where her brothers, sensing no danger, are discussing the invitation to her husband's court:

> 'What do you think the lady meant
> when she sent us a ring
> wrapped in the heath-ranger's coat?   [wolf]
> I think she offered us a warning.
> I found a hair of the heath-ranger
> twisted round the red ring.

Codex Regius of the Poetic Edda, *Voluspá.*

> Our way is wolfish
> if we ride on this journey.'

Nevertheless, their masculine pride forces them to take up the challenge. Guðrún tries once more to send them back, by intercepting them on their arrival to Atli's court:

> 'You should have stayed in the saddle
> through sun-lit days,
> made the Norns weep
> at the corpses' forced pallor,
> made the shieldmaids of the Huns
> try their skill at the harrow –
> while Atli himself
> you should have brought into the snake-pit.
> Now the snake-pit lies waiting
> for Hǫgni and you.'

Hǫgni's heart is cut out of him alive and Gunnarr dies in the snake-pit, neither having revealed to Atli the whereabouts of the Niflung treasure.

Guðrún welcomes Atli on his return from having killed her brothers in a parody of the usual welcome of the hostess for the returning warrior:

> Then Guðrún came out
> to meet Atli
> with gilded cup,
> 'You may take and eat, sire,
> in your hall
> joyfully from Guðrún's hands
> young beasts gone to the shades.'

Although Atli does not yet know it, the 'young beasts' are in fact his sons. Guðrún gets him drunk and then tells him the awful news, in a speech which contrasts the grisly meal with happy family memories:

> 'You are digesting, proud one,
> slaughtered human meat,
> eating it as ale-morsels,
> sending it to the high-seats.
>
> You will not again call
> to your knee
> Erpr or Eitill,
> both merry with feasting –

146

> you will not see again
> at the centre of the dais
> the bounteous princes
> fitting shafts to their spears,
> clipping manes,
> or cantering their horses.'

At this a great moan arises among the Huns and all bewail the news

> save only Guðrún
> who never wept
> for her brothers, fierce as bears,
> and beloved sons,
> young, untried by life,
> whom she bore to Atli.

Although Guðrún is distressed at what she has done, the implication is that she had no choice, that it was a necessary sacrifice to take revenge for the, to her, equally if not more distressing death of her brothers. Guðrún completes her revenge by stabbing her husband in bed and setting the hall on fire, with all his followers in it. The poem concludes

> The whole tale is told:
> never after her
> will any wife go thus in armour
> to avenge her brothers.
> She caused the death
> of three kings
> of a nation,
> bright lady, before she died.

Although Guðrún's tragedy is great, she is a larger-than-life heroine who has taken on herself the male prerogative of vengeance. The final verse sums up the admiration such a heroine could occasion.

Not all the female characters who suffer from male rivalries are able to act heroically as Guðrún did, and the oldest poetry of the *Edda* also has sympathy for women who are purely victims. The heroic poem *Vǫlundarkviða* is not a part of the Sigurðr cycle, but is also based on an old legend known from other parts of the Germanic world, especially Anglo-Saxon England. The smith Vǫlundr, who is hamstrung by the wicked king Níðuðr, takes his revenge on the king's children. The two sons are killed and their skulls made into cups and their teeth into jewellery. Vǫlundr then makes the king's daughter Bǫðvildr drunk and rapes her, making her pregnant. Vǫlundr's moment of grim triumph is when he flies away with the set of wings he has made for himself:

Laughing, Vǫlundr rose into the air,
crying, Bǫðvildr went from the island.

Women in myth and reality

The unfortunate Bǫðvildr and the rather passive and decorative goddesses in Norse mythology suggest that females did not count for very
much in the Viking Age. On the other hand, they could exercise power,
if they had wisdom or strength of character, and there was admiration
for women who could behave like men, like Skaði and Guðrún. Female
figures could also be feared, for their sexuality (the troubles the gods
had with the giants were often caused by Freyja's desirability), or for
their knowledge (such as the sibyl in *Vǫluspá*). But in what way do
attitudes to goddesses and heroines in mythology and literature reflect
attitudes to women in real life? Were power and wisdom restricted to
fictional women, safely contained by the unreality of mythology or the
distance of heroic legend? There is never an easy correlation between
literature and life, but looking at some Viking Age poetry that does
purport to deal with real people, rather than gods and superhuman
heroes, may bring us closer to an answer.

WOMEN AND SKALDIC POETRY

Skalds and their verse

Of all the cultural products of the Viking Age, it is skaldic poetry which
comes closest to our image of that period as masculine and military.

The Old Norse word *skáld* means 'poet'. While much Old Norse
poetry is anonymous, the term 'skaldic' is thus used for the kind of
verse that is typically by named poets. This poetry was composed in a
fairly rigid verse form which was unique to Scandinavia, where it was
productive from the Viking Age through to the fourteenth century,
although in the Middle Ages it was practised mostly by Icelanders.

The earliest skaldic verse was composed at the courts of the Viking
Age rulers of Scandinavia. The skalds were professional poets, their job
to praise the king or chieftain and to entertain the court. In return they
received handsome financial rewards. The most common themes of
such poems were the military exploits of the ruler at sea and on land.

The ruler was often praised for his generosity, not only because this was a highly valued quality, but also as a reminder by the poet of the fee he expected in return. As well as praising a living ruler, poets could be commissioned to compose a eulogy in memory of a dead one.

Skaldic poetry could encompass wider themes than just martial praise. A ruler who had military success soon acquired power, and many descriptions of battles also suggest their political and historical consequences. In a largely oral society, skaldic poems were thus a way of recording as well as praising the achievements of a ruler. Descriptions of seafaring provide some of the most effective skaldic verse which often transcends its rather dreary military context. Poems on mythological themes for the entertainment of the audience were also popular from an early stage. Later, skaldic forms could be used for verse on almost any subject and we have scurrilous verse, love poetry, dream visions and Christian praise poetry from medieval Iceland where the genre continued to be practised until well into the Middle Ages.

This long popularity of skaldic verse forms can make it difficult to distinguish between Viking Age and later compositions. Apart from verses in runic insriptions Old Norse poetry is preserved in Icelandic manuscripts of the thirteenth century or later and there is thus never any guarantee that a given verse is genuinely as old as the Viking Age; there is always the possibility that it was composed much nearer the time when it was written down. This is certainly true of many of the skaldic verses attributed to Viking Age poets and presented as if they were Viking Age compositions which adorn the Icelandic family sagas. Nevertheless, scholars agree that there is a substantial body of skaldic verse composed in the Viking Age by poets whose names were remembered, which was orally transmitted until it came to be written down in medieval Iceland. Although the dating of skaldic poetry is notoriously difficult, there is broad agreement on the categories of verse that are likely to be genuine and those that are, at the very least, doubtful. Verses preserved in the *konungasögur*, or sagas of the kings, and in poetological treatises such as Snorri's *Edda*, are likely to be genuine. All others must be assumed to be doubtful.

The 'doubtful' skaldic verse must be treated in the same way as other medieval Icelandic literature: as a particular view of the Viking Age filtered through the minds of the Christian Icelanders who wrote it. 'Genuine' skaldic verse, on the other hand, is the literary expression of the concerns of people living in the Viking Age and indispensable to an understanding of the period.

The skald's craft

Poetry is designed to be remembered. Metrical structures and devices such as rhyme make verse easier to remember than prose. The more rigid the rules of metre and rhyme are, the more likely the verse is to have been preserved accurately in oral tradition. The rules of skaldic verse are about as strict as they can be, thus greatly aiding its preservation.

Skaldic poetry is stanzaic, and could consist either of a single stanza or of two or more stanzas strung together into a longer poem. The basic skaldic stanza has eight lines of six syllables each (although it falls naturally into two halves and sometimes only four lines are preserved). Within this tight framework of 48 syllables the poet had to juggle the metrical demands of alliteration and rhyme, and the stylistic demands of an elaborate poetic language. Each of the eight lines contains two rhyming syllables, with full rhyme in lines 2, 4, 6 and 8, but only half-rhyme in lines 1, 3, 5 and 7. Lines 1 and 2, 3 and 4, 5 and 6, and 7 and 8 were joined in couplets by alliteration, according to the standard practice of early Germanic poetry. Thus, two words in the odd-numbered line and one in the even-numbered line had to begin with the same sound, and this sound had to be at the beginning of the even-numbered line. The following verse has been marked to demonstrate these rules – alliteration is marked in **bold**, half-rhyme by <u>single underlining</u>, full rhyme by <u>double underlining</u>:

1 Var<u>ð</u>a **g**ims sem <u>gerð</u>i
2 **G**er<u>ð</u>r bjúglimum h<u>erð</u>a,
3 **g**n<u>yr</u> óx Fjǫlnis f<u>úra</u>,
4 **f**ar<u>l</u>ig sæing j<u>arl</u>i,
5 **þ**ás **hr**ingf<u>ó</u>um **H**a<u>ng</u>a
6 **hr**y<u>n</u>serk, viðum br<u>yn</u>ju
7 **hr**u<u>ð</u>usk riðmarar R<u>óð</u>a
8 **r**a<u>st</u>ar, varð at k<u>ast</u>a.

(see p. 151 below for translation)

Not only did poets have to mind their syllables, they also made extensive use of an elaborate poetic language. Most poets used special poetic words for otherwise everyday things that were not used in prose (known as *heiti*), and elaborate metaphorical constructions called 'kennings' that are familiar from poetry in other languages, but nowhere so consistently developed as in skaldic verse. The wide range of synonyms that *heiti* and kennings provided poets made it easier for them to find words with the appropriate alliteration and rhyme to fit into their metrical jigsaw puzzles.

Women in a man's world

The world of skaldic verse

It is not easy to see that there could be any room for women in this poetic world of kings and battles, swords and carrion birds, ships and sailing. Indeed, the number of Viking Age skaldic stanzas that make any reference to women is very small indeed. Since skaldic poetry appears to represent a real, if somewhat idealised and formalised, world, we have to conclude that this was an important aspect of Viking Age life in which women played little or no part. Yet if we look more carefully at some skaldic stanzas, we find references to women indicating that they were considered a part of the larger world that sanctioned and demanded military action, and that also suffered from it.

Skaldic verse is action poetry, it tends to the descriptive rather than the narrative and is good at painting word-pictures of the heat of battle or of a ship at sea, or at cataloguing the achievements of a hero. The larger context in which all this takes place, the country for which a battle is fought, the reason for a sea-voyage, the audience of a praise poem, are all in the background, on the horizon of the poetic scene. It is at this edge of the specific and limited masculine world of the skalds that we find women.

The ironic contrast

The poem quoted above (p. 150) to illustrate skaldic metre is an example of this placement of women beyond the immediate military scene of a skaldic poem. It can be translated as follows:

Not like when a beautiful	
fire-goddess with bent shoulder-limbs	[woman; arms]
made for the jarl a bed	
(din-of-Óðinn's-fires increased),	[battle]
was when he cast off the few-ringed	
resounding shirt of Óðinn,	[mail coat]
the steeds of the sea-leagues	[ships]
were cleared of mail-coat-trees.	[warriors]

The stanza is from a panegyric on the Norwegian jarl Hákon, who lived in the second half of the tenth century, celebrating his most famous victory in the battle of Hjǫrungavágr, by an Icelandic poet, Tindr Hallkelsson. This stanza explores the contrast between the rage of battle and the comforts of home life. Thus battle is the 'din of the fires of Óðinn' (Óðinn is the god of war, his 'fire' a flashing sword). Warriors are 'mail-coat-trees' and Hákon's prowess is emphasised by the fact that he is fighting without his ('few-ringed', worn) chain mail ('resounding shirt of Óðinn'). The ships (of his opponents) are swept clear of their fighters just as Hákon throws away his armour. This noisy scene is contrasted with the home in which a woman ('goddess of the [hearth-] fire'), with her bent arms (suggesting an embrace) prepares a bed for the warrior. On one hand, the implication is that real men are out there in the thick of things, not lolling about at home with women. On the other hand, there is also the hint that warriors long to be doing just that and that whoever wins the battle will be the lucky one who can go home to such comforts afterwards. Thus women become the focus of male ambivalence about war. It must be said that this modern-seeming doubt is hardly common in skaldic poetry, which more usually glories in the violence of battle without underlining the attractiveness of the quiet alternative.

Cheering them on

More often we see women on the sidelines, as helpers, instigators and approvers of the masculine behaviour described in skaldic verse.

They could help in a practical way by making the cloth for the sails of a ship, as in this half-stanza from a praise poem by Óttarr the Black:

> You scored with planed rudder
> the splash-high waves; the sail
> spun by women played on
> the launch-reindeer's mast-top.   [ship]

Women were expected to admire the spectacle of men setting out for war. In this series of verses by Þjóðólfr Arnórsson describing the departure of the naval levy from Trondheim under the leadership of Haraldr the Hard-ruler, the king's ship is compared to a dragon:

> Fair lady, I saw the ship launched
> from the river into the sea.
> See where the long-sided warship

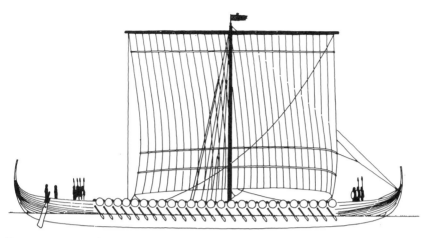

Reconstruction of a viking warship (based on Skuldelev 2).

<blockquote>

lies, splendid, off the shore.
The bright dragon's mane above
the cargo shines, since he was launched
from rollers, his decorated
neck is burnished with gold.

</blockquote>

<blockquote>

The troop-lord casts off the long   [Haraldr]
tarpaulin on Saturday,
where splendid widows from the
city see the dragon's side.
The young king steers out of the Nid
the brand-new ship westwards,
while the oars of the sailors
splash into the sea.

</blockquote>

<blockquote>

The prince's band can pull
their oars straight out of the sea.
The widow looks and admires
the wondrous flight of the oars.
Madam, there'll be much rowing
till the tarred sea-tools fall apart.   [oars]
The four-edged pine allows that   [oar]
while there still is full peace.

</blockquote>

Skaldic verses are often presented as if they were declaimed by the poet in the middle of the event he is describing. A poet in the thick of battle may remember the woman who urged him to fight, as did Haraldr (one of several kings of Norway who were also remembered as poets) in this last verse before he fell in the battle of Stamford Bridge in 1066:

We won't creep from weapon-crash	[battle]
behind curved shield in battle,	
thus did command the loyal	
lady of the hawk's land.	[arm]
Necklace-bearer once bade me	[woman]
hold high my helmet-support	[head]
in the weapon-din where	[battle]
war-icicles met skulls.	[swords]

The literary motif of women, behind the scenes, urging their men into battle, is common and Haraldr may not have had any particular woman in mind.

Having urged men into battle, women become the arbiters of how well they perform there. This anxiety to be seen to be performing heroically by a woman is expressed in a half stanza by the Icelander Skúli Þorsteinsson, who fought on the winning side in the battle of Svold in the year 1000:

Valkyrie of the drink-vessel	[woman]
won't have seen me in the rear	
of the regiment when I gave	
gory wounds for the dawn-flier.	[raven]

The idea of women as observers of a battle (rather like medieval ladies at a tournament) is explored in the anonymous poem *Liðsmanna-flokkr*, describing Cnut's capture of London in 1016:

The pure widow living in	
the stone house will look out and see	
(weapons often glow above the head	
of the oft-helmeted leader)	
the victory-eager Danish	
chief with energy attack the	
town's defenders, blood-icicle	[sword]
crashes on British mail-coats.	
Drink-horn-valkyrie on the bank	[woman]
of the Thames each morning sees	
helmet-spoiler red with blood	[weapon]
(Óðinn's seagull won't starve).	[raven]

Telling women all about it

Even if a woman could not actually witness the hero's prowess in battle, she could still be told about it and so have a basis for her admiration.

Another stanza from *Liðsmannaflokkr* addresses an anonymous woman
directly to tell her of recent battles:

> Every day Hǫgni's door   [shield]
> indeed became quite bloody,
> goddess, when early we fought   [woman]
> in the fray with our leader;
> since hard-fought fight is now
> finished, we can sit in
> fair London, o land   [woman]
> of the sun of the sea.   [gold]

(The 'sun of the sea' is gold, and its 'land' is a woman, the woman
who is being addressed in this stanza).

This boasting of one's achievements to a listening woman could also
take place in a more peaceful context. The Icelandic poet Sigvatr
Þórðarson went on a diplomatic mission to Sweden and composed a set
of verses about his journey. In this stanza, having just received the gift of
a ring, he boasts to a local woman:

> These dark Icelandic eyes,
> woman, have led me far
> along the hard road
> to the shining ring.
> Mead-goddess, my foot   [woman]
> has gone full boldly
> on ancient ways unknown
> to your husband.

Women as victims

In skaldic verse, battle is usually an all-male affair, the victorious heroes'
victims are the warriors on the losing side. But we do get glimpses of
more wholesale warfare, usually abroad, where the female population
also suffers. In a panegyric on the Norwegian king Magnús the Good,
Þjóðólfr Arnórsson described the impact of his campaign against the
Danish king Sveinn:

> The girls of Sjælland asked as one
> who brought the battle standard,
> it is true too that many
> men had blood-reddened shields.
> The wealth-bearers' fate was   [women]

> to run through the forest.
> Very many refugees
> raced over to Ringsted.

New views

Towards the end of the Viking Age, women appear in skaldic verse in new roles. Sigvatr, court poet to King Óláfr the Saint who was responsible for Christianising Norway, was a convert himself and a close friend of the king. When the king became godfather to Sigvatr's daughter, the proud father composed this verse:

> Lord, glorious is thy will,
> help him who lifted my
> daughter out of heathendom
> and gave her the name Tófa,
> under water the wise
> brave brother of Haraldr   [Óláfr]
> held my child, I was very
> cheerful that morning.

When Sigvatr is praising the king as a godfather, not as a warrior, we are in a new world.

Sigvatr outlived his patron to compose verse for his son Magnús the Good. He also composed the only skaldic panegyric in praise of a woman, Ástríðr, wife of Óláfr and stepmother of Magnús. Ástríðr was a daughter of the Swedish king, Óláfr Eiríksson, and Sigvatr had played a large part in arranging her marriage to Óláfr Haraldsson. Ástríðr and Óláfr had only one daughter, Úlfhildr; Óláfr's son and successor, Magnús, was the son of a concubine. After Óláfr's death at the battle of Stiklestad, Ástríðr went home to Sweden and Magnús into exile in Russia. When Magnús returned to Norway to claim his patrimony, he was fully supported by his stepmother. Sigvatr's poem praises her for this:

> I will praise well with my poem
> Óláfr's daughter, wife of the stout,
> victorious warrior,   [Óláfr]
> for her many bright presents.
> A substantial army of Swedes
> came east to the thing at Hangrar   [assembly]
> when Ástríðr announced the cause
> of the son of Óláfr.   [Magnús]

Good advice-giver, she could
hardly have dealt better with
the determined Swedes had
bold Magnús been her own son.
She, with the mighty Christ,
was the main reason that King
Magnús could take up all the
inheritance of Haraldr.

Generous Magnús owes Ástríðr
a reward for her bold deed,
we're glad for it, it gave
a great realm to the friend of men.   [Magnús]
Woman of wise advice has
helped her stepson as few
others would, true words I make
to honour the lady.

The poem shows the queen acting in the public arena, persuading her compatriots the Swedes to help her stepson recover the kingship of Norway and, most importantly, succeeding. The sagas in which this poem is preserved tell us that when the men of the Danish king Sveinn (who was ruling Norway at the time) saw the hordes of Swedes, there was no resistance to Magnús and he became king very easily. It is both high praise indeed and something totally new when the poet ascribes this important political development entirely to the actions of a woman, helped of course by the might of the new Christian god.

But then Sigvatr was clearly partial to his protegée, the wife he had found for his patron and hero, St Óláfr. The sagas tell us that King Magnús had his natural mother Álfhildr brought to court and that there was some rivalry between the old king's queen and his concubine. Sigvatr gave this advice:

Álfhildr, let Ástríðr take
precedence over yourself,
your status has anyway
improved, and it is God's will.

What about romance?

Love in Viking Age skaldic verse is most notable by its absence. The implied contrast with war is usually to the disadvantage of love. Haraldr the Hard-ruler, on a campaign in Denmark, composed this verse:

> The linen-oak, song-goddess,   [woman]
> sings lullabies to her
> husband, while we lie at
> anchor in the Randersfjord.

The husband is clearly going to get a shock when he gets up from his dilly-dallying and finds the Norwegian army at his door!

But in the late Viking Age we find romance creeping into skaldic verses, especially those attributed to three eleventh-century kings of Norway: St Óláfr, his half-brother Haraldr the Hard-ruler, and his son Magnús the Good. Óláfr is said to have composed this verse about the Swedish princess Ingigerðr who was to have married him, but was instead married off to Yaroslav, Prince of Kiev:

> I stood on a mound, watching
> a fair mount bear the woman,
> the beautiful-eyed wife
> caused me to lose pleasure;
> friendly woman, goddess of the   [woman]
> hawk's ground, quickly drove the horse
> out of the yard; each man is
> haunted by one mistake.

A number of sagas of Icelanders have poets as their heroes, with the poet's unhappy love-affair as a major element of the plot. These sagas (*Kormáks saga, Bjarnar saga Hítdœlakappa, Gunnlaugs saga, Hallfreðar saga*) all contain romantic verses by the hero in praise of his beloved. It is however doubtful that these are genuinely Viking Age poems that reflect the attitudes of that period. Although the people of the Viking Age must have experienced love between man and woman, it is only at the end of the period that the literary expression of that love in skaldic verse became possible, and then under the influence of foreign literary taste. The skald sagas reflect this later development rather than the attitudes of the tenth and eleventh centuries that they purport to describe: it is likely that their love-verses were composed in the twelfth century or later, if not at the time when the sagas were written in the thirteenth.

158

Women and poetic language

Heiti

The verses translated above have already suggested the elaborate poetic language used by the skalds which, along with the complex metre, make it impossible to translate their poetry in a way which puts the full flavour across.

Heiti, which are simply poetic words for ordinary things, are easier to give an idea of, since there are parallels in English – who but a poet would say 'mount' for 'horse', or 'maid' for 'girl'? A wide range of synonyms enabled the poet to choose the word that fit the metrical scheme. Sometimes, the metrical needs overcame logic and the word chosen was not always the most appropriate. The normal word for a woman, *kona* could be used, but more common were *mær* ('maiden') and *ekkja* ('widow'), short and easy to fit into a variety of rhyme and alliteration schemes. Both should probably just be translated 'female person', but there is always the possibility of reading the original meaning of the word if it improves the poem. The 'pure widow' who looks out of her window in *Liðsmannaflokkr* could be any woman, but it adds to the effect of the poem to think of her as a woman newly widowed, one who has just watched her husband being killed by Cnut's army.

Kennings

More revealing about Viking Age attitudes to women are the kennings used for them. Kennings are a special, compressed form of metaphor common in skaldic verse but known elsewhere. The classic example of a kenning is when a camel is called 'the ship of the desert'. The metaphorical process can be explained as follows: A camel is a mode of transport just like a ship. But a camel is not really a ship and if we just call it a ship, no one will know what we mean, so we add a determinant, in this case, the desert. Thus, a camel is a mode of transport (ship) that is used in the desert. The dryness of the desert adds an extra piquancy to this particular kenning.

Skalds had kennings for most of the things described in their poetry, including these examples from the poems quoted earlier:

sword:	fire of Óðinn
	icicle of war
	icicle of blood

mail coat:	shirt of Óðinn
battle:	din of swords
	crash of weapons
raven:	seagull of Óðinn
ship:	steed of the sea
	reindeer of the launch rollers
leader:	lord of troops
	friend of men
head:	support of the helmet

Kennings could be embedded in one another to create complex kennings. Thus, the 'din of swords' means battle, but a sword could be
called the 'fire of Óðinn' (from its flashing appearance and because
Óðinn is the god of war), so that battle could become the 'din of Óðinn's
fires'.

Kennings divide into two types. In the classic kenning, the base word
is something which, logically, the referent is not (a ship is not a horse, a
sword is not an icicle, a raven is not a seagull) and yet the two have
something in common (ships and horses are modes of transport, swords
and icicles look similar, ravens and seagulls are both birds). The determinant then helps to specify what is meant (a horse of the sea is a ship,
an icicle of war is a sword, a seagull of Óðinn is a raven). The other kind
of kenning, however, tells us something that is true: a head is a support
for a helmet, a leader is a friend of men.

Kennings for people most commonly have one of two kinds of base
words. The base word can be the name of a god or supernatural being.
Thus a man can be a 'god of battle', with any one of a number of gods'
names. Also very common is the use of a word meaning tree (often a
particular kind of tree), presumably deriving from their similar shape.
Thus a man is a 'mail-coat tree'.

While the determinants for men often refer to their military prowess,
the determinants in kennings for women may refer to their domestic
function. Thus we had, quoted above, 'mead-Nanna' where Nanna is
the name of a goddess, and 'valkyrie of the drinking vessel'. We have
already seen how valkyries welcomed dead warriors in Valhall, a surviving warrior would expect to be welcomed in the same way at home
by his wife. Woman's role as hostess complements the male role of
warrior: in Tindr's verse the 'Gerðr (goddess) of the hearth-fire' was
explicitly contrasted with the male activities of war.

In a heroic society a woman was also important as a living symbol of
her husband's wealth and we often find women defined in terms of

their gold and jewellery. 'Necklace-bearer' and 'wealth-bearer' suggest a woman weighed down by her riches. Gold, silver and jewels give the skaldic poets a chance to show off their talents, for there are all sorts of complicated kennings for them that can be incorporated into the woman-kennings. Thus, in the legend told by Snorri (and which is also familiar from the *Nibelungenlied*), the treasure of the Niflungs was thrown into the Rhine, so that gold can be called the 'fire' or 'sun' (because it shines) of any kind of water (for instance 'the sea'). A woman who is the 'land of the sun of the sea' is thus a sort of background for a lot of gold. The idea of gold and silver bracelets gives rise to a lot of kennings involving arms. The arm is the 'hawk's ground' and a 'Gefn (the name of a goddess) of the arm' is a woman. This does not however imply that women actually practised hawking. It is in fact shorthand for a full kenning in which gold is called the 'fire of the hawk's ground (arm)' and a woman is a 'goddess of gold'.

Like the kennings for men, those for women could also have the name of a tree as a base-word (Old Norse being a language with grammatical gender, the poets used feminine tree nouns for women and masculine ones for men). In Haraldr's verse quoted above, a woman is an 'oak of linen', referring to her linen headdress. The metaphor of a person as a tree could be further developed, so that the 'branches of the shoulders' is a kenning for 'arms', as in Tindr's verse.

Women skalds

Given the overwhelming maleness of skaldic poetry, it is surprising to find that medieval Icelandic traditions record some skaldic poets who were women. Their numbers are not great, especially if we discount the almost certainly fictional skaldic utterances by the occasional female character in the Sagas of Icelanders. Leaving them out, there remain four named Viking Age women who were remembered by medieval Icelanders as poets and whose verse is preserved in historical sagas.

We know little enough about these four as poets (in two cases only one stanza or just half a stanza survive) and in three of the four cases very little about them as women. The exception is Gunnhildr, known as 'mother of kings', the wife of Eiríkr Bloodaxe, king of Norway and sometime king in York during his exile from Norway. Our picture of Gunnhildr derives from later Icelandic texts: she was a favourite hate-figure of the Icelandic saga-writers and there are unflattering portraits of her in *Egils saga, Laxdœla saga* and *Njáls saga*. Leaving aside these sagas' accusations of nymphomania and witchcraft, even the more historical kings' sagas show her as a malevolent, scheming, arrogant woman who outlived her husband to return to Norway and attempt to further the royal ambitions of their sons there before she was once again and for the last time driven into exile in Scotland. It is difficult to penetrate beneath this misogynist picture to discover any facts about Gunnhildr, we are not even sure whether she was Norwegian or Danish. But in one history of the kings of Norway, the thirteenth-century *Fagrskinna*, she is remembered as having had some interest in poetry. After the death in battle of Eiríkr Bloodaxe in England in 954, his widow 'commissioned a poem about him'. This poem, the *Eiríksmál*, describes how Eiríkr is welcomed to Valhall by Óðinn.

Eiríkr and Gunnhildr had been driven into exile in England by his half-brother, Hákon the Good, the youngest son of King Haraldr Finehair of Norway. Haraldr was credited in Icelandic tradition with twenty sons and most of them aspired to the throne. As the eldest, Eiríkr succeeded his father for a time while Hákon was abroad in England, but Hákon soon returned to make his claim. It is at the time of Hákon's return to Norway that Gunnhildr is credited with a half-stanza. There had been a shipwreck and it was thought that Hákon had perished, but Gunnhildr, with her powers of prophecy, knew better, and announced his safe arrival in the fjords of western Norway thus:

> Hákon rode plank-horse onto   [ship]
> the back of the waves from the west;
> the king let the prow bite the surf
> and the prince has reached the fjords.

It is unlikely that Gunnhildr would have dignified the claim of her husband's deadly rival to rule Norway by commemorating it in skaldic verse and the attribution of the poem to her may be apocryphal. Taken out of its prose context, the half-stanza could be from a standard skaldic poem in praise of Hákon, mistakenly attributed to Gunnhildr.

Also connected with political machinations in Viking Age Norway is the verse attributed to Hildr Hrólfsdóttir. Hildr was married to a close associate of King Haraldr Finehair and was the mother of Gǫngu-Hrólfr ('Walking-Hrólfr'), whom Icelandic tradition believed to have been the same man as Rollo, the legendary viking founder of Normandy. In *Heimskringla*, the Icelandic historian Snorri Sturluson tells how Hrólfr, in his youth, got on the wrong side of King Haraldr, and was exiled by him

Gold hoard from Hon, Buskerud, Norway.

for threatening the order recently established in the country by the king. Snorri presents Hildr as going to the king and begging for mercy for her son in the following words:

You forsake Nose's namesake   [Hrólfr]
now you drive out like a wolf
the wise brother of farmers.   [Hrólfr]
Why, king, behave thus badly?
It's bad to out-wolf such a wolf

of the slain-board of Óðinn,
he will not be easy on the royal herds
if he runs to the woods.

(board of the slain of Óðinn = shield; wolf of the shield = warrior)

Snorri's interpretation of this episode is highly coloured by thirteenth-century attitudes, with the anxious mother interceding for her son. His description of her feminine pleading contradicts the tone of the verse itself which is quite ugly and threatening. It is likely that the verse is genuinely old and genuinely by Hildr – it gives us a rare insight into the conduct of Viking politics.

The other two female poets of the Viking Age whose names and poems have been preserved for posterity were also interested in public affairs. Their figures are shadowy, but their poems speak clearly enough. About Jórunn we know nothing more than her name and the fact that she was given the nickname of 'skald-maiden'. There is no indication of whether she was Norwegian or Icelandic, or even when she lived. Her verses survive because they record an incident during the lifetime of Haraldr Finehair. Even before his death, his sons were jockeying for position. *Heimskringla* described an attack by one of Haraldr's sons, Hálfdan the Black, on his brother, Eiríkr Bloodaxe. This angered Haraldr, who prepared to retaliate against the attacker. The situation was defused by a poet called Guthormr Sindri, a court poet and great friend of both Hálfdan and Haraldr. Guthormr composed poems in praise of both of them and refused the skald's traditional payment, desiring only that they should be reconciled. Guthormr's mollifying verses are not recorded, but we have the tribute of another poet, Jórunn, in which she describes the royal conflict and the way in which the 'trouble of the princes ceased' because of Guthormr Sindri's poetic intervention. The poem is quite difficult to understand and extremely difficult to translate, but the following should give the flavour:

Harald frák, Halfdan, spyrja	Halfdan! I'm told Haraldr Finehair heard
herðibrǫgð, en lǫgðis	about those deeds of darkness,
sýnisk svartleitr reyni	and that poem seems darksome to
sjá bragr, enn hárfagra.	the adventurer of the blade.
	[adventurer of the blade = warrior]
Bragningr réð í blóði,	The ruler let weapons redden
beið herr konungs reiði,	in the blood of the rascal crowd,
hús lutu opt fyr eisum,	the folk endured the king's anger

óþjóðar slǫg rjóða;
því at ríkr konungr rekka,
reyr undlagar dreyra
morðs þá er merkja þorðu
magnendr, bjósk at fagna.

and many a house fell in flames;
because the powerful king of
warriors prepared to rejoice
when the quickeners of death dared
to blot with blood the wound-sea's reed.

[quickeners of death = warriors]
[sea of the wound = blood; reed of blood
= sword]

Hvar vitu einka ǫrvir
ǫrveðrs frama gǫrvan
tinglrýrǫndum tungla
tveir jǫfrar veg meira
en geðharðir gerðu
gulls landrekar þollum
(upp angr um hófsk yngva)
óblinds fyri lof Sindra?

Where do equally battle-quick
chieftains two know greater honour,
grandeur granted the destroyers
of the planet of the prow-boss,
than was given the firs of gold
by toughminded kings because of
the praise of clearsighted Sindri?
The trouble of princes ceased.

[planet of the prow-boss = shield;
destroyers of shield = warriors]
firs of gold = men]

Hróðr vann hringa stríðir
Haralds frammkveðinn ramman;
Gotþormr hlaut af gæti
góð laun kveðins óðar;
raunframra brá rimmu
runnr skjǫldunga gunnar;
áðr bjósk herr til hjǫrva
hreggs dǫglinga tveggja.

The enemy of rings performed
Harald's potent panegyric;
Guthormr got from the sovereign
good pay for recited poem;
the battle-tree ended bloodshed
between truly successful kings;
the armies of the two princes
had prepared for the storm of swords.

[enemy of rings = (generous) man]
[battle-tree = warrior, man]
[storm of swords = battle]

Even a translation can give some idea of Jórunn's stunning effects and her deliberately ironic use of poetic language. Thus, in the last stanza, Guthormr is called an 'enemy of rings', a standard kenning implying financial generosity, usually used for a ruler. But Guthormr is actually not only on the receiving end of royal generosity, but is also renouncing the poet's usual reward for pay of a more intangible kind. Then, he is called a 'tree of battle', again a common kenning for a warrior, precisely while he is being praised for ending bloodshed. It is a poem about the power of poetry, which cunningly makes use of the traditional language and preoccupations of skaldic verse to subvert its more usual subject matter. Jórunn was a talented poet and we can only wish that more of her verse had been preserved.

The last recorded poetic female of the Viking Age lived in Iceland at the time of its imminent conversion to Christianity, very late in the tenth century. She was called Steinunn, and was remembered as the mother of a poet called Refr Gestsson. Since poetry seems to have run in the family, it is likely that she composed more verse that is now lost. Certainly that which is preserved shows she had a talent for poetry.

Two of Steinunn's stanzas are preserved in a narrative recounting the altercations between Christian missionaries in Iceland and a number of adherents of the heathen faith, all of whom were poets. This narrative is preserved in several versions and was clearly popular with medieval Icelanders. Although they must have identified with the ultimately successful Christians, they also enjoyed the clever verses of the heathens. The missionaries, being foreigners, did not have this entertaining talent. The German missionary Þangbrandr kills a number of poets who composed scurrilous verses about him and the climax of the story comes when he attempts to leave Iceland. He is foiled by the wreck of his ship in a storm off the coast of Iceland. This is described in these two verses by Steinunn, in which she contrasts the power of Christ to protect his servant unfavourably with the power of her god, Þórr, to cause the shipwreck in the first place:

Þórr brá Þvinnils dýri
Þangbrands ór stað lǫngu,
hristi borð ok beysti

Þórr altered the course of Þangbrand's
long horse of Þvinnill, he tossed and
bashed the plank of the prow and
    smashed

barðs ok laust við jǫrðu;
munat skíð um sæ síðan
sundfœrt Atals grundar,
hregg því at hart tók leggja,
hánum kennt, í spánu.

it all down on the solid ground;
the ski of the ground of Atall
won't later be buoyant on the sea
since the baleful gale caused by him
splintered it all into kindling.

[Þvinnill = a sea-king; his horse = a ship]
[plank of the prow = a ship]
[Atall = a sea-king; his ground = the sea;
a ski of the sea = a ship]

Braut fyrir bjǫllu gæti
(bǫnd ráku val strandar)
mǫgfellandi mellu
móstalls vísund allan;
hlífðit Kristr, þá er kneyfði
knǫrr, málfeta varrar;
lítt hygg ek at Guð gætti
Gylfa hreins at einu.

The killer of ogresses' kin
pulverized fully the mew-perch
bison of the bell's guardian
(the gods chased the steed of the strand);
Christ cared not for sea-shingle
stepper when cargo-boat crumbled;
I think that God hardly guarded
the reindeer of Gylfi at all.

[ogresses' kin = ogres, giants; their killer
= Þórr]
[perch of the mew = the sea; bison of the
sea = a ship]
[guardian of the bell = a priest, i.e.
Þangbrandr]
[steed of strand = a ship]
[stepper of the sea's shingle = a ship]
[Gylfi = a sea-king; his reindeer = a ship]

Steinunn is working within a tradition of skaldic praise poetry in which it was usual to show the hero making a successful sea-journey in spite of bad weather, storms and high seas. Her copious use of kennings for the sea and for ships shows that she was fully conversant with this type of seafaring poetry. Yet she inverts the convention by describing a failed voyage – Þangbrandr does not manage to leave Iceland – and the poem becomes the antithesis of a praise poem. Like Jórunn, she uses the full panoply of skaldic technique to do the opposite of what skaldic verse normally does.

There is hardly enough evidence to generalise about women's poetic activities in the Viking Age. It is remarkable that women composed poetry at that time at all. Although the attributions of these poems derive from thirteenth-century (or later) Icelandic traditions, we cannot call these into question without doubting most of the attributions of Viking Age skaldic verse. The evidence for female poets is as good as, if not as copious as, that for male poets.

These four women poets took politics and public events as the subject matter of their verse. It is striking to the modern eye that we do not see any evidence of what we might imagine were typically 'female' preoccupations in their poems. This may just be because not enough of them are preserved, for what interest would the writers of the kings' sagas (who were primarily responsible, along with Snorri in his *Edda*, for transmitting Viking Age poetry) have in poems that saw the world through female eyes? The pessimistic view would be that female poets in the Viking Age had to work within the closely-defined genre of skaldic verse and had to produce texts that appealed to a largely male audience. Thus, they either never bothered to produce work that did not fit the mould or, if they did, then it was neglected and forgotten precisely because it did not fit. Yet we cannot complain that we have *no* insight into how a Viking Age woman might have seen the world around her. Hildr, Gunnhildr, Jórunn and Steinunn have all given us that insight.

The last two have even done it in a way that shows they had the talent to use rigid skaldic conventions for their own ends. If their poems do not fit in with our preconceptions of what a 'woman's-eye view' of the Viking Age might be like, that is hardly their fault.

THE AUDIENCE OF VIKING AGE POETRY

Who were the poems for?

It is clear that the earliest skaldic poetry was composed for an audience that was largely aristocratic, largely military, above all, largely male. This is obvious from what we know about the poets and the circumstances of composition, but is also strongly suggested by the poetry itself. The above selection of references to women in genuinely Viking Age poetry, although not exhaustive, is very nearly so. In the vast corpus of skaldic poetry, women are marginalised, whether as subjects of the poetry, as addressees, as real or fictional admirers of male militarism, or as poets. It is unlikely that any audience that contained a substantial proportion of women would sustain interest in such an art form for very long, however brilliantly wrought the verses.

Eddic poems, by contrast, are full of female figures. The verse forms of Eddic poetry are simpler, suggesting a less specialised, broader, audience. The subject matter of the poetry ranges widely, from comedy to tragedy, again suggesting a wider audience. The Eddic poems are all anonymous, leaving room for speculation about the circumstances of their composition. All of these points suggest that the Eddic tradition was one in which women could also take part.

Many things have to be taken into consideration in evaluating this suggestion. Is it naive, for instance, to assume that poems which have prominent female characters, which pay attention to clothing and appearance, which emphasise female tasks and which display female emotions are necessarily part of a tradition of poetry composed or transmitted by or for women? The problem of the chronology of the Eddic poems has already been mentioned. Most of the poems which show this feminine sensibility are those which are generally considered to be late, post-Viking Age products of a romantic trend that can be discerned elsewhere in Norse literature. The very anonymity of the poems raises questions. Is each recording of an Eddic poem just one 'performance' of a poem that lived, ever-changing, in oral tradition, or are they poems like modern poems, or even skaldic poems, very firmly implying the figure of a poet? And to what extent can such poetry, very obviously based on old and traditional material, be taken as representing the attitudes of the audience for which it was composed? How long can values remain fossilised in living literary texts when the audience of those texts no longer shares those values?

Scholars are a long way off agreeing on the answers to any of these questions, at least as far as they affect the poems of the *Edda*. But one example will illustrate both the difficulties of using such literary material and the potential benefits.

Helgi and Sigrún

The Helgi poems

The way texts can reflect different attitudes is most easily demonstrated when we have the same story told in more than one version. There are a number of examples of this among the poems of the *Edda*, but the two poems about Helgi Hunding-slayer (known as *Helgakviða Hundingsbana I* and *Helgakviða Hundingsbana II*) are particularly illuminating, since there is some overlap of verses as well as of subject matter and they are obviously in the same tradition. Both poems belong to the 'heroic' section of the *Poetic Edda* and are loosely connected with the cycle of poems about Sigurðr. There is no clear consensus among scholars about their chronology or even place of origin. The second poem is confused in its structure and it is often assumed that it was somehow mangled in transmission, whether oral or literary.

Both poems tell the story of the hero Helgi, son of Sigmundr the Volsung (and thus half-brother of Sigurðr). Both mention, briefly, the killing of Hundingr from which he gets his nickname. The narrative interest, however, is concentrated on the battle in which Helgi, at the insistence of Sigrún, daughter of the king Hǫgni, kills another king, Hǫðbroddr, whom her father had wished her to marry.

The plot and the main characters are the same, but there the similarity ends. The first Helgi poem begins with the birth of the hero and dwells at length on his youthful exploits, ending just after the battle when Sigrún prophesies a glorious future for him in which she, of course, also plays a part. The poem is strong on descriptions of the glory of Helgi and his fleet, and emphasises his prowess and the number of his followers. The language is more elaborate and closer to the skaldic style than is usual for Eddic poems and many scholars would see it, in effect, as a praise poem, though for a legendary hero and not a real one. Sigrún plays a small, but significant, role in it. She provides the cause of his great triumph. She is a valkyrie who protects his expedition, and she pronounces the final victory and prophesies the hero's successful future.

In the second Helgi poem we do not hear of Helgi's birth and youth, but we do get a burlesque account of how Helgi had to dress up as a serving-maid to escape from Hundingr. There is more emphasis on the attraction between Helgi and Sigrún, and on her conflicts with her family for not wanting to marry Hǫðbroddr. In the battle with Hǫðbroddr, Helgi kills not only him, but also Sigrún's father and one of her brothers. The poem continues beyond this battle and tells how her surviving brother Dagr took revenge by killing Helgi. It ends with Sigrún spending a last night with the ghost of Helgi in his burial mound. This last motif ('the dead lover's return') is well known from folklore and literature throughout Europe. While it may not originally have been a part of the Helgi story, it is essential to the interpretation of this story found in the second Helgi poem, which elevates the conflict into a tragic one in which a woman is torn between loyalty to her own family and to her husband.

Thus, the first poem shows the triumphant Helgi, the second shows the tragic Sigrún. In the first poem, Sigrún is also a triumphal figure, her strength contributing to Helgi's. In the second poem, Sigrún's tragedy leads to Helgi's downfall as well as her own. This becomes clear if we compare the treatment of some key scenes in the two poems.

The meeting of Helgi and Sigrún

In the first poem, Sigrún appears out of the blue during Helgi's battle with Hundingr, along with some other valkyries:

> Their mail-coats were splattered with blood.
> Rays shone from their spears.

Helgi asks them if they want to go home with him that night. Sigrún's answer is short and to the point:

> 'I think we have other things to do
> than to drink beer with the ring-breaker.'   [generous man]

She tells him that her father has promised her to the 'fierce son of Granmarr' and that he will come to fetch her in a few nights' time unless Helgi challenges him. Helgi immediately promises to take on Hǫðbroddr in battle. The scene is unemotional and the conversation factual.

In the second Helgi poem, their meeting also takes place just after he has killed Hundingr. Sigrún runs up to him and kisses him, and 'then the prince liked the woman'. She, we are told, had 'loved him with all her heart' even before they met. She tells him that she has been betrothed to Hǫðbroddr, but that she faces the 'anger of kinsmen' because she has gone against her 'father's dearest wish'. Helgi's reply is comforting and a bit patronising:

> 'Never mind the wrath of Hǫgni,
> nor the evil thoughts of your kin!
> You, young maid, will live with me,
> your kin, good one, will be where I am.'

Sigrún, the valkyrie

Sigrún is a valkyrie who follows Helgi in battle and brings him victory, and this is made clear in the first Helgi poem. As well as her martial appearance when she first meets Helgi on the battlefield, she is deliberately associated with the battle raging around them in her conversation with him:

> From her horse, Hǫgni's daughter
> (the clash of shields concluded) told the leader:
> 'I think we have other things to do
> than to drink beer with the ring-breaker.'   [generous man]

As Helgi's fleet sails to challenge Hǫðbroddr, Sigrún flies above them:

> And Sigrún, from above, battle-bold,
> protected them and their journey;

At the end of the battle, the valkyries come to apportion victory and Sigrún has the last word:

> Helmeted creatures came down from the air   [valkyries]
> (roar of spears grew) protecting the prince;
> then Sigrún said (wound-creatures flew,   [valkyries]
> wolves ate the food of Óðinn's raven):   [carrion]

171

> 'Leader, you'll thrive and have glory,
> descendant of Yngvi, you'll enjoy life,
> since you have felled the staunch
> chief, who caused the king's death.

> 'King, both gold rings and
> the rich maiden suit you well;
> king, you'll thrive and enjoy both
> Hǫgni's daughter and Ringsted,
> victory and land; the battle is over.'

In the second Helgi poem, Sigrún's role as a valkyrie is much less explicit. When Sigrún is searching for Helgi, she tells his lieutenant that she knows all about his victory over Hundingr because:

> 'I was not far away, captain of the troop,
> yesterday morning when the lord's life ended'

All other references to Sigrún's valkyrie career are in the prose passages inserted into the poem, which are not an integral part of it, but depend on a scribe or redactor's knowledge of traditions about Helgi.

The tragedy of Sigrún

With less emphasis on battles and Helgi's martial prowess than the first poem, the second Helgi poem develops an aspect of the story that is totally absent from the first, the personal tragedy of Sigrún. Her first meeting with Helgi emphasises both her emotional state and the personal dilemma of conflict with her family. Both of these themes are highlighted later in the poem, along with a sense of her inability to control events, unlike the very determined Sigrún of the first poem.

After the death of Hǫðbroddr, Sigrún exclaims joyfully that she will never have to 'sink into his arms', only to have her pleasure dashed by Helgi's announcement that he has killed her father and brother. His attempt to console her in her distress receives this reply which makes clear her dilemma:

> 'If I could, I would choose to bring to life the dead,
> and yet hide myself in your embrace.'

This is the classic dilemma of woman in a heroic society, divided in her loyalties. The conflict is brought to a head when her surviving brother, Dagr, kills Helgi out of vengeance for their father, despite their earlier reconciliation. His announcement of this killing again emphasises her emotional state:

> 'I am reluctant, sister, to tell you sad news,
> because I prefer not to make my sister weep'

Sigrún, however, summons her strength of character and, far from weeping, puts a virulent curse on her brother. But again, she is patronised. Dagr tells her she is 'mad' and 'out of her wits' to curse *him*, for it is Óðinn that is responsible for all the trouble, and he offers her money in compensation. Sigrún breaks into a lament for the dead Helgi, which concentrates on his powers as a warrior and a leader of men:

> 'Helgi towered over other princes
> like the well-shaped ash over a thorn,
> or the dew-sprinkled deer calf
> moving taller than all animals,
> its horns glowing in heaven itself.'

This imagery is not of the Viking Age, nor is the gruesome encounter between Sigrún and the ghost of Helgi in the grave:

> 'I want to kiss the dead king before
> you throw off your mail-coat;
> your hair, Helgi, is matted with hoar frost,
> the leader is all sprinkled with corpse-dew,   [blood]
> Hǫgni's son-in-law's hands are rain-cool'

Helgi replies that each tear that she sheds falls as a drop of blood on his breast. They spend the night together, but Helgi has to ride away before dawn and she never sees him again.

The female dilemma

In the first Helgi poem, it appears to be no problem that Sigrún does not marry the man her father chose for her, as long as Helgi gets him out of the way by killing him. The second Helgi poem, however, emphasises that Sigrún has transferred her loyalties from her own family to her husband. Guðrún had a similar conflict of loyalties in *Atlakviða*, however her primary allegiance remained with her brothers rather than her husband and sons. The second Helgi poem presents us with a woman whose love for her husband is greater than her loyalty to her family. In this poem, Sigrún is a rather weak character who can only express this loyalty emotionally. But in some thirteenth-century Sagas of Icelanders (especially *Gísla saga*), we find an exploration of these conflicts expressed through female characters who are more forceful and able to take more practical actions to express their loyalty.

This suggests that the second Helgi poem, with its interest in female dilemmas and emotions, represents post-Viking Age concerns and attitudes. Its interest in gender roles is also demonstrated by the curious incident when Helgi has to dress up as a serving maid to elude Hundingr, who is chasing him. Hundingr, like the giant in *Þrymskviða*, suspects from his 'sharp' eyes that he is not a woman, but Helgi is saved by the explanation that he was once a valkyrie:

> 'she strode above the clouds
> and dared to fight like a viking,
> before Helgi captured her'

The valkyrie motif, which in the first Helgi poem was quite serious, is here a bit of a joke.

The exploration of 'female' problems and the interest in the boundaries between gender roles of much Old Norse literature contrast with most Viking Age skaldic poetry and with poems such as *Atlakviða*. In these, women are either not present, or they are present on the sidelines, or they behave essentially like men. When specifically female behaviour is defined and explored, when it is put at the centre of literary interest, when the boundaries between the sexes become a problem, we sense we are in a new world where the gender balance has somehow changed. Literary explorations of femaleness and maleness indicate this change, although they may not reflect exactly what has happened.

This change in balance may just be a result of greater female participation in, or interest in, the literary activities which reflect it. Thus, poems like the second Helgi poem suggest there was a female audience for such literature, perhaps even that it was composed or transmitted by women. However, the female characters are rarely seen from within, they most often show the male's attempt to come to terms with a new situation. Thus, I believe there is a more fundamental, historical change behind these literary developments. Literary history suggests that those texts which emphasise gender roles are likely to be those which come at the very end of, or even after, the Viking Age: there is nothing in *Þrymskviða*, *Lokasenna* or the second Helgi poem that conclusively proves they are very old. As we shall see in the next chapter, such themes are also a prominent feature of the post-Viking Age prose literature of Iceland.

The runic inscriptions of the late Viking Age, particularly in Sweden, show how women could come into a new prominence where previously they had been invisible. In the areas of Sweden, such as Uppland, which have the most inscriptions mentioning women, the vast majority of the inscriptions are overtly Christian. It is clear that Christianity brought about all sorts of social changes and many of these radically altered the lives of women. Whether these changes were for good or ill, they certainly impinged on the lives of men and it is their confusion that finds literary expression in the literature of the post-Viking period.

CHAPTER VI

Warrior Woman to Nun – Looking Back at Viking Women

WARRIOR WOMEN

'Not the couch but the kill'

There were once women in Denmark who dressed themselves to look like men and spent almost every minute cultivating soldiers' skills; they did not want the sinews of their valour to lose tautness and be infected by self-indulgence. Loathing a dainty style of living, they would harden body and mind with toil and endurance, rejecting the fickle pliancy of girls and compelling their womanish spirits to act with a virile ruthlessness. They courted military celebrity so earnestly that you would have guessed they had unsexed themselves. Those especially who had forceful personalities or were tall and elegant embarked on this way of life. As if they were forgetful of their true selves they put toughness before allure, aimed at conflicts instead of kisses, tasted blood, not lips, sought the clash of arms rather than the arm's embrace, fitted to weapons hands which should have been weaving, desired not the couch but the kill, and those they could have appeased with looks they attacked with lances.

This is how Saxo Grammaticus, writing in flowery Latin his *History of the Danes* in about 1200, described warrior women in Viking Age Denmark. He used this digression to explain the good number of references to such warrior women in the first part (Books 1–9) of his *History*, dealing with Denmark's legendary past.

Thus, we hear of 'Sela, a warring amazon and accomplished pirate', and of

Lathgertha, a skilled female fighter, who bore a man's temper in a girl's

176

body; with locks flowing loose over her shoulders she would do battle in the forefront of the most valiant warriors.

There are women warriors at the great battle of Brávellir, an event long remembered in Norse legend, in which the aging Danish king Harald War-tooth lost to his Swedish nephew Ring. Hetha and Visna, 'whose female bodies Nature had endowed with manly courage', and Vebiorg, 'instilled with the same spirit', lead companies of men on the Danish side, with Hetha in charge of the right flank of Harald's army and Visna his standard-bearer. Visna and Vebiorg are killed in the battle, but Hetha survives to be given part of Denmark to rule under the victorious Ring. She does not last long, however, because 'the Sjællanders, who had had Harald as their captain, thought it a disgrace to be subject to a woman's laws. . .'

It is characteristic of Saxo's woman warriors that they are ultimately defeated. Even the formidable Rusila, who 'had had frequent clashes with her brother Thrond for the throne of Norway' and had 'set her sights on nothing less than the sovereignty of Denmark' eventually succumbs to the Danish king, despite a series of military successes. Like 'the girl Stikla', many a woman 'stole away from her fatherland, preferring the sphere of war to that of marriage', but usually they ended up married all the same.

A prince called Alf, despite overcoming two deadly snakes to win the princess Alvild, cannot marry her straight away, although both the girl and her father are willing. Her mother poisons her mind against her suitor and

> she changed into man's clothing and from being a highly virtuous maiden began to lead the life of a savage pirate. Many girls of the same persuasion had enrolled in her company by the time she chanced to arrive at a spot where a band of pirates were mourning the loss of their leader, who had been killed fighting. Because of her beauty she was elected the pirate chief and performed feats beyond a woman's courage.

Alf and Alvild eventually meet up in battle, where

> he laid hands on her more lovingly and compelled her to change back into feminine clothing; afterwards she had a daughter by him, Gurith.

Later, Gurith follows in her mother's footsteps by taking part in battle herself, although with less effect. Her husband is killed in the battle and her son 'Harald consequently reckoned his mother's aid had brought him more embarrassment than assistance.'

As a Christian, a cleric and a man, Saxo did not approve of women warriors, that much is clear. Like many a churchman, he saw only one possible role for women, that of a sexual being. To Saxo, therefore, women warriors who refused this role are further examples of the chaos and disintegration of the old heathen Denmark, before the church and a stable monarchy brought in a new order. Book 10 of Saxo's history recounts the national conversion of Denmark and there are no women warriors in Books 10–16, only the mothers, sisters, wives, concubines and daughters of Danish and other kings.

In these last seven books, Saxo was writing recent, contemporary history, and these form the main part of his work. He had good access to information about this period through his connections with both the church and the aristocracy, as well as through his predecessors in Danish history-writing. Books 1–9 form a lengthy introduction to Saxo's contemporary history and contain a rich variety of tales and legends, generally considered to be largely fictional. The sources of these are not fully understood, for scholars have yet to plumb all the depths of Saxo's narrative. But it is clear that, writing in Latin, Saxo was influenced by classical models. His warrior women owe a lot to classical concepts of amazons. They may also be compared with female warriors like Camilla in the *Aeneid*, whose

> girl's hands had never been trained to Minerva's distaff and her baskets of wool, but rather, though a maiden, she was one to face out grim fights. . .

Yet Saxo's warrior women are not just a classical fiction transplanted to northern Europe. Saxo drew much of his material from native Scandinavian sources and notes particularly, in his preface, the 'diligence of the men of Iceland', adding that he had 'scrutinised their store of historical treasures and composed a considerable part of this present work by copying their narratives.' Thus, many of Saxo's fantastic tales in the first nine books have parallels in Old Norse literature, although it is rarely easy to trace the connections between Saxo and the extant Icelandic texts. Despite their amazon heritage, then, Saxo's women warriors must be seen in the context of Old Norse traditions preserved in Icelandic literature.

Valkyries and warriors

A point of contact is provided by Saxo's tragic love story of Hagbarth, who desires to win the princess Signe from his rival Haki, despite having killed her brothers. To gain access to her, he 'dressed himself in woman's clothing' and 'to advance a plausible reason for his expedition he professed to be a fighting-woman of Haki's, coming from him on embassy...' When Signe's maidservants marvel at why his 'legs were so hairy and his hands not very soft to the touch', both Hagbarth and Signe have fun in further deceiving them, asserting that 'it wasn't the custom of one of Haki's warrior slaves to devote herself to women's chores but to hurl spears and lances with a blood-stained right arm'.

Although the situation is different, this scene is reminiscent of *Helga-kviða Hundingsbana II* where Helgi disguises himself as a woman. He too is asked why he is so masculine:

> 'More fitting is to that hand
> a sword-hilt than a mangle.'

Helgi explains that this is because of his past as a warrior woman who 'dared to fight like a viking'.

We have already seen that the Helgi poems form a part of Icelandic traditions about valkyries. In them, the mythological valkyries who allot death on the battlefield and serve drinks in Valhall have developed the additional role of guardian and tutor to the hero. Although of martial appearance and present during battles, the valkyries of the Helgi poems and of other Icelandic texts are not actually shown fighting. Indeed, it is hard to imagine the rather pathetic Sigrún of *Helgakviða Hundingsbana II* taking part in a battle. But Helgi in disguise shows that the idea of a woman warrior was not inconceivable to the Icelandic audience of the *Poetic Edda*.

Saxo emphasised warrior women who fought on their own account, but on at least one occasion he shows one of these giving more intangible help to the hero. Lathgertha, who had been both married to and divorced from the hero Regner Lothbrog, could still come to his assistance in battle and

with a measure of vitality at odds with her tender frame, roused the mettle of the faltering soldiery by a splendid exhibition of bravery. She flew round the rear of the unprepared enemy in a circling manoeuvre and carried the panic which had been felt by the allies into the camp of their adversaries.

Lathgertha's ability to fly shows her kinship with the valkyries of the Helgi poems. That Saxo knew about valkyries is shown by a passage in which he describes some 'forest maidens' whose

> special function was to control the fortune of wars by their guidance and blessings. They were often invisibly present on the battlefield and by their secret help afforded the desired outcome to their favourites. . .

Although Saxo's warrior women are related to the valkyries of Norse myth and legend, they represent a typically medieval view of such past beliefs. Valkyries can only turn into amazons when they are no longer a part of the belief structures of a society, although they may then represent new belief structures, in Saxo's case a typically Christian view of women. The heroic fantasy of the protective valkyrie we find in Eddic poetry and Saxo's misogynist fantasy of warrior women may be easy enough to recognise for the products of the male imagination that they are. But there has always been a temptation to regard the female characters of Icelandic prose literature as a more realistic portrait.

OLD NORSE LITERATURE

Saxo wrote in Denmark and in Latin, but the great bulk of literature preserved from medieval Scandinavia is in the vernacular and in Icelandic manuscripts. In fact, 'Old Norse literature' is nearly synonymous with 'Old Icelandic literature'.

Scandinavians were not entirely illiterate in the Viking Age for they knew runes, but they did not regularly write lengthy texts until after the conversion to Christianity and the introduction of the Roman alphabet, along with the technology of producing manuscript books. Although the language of the Church was Latin, the Scandinavians followed the example of the Anglo-Saxons and used the new alphabet to write their own language as well. By the mid-twelfth century, we know that Icelanders were writing 'laws, genealogies' and 'sacred writings' in Icelandic, as well as 'that historical lore which Ari Thorgilsson has recorded in his books'. This early use of the vernacular for religious and practical purposes led, in Iceland, to the development of an extensive and varied literary culture that flourished throughout the Middle Ages. As Saxo put it:

> since the barrenness of their native soil offers no means of self-indulgence, they pursue a steady routine of temperance and devote all their time to improving our knowledge of others' deeds, compensating for poverty by their intelligence.

Any study of the Viking Age has to come to terms with the testimony of Old Icelandic literature and it would be almost impossible to write about the period without taking this into account. Icelandic texts already quoted in this study include: historical works such as Ari Þorgilsson's *Íslendingabók* and that comprehensive account of the settlement of Iceland, *Landnámabók*; that indispensable guide to Norse mythology, the *Edda* of Snorri Sturluson, the important collection of myth and legend in the *Poetic Edda*, and the testimony of Viking Age skaldic poetry preserved mainly in the historical sagas of Norwegian kings.

These works are extant in Icelandic manuscripts of the thirteenth century or (usually) later. None of them preserves the original version of the text: all of these works were first put into writing earlier than the manuscript evidence would suggest. However, since none of them could have been put into writing before the general introduction of writing to Iceland, probably around 1100, their relevance to the study of the Viking Age derives from the fact that they appear to depend on traditions that go back to the Viking Age. In the case of poetry, both Eddic and skaldic, this is unproblematic, in theory at least, for the mnemonic structures of verse indicate that it can be preserved in an oral tradition as well as a written one. The myths told in Snorri's *Prose Edda* depend partly on such extant poetry and partly on mythological narratives in verse or prose that, although not preserved today, must have been widely known then. Both iconographic sources and the kennings of skaldic poetry presuppose knowledge of myths such as those recorded by Snorri. Ari, in his *Íslendingabók*, tells us that much of his material came from reliable oral historical tradition, and both he and the compilers of the versions of *Landnámabók* made use of the genealogical lore which has always been a feature of Icelandic culture. Although difficult to pin down, it is nonetheless clear that there was some kind of oral tradition stretching back to the Viking Age behind much of Iceland's medieval literature.

But none of these texts can be used directly as evidence for the history and culture of the Viking Age, they first have to be put through a sifting process in which they are studied as the literary products of twelfth- and thirteenth-century Iceland. Recent scholarship has emphasised this contemporary aspect of Old Icelandic literature rather than its value to Viking Age studies.

One branch of Old Icelandic literature, now generally studied as high medieval literature rather than as a source for the Viking Age, is the group of Sagas known as *Íslendingasögur*, or Sagas of Icelanders. They are generally viewed as self-conscious fiction, as precursors of the realistic novel in prose, not otherwise known in Europe until many centuries later. Despite this modern emphasis on their fictionality, it remains true that the Sagas of Icelanders purport to deal with historical characters and real events, and to provide a picture of life in Iceland in the late Viking Age, from the late ninth to the early eleventh century. For this reason, they have greatly influenced modern views of the Viking Age.

This is particularly true in our understanding of the role of women. If modern readers have a picture of Viking Age women at all, it is of the strong-willed, free and dominant women they know from the Sagas of Icelanders. This myth is the two-way mirror through which we inevitably see the women of the Viking Age. Indeed it is fair to say that much of our view of that period is, for good or ill, highly coloured by the detailed narratives of the Icelandic sagas. Even those who dismiss the evidence of the sagas are subconsciously influenced by them. Thus any study of women in the Viking Age must confront the myth promulgated in the Icelandic sagas.

WOMEN IN THE SAGAS OF ICELANDERS

The troublemaker

Many of the female characters in these sagas are thoroughly unpleasant. An example is Freydís, daughter of the Greenland chieftain Eiríkr the Red. She appears in two sagas, *Grœnlendinga saga* (The Greenlanders' saga) and briefly in *Eiríks saga rauða* (Eiríkr the Red's saga), which describe the settlement of Greenland by emigrants from Iceland, and the

Spindle-whorl of Viking-Age type found at L'Anse aux Meadows, Newfoundland.

remarkable voyages some of these Greenlanders made to 'Vínland', somewhere in North America. These sagas illustrate the important historical kernel there can be in such texts. Scholars had long known that Norse people discovered North America some five hundred years before Columbus, but the only evidence was in these two sagas and in a few stray references in other texts. The saga descriptions of the voyages of exploration by Greenlanders and Icelanders to the place they called Vínland were spectacularly vindicated in the 1960s by the archaeological discovery of a Norse settlement at L'Anse aux Meadows in Newfoundland.

The last of a series of voyages to Vínland related in *Grœnlendinga saga* occurs when two Icelandic brothers, Helgi and Finnbogi, arrive in Greenland. Freydís 'asked them if they would sail their ship to Vínland, and go halves with her on all the profits they made there.' It is clearly a business arrangement, for North America was a good source for raw materials, particularly timber, unavailable in Greenland and Iceland. We soon learn, however, that Freydís can be up to no good. Despite an agreement that each party would have thirty 'able-bodied men' on board ship, Freydís takes thirty-five, giving her an advantage that the brothers do not discover until they reach Vínland.

Things go from bad to worse in Vínland itself. Freydís throws the brothers out of the houses her brother Leifr had built on an earlier voyage there and discord mounts over the winter, until the two groups are no longer speaking to each other. Then one day Freydís gets up early and, dressed in her husband's cloak, goes over to the others and demands that they trade ships with her, 'because you have a bigger ship than I do, and I would like to get away from here'. No doubt relieved at the prospect of seeing the last of her, Finnbogi agrees. Freydís goes home and wakes up her husband Þorvarðr. She tells him that she has offered to buy the brothers' ship, but that they have beaten and maltreated her. By these lies, and by threatening Þorvarðr with divorce, she persuades him to take revenge on the brothers for her. Þorvarðr and his men surprise the others still asleep, tie them up and drag them out of the house one by one:

> Freydís had each one killed as he came out. Soon all the men were killed and only women remained, but nobody wanted to kill them. Then Freydís said, 'Get me an axe.' This was done. She then struck at the five women there and left them dead.

Freydís got what she wanted, which was great profit from the venture:

> In early spring, they loaded the ship that had belonged to the brothers with as much produce as they could get hold of and as the ship could bear.

She bribed her crew to keep quiet about this awful deed, but eventually the secret leaked out and reached her brother Leifr, who 'thought this a dreadful story'. Yet he is strangely reluctant to punish her in any way, only predicting that there would be 'little prosperity' for her descendants. 'Afterwards', we are told by the narrator of the saga, 'no one thought anything but ill of her and her husband.'

The laconic style of the Icelandic sagas does not give much away. We are not told know why Freydís behaved in this way and the condemnation of her deeds is not as great as we might expect. But if we read the saga carefully, we can see that there is some point to this rather sensational story.

Towards the beginning of the saga, we are introduced to Eiríkr's children, including Freydís, married to Þorvarðr:

> They lived at Garðar, where the bishop's seat is nowadays. She was a very haughty woman, but Þorvarðr was not a very imposing person; she had been married mainly for money. The inhabitants of Greenland were heathen at that time.

We are told three important things in this introduction. Freydís is a *svarri mikill*, a 'very haughty woman', and we get a clear hint of her interest in money. These two characteristics explain her behaviour in Vínland. Thirdly, we learn that she lived at a place that later became Greenland's bishop's seat. Freydís is not a Christian and does not become one during the saga, unlike most of the other characters. Leifr (who is credited with introducing Christianity to Greenland) made a significant remark when he said that none of her offspring would prosper. This contrasts Freydís with another of the female characters in the saga, Guðríðr, who turns out to be the ancestor of several Icelandic bishops. Guðríðr, we are told, 'was an imposing woman to look at; she was an intelligent woman and knew well how to behave amongst strangers'. She also travelled to Vínland, and ended her days as a nun.

Freydís, like Saxo's warrior women, wears men's clothes and wields weapons. And like them, she represents the bad old days, the heathen past that, according to the author, is now mercifully gone and replaced by the light of Christianity. For the author and the audience of *Grœnlendinga saga*, this contrast between past and present was embodied in the contrast between the domineering and strong-willed Freydís, and the good wife and mother Guðríðr.

Iceland's vengeful housewives

Hallgerðr and Bergþóra

While *Grœnlendinga saga* and *Eiríks saga rauða* concentrate on events that took place in Greenland and Vínland, most Sagas of Icelanders are firmly rooted in the landscape of Iceland. Probably the best known of these is the monumental *Njáls saga*.

The longest of the Sagas of Icelanders, with a complex plot and a large cast, *Njáls saga* has a number of interesting female characters involved in its intricate chain of feud and counter-feud.

In the very first chapter of the saga, we meet Hallgerðr, daughter of Hǫskuldr, who was 'pretty to look at and tall, and had hair as beautiful as silk, so long that it reached her belt'. When her father tries to show her off to his half-brother, he is told

'The girl is beautiful enough, and many will have to pay for this; what I don't understand is where thief's eyes have come into our family from.'

Thus our very first meeting with Hallgerðr anticipates the climactic scene in ch. 77 when her third husband, Gunnarr, dies in an ambush at his home. Gunnarr is Iceland's foremost archer, but he can no longer defend himself when his bowstring is cut and Hallgerðr refuses to give him two locks of her hair to make a new one. The ambush in which he dies is the culmination of a feud which was sparked off by Hallgerðr's theft of food from a neighbour. The very seed of Gunnarr's destruction is contained in that first description of Hallgerðr.

Hallgerðr is paired in the saga with Bergþóra, the wife of her husband Gunnarr's close friend Njáll. Bergþóra is a different character altogether, she is 'a great lady and noble-minded, but somewhat severe'. The strong-willed wives of the two chief men of the district are bound to clash, and they do. Soon after Gunnarr marries Hallgerðr, they are invited to a feast at Njáll's farm. Hallgerðr immediately sits in the seat of honour, but is removed by Bergþóra to make way for her daughter-in-law, wife of her youngest son. This is meant as an insult, and is taken as such, and from this unseemly squabble arises a long and destructive feud, which is not fully worked out until most of the main characters in the saga are dead. Hallgerðr and Bergþóra alternately send members of their households to assassinate members of the rival household. The vengeance is stepped up in each round, they start by sending slaves to kill slaves, but eventually their husbands and sons become involved, and the feud grows to include many more people than just the members of the two households.

A detailed study of *Njáls saga* would require more space than is available here. But a closer look at how these two women are presented in the saga can reveal the attitudes of thirteenth-century Icelanders to their female ancestors of two centuries earlier.

Despite the epic scale and grand tragic themes of many *Íslendingasögur*, the stories are firmly anchored in the everyday lives of Icelandic farming communities in the Viking Age. Although a hierarchical and stratified society, it was nevertheless one in which both chieftains and slaves had to work to ensure their continued existence in a harsh climate with poor agricultural conditions. The realism of the sagas means that the feuds, killings and lawsuits take place against a background of everyday life and work. In the society portrayed by sagas such as *Njáls saga*, women such as Hallgerðr and Bergþóra were *húsfreyjar*, not just 'housewives', but the mistresses of large farms. Such women had sole responsibility for the provision of food to large numbers of people. With the men often away, the housewife also had considerable power over the day-to-day running of the farm. But it is clear that their power depended on the standing of their husband, and on how much responsibility he was willing to give his wife. A man looking for work asks Bergþóra, 'Do you have any say here?' She can reply, 'I am Njáll's wife . . . and I have no less say in the household than he does.'

Hallgerðr, on the other hand, does not find it easy to reach the same level of trust with her husbands and her housekeeping methods usually lead to trouble. Her first marriage was a disaster from the start, for her father, anxious to get rid of his difficult daughter, married her off without consulting her to a man she considered beneath her. Her housekeeping is wasteful and, in a confrontation about her extravagance, her husband slaps her. He pays for this with his life, when Hallgerðr's uncle and protector, Þjóstólfr, kills him. Hallgerðr's second marriage was much happier, for she liked the bridegroom and was fully consulted about the marriage. Hallgerðr shows considerable restraint, she does not at first take charge of the household, which they share with her husband's brother. When he moves out, she runs the household in a way that is 'generous and lavish', but the two of them get on well. Unfortunately, her second husband also succumbs to a quarrel with Þjóstólfr.

We sense there will be trouble in her third marriage, to Gunnarr, when we are told immediately after an account of their wedding that 'Hallgerðr took charge of the household and was lavish and domineering.' Yet her fourteen-year-old daughter, whom Hallgerðr had married off spontaneously at her own wedding feast, 'was an excellent housewife'. Like Hallgerðr's first husband, Gunnarr's downfall can be traced to his criticisms of her housekeeping. One winter when there was a great famine in Iceland, Gunnarr handed out his own stocks of hay and food until he had none left. He goes to a neighbour who has not been so generous to ask whether he might buy hay and food from him. The neighbour refuses and Gunnarr gets what he needs from Njáll in the end. But Hallgerðr sends a slave to steal the neighbour's food, particularly cheese and butter, telling him to cover his tracks by setting fire to the storehouse. Gunnarr sees cheese and butter on his table and asks where they came from. Hallgerðr's reply is that

'it's not for men to bother about preparing food.' Gunnarr grew angry and
said, 'It is bad if I am the accomplice of a thief,' and slapped her face.
[ch. 48]

The theft is uncovered and sets off the feud which ultimately leads to
Gunnarr's death. And it is this slap Hallgerðr reminds her husband of
when refusing him her hair for a bowstring.

Bergþóra, by contrast, presumably runs her household efficiently, for
it occasions no comment. Apart from employing servants, we see her
serving food, for instance at Gunnarr's wedding. Most memorably, on
the night before she is burned alive in her house along with her husband
Njáll, their sons and a grandson, she serves them with a last supper:

'Now you should each choose what you would most like to eat tonight,
because this evening will be the last on which I serve food to my household.' [ch. 127]

Unlike Hallgerðr, whose life is marked by conflict with her husbands,
Bergþóra remains a loyal wife to the end. Given a chance to leave the
burning house, she makes this statement:

'I married Njáll young, and I have promised him that we would both have
the same fate.' [ch. 129]

Although their roles as wives and housewives differ, Hallgerðr and
Bergþóra play similar parts in the feuds which make up so much of the
saga. In fact, they both act out the role most commonly assigned to
female characters in the Sagas of Icelanders, that of the woman who has
to goad the male members of her household into starting or continuing
a feud. The sagas can give the impression that because of men's essentially peaceful natures, there would have been no feuds were it not for
the incitement of women. This is expressed clearly in *Njáls saga* at the
height of the Hallgerðr/Bergþóra feud:

When Njáll came home, he reprimanded Bergþóra, but she said she
would never give in to Hallgerðr. Hallgerðr was very angry at Gunnarr
for having settled over the killing. Gunnarr said that he would never
deceive Njáll or his sons. She raged at this, but Gunnarr paid no attention.
The men made sure that nothing happened that year. [ch. 37]

Yet when the men get more involved in the feud themselves, they do
not condemn the women, indeed they accept their goading and are

quick to take vengeance. Hallgerðr insults Njáll and his sons by calling them 'Old Beardless' and 'Little Dung-Beards' and persuades her husband's kinsman Sigmundr to compose some mocking verses on this subject. When the news reaches Bergþóra, she addresses her menfolk at the table and refers to the scurrilous nicknames as 'gifts':

'Gifts have been given to you, father and sons, and you will be disgraced by this unless you repay them.' [ch. 44]

Her eldest son, Skarpheðinn, at first replies laconically, 'We are not like women . . . flying into a rage about everything' but, before the night is out, Sigmundr is dead, killed by the sons of Njáll. Njáll tells Bergþóra that she has 'goaded them into doing something', but he does not condemn either this or the killing. Indeed, when his sons return, he is pleased at the news.

Bergþóra's devotion to her family's honour even extends to calling for vengeance for the death of her husband's illegitimate son together with her rival, his mother Hróðný:

Hróðný said, 'I ask you, Skarpheðinn, to avenge your brother. Even though he was not legitimate, I am sure that you will succeed and that you are the one who will try hardest.' Bergþóra said, 'You behave in a strange way, you kill when there is little to compel you, but with this you chew over and brood on it so that nothing comes of it . . . now is the time to act, if you want to.' [ch. 98]

Hallgerðr and Bergþóra illustrate aspects of the two roles most frequently assigned to female characters in the Sagas of Icelanders: on one hand, the proud, strong-willed woman who is frequently the catalyst for, if not the cause of, trouble; on the other hand the fierce guardian of her family's standing and honour, the voice of conscience that reminds men of their duty. Both these roles are clichés that recur in the Sagas of Icelanders and the role of the inciter is the one in which we most frequently meet female characters in the sagas.

The female inciter

It has been suggested that the female inciters of the sagas reflect a real situation in the Viking Age and later in which women could participate in Icelandic public life by playing this rather grisly role. Since there was no higher public authority to enforce the law, social control was maintained by the feud system, which kept a balance between competing, but roughly equal kin groups. According to this theory, in a society which practised blood-feud there was a division of labour between the women, whose task it was to keep track of their family's standing in the community and to initiate retaliation when this standing had been diminished in some way, and the men, whose task was to carry out this retaliation, or arrive at a settlement which gave satisfaction to both parties.

Although an interesting theory, the idea that it was women's positive duty to incite men to bloodshed does not really explore the way in which the sagas reflect social realities in either Viking Age or medieval Iceland. The laws deal, not unnaturally, with *legal* retributions for injuries, not the informal ones of feud. And women took no part in the legal process. Although the sagas present an alternative to the legal process, a way in which women could participate in public life, there is no evidence that this alternative existed outside literature. The female inciters of the sagas are literary clichés. Most sagas follow a fairly standard formula in developing their feud plots and one of the constant elements of this formula is that of the female inciter. An episode from *Njáls saga* indicates that this literary cliché is one which blames women, rather than empowering them, and that this blame comes from men.

Hildigunnr, whose husband Hǫskuldr has been killed by the sons of Njáll, welcomes her nearest male relative, her uncle Flosi, to her house. As the men sit down to eat, she enters the room weeping:

> Flosi said, 'You are heavy-hearted, kinswoman, now that you are weeping, and yet it is good that you weep for a good husband.' 'Will you take on the prosecution or give me other help?' she asked. Flosi said, 'I will prosecute your case to the full extent of the law or arrange for such a settlement that good men will admit that we are honoured in all ways.' She said, 'Hǫskuldr would have avenged you, if he had had to prosecute your death.' [ch. 116]

She caps her speech by throwing the bloody cloak in which Hǫskuldr had been killed over her uncle. He is very angry:

> 'You are a monster, you want us to do that which will be worst for us all. "Cold are the counsels of women." '

And Flosi rushes out to start on a remorseless chain of vengeance which leads to the burning of Njáll and his sons in their house, with the equally remorseless vengeance of Njáll's son-in-law in his turn, until most of the protagonists are dead and the saga reaches an exhausted end.

Flosi's proverbial statement 'cold are the counsels of women' sums up the Icelandic male attitude. In the mindlessly violent world of thirteenth-century Iceland, people's concerns and anxieties found literary expression in the sagas. Someone had to be blamed and the strong-willed women of the sagas, safely anchored in the Viking past, provided a scapegoat. The female inciters of the sagas functioned rather like their literary predecessors, the valkyries. They were a useful and colourful myth that accounted for the horrors of violence while removing the blame for it from male shoulders.

Conflict of loyalties and the women of Gísla saga

The female characters of *Njáls saga* never wield weapons, but some saga women show affinity with their literary sisters in Eddic poetry by attempting to wreak vengeance themselves.

Gísla saga tells how Þórdís, distraught with grief at the killing of her brother Gísli, welcomes his killer Eyjólfr at her table:

> when she brought the food in, she dropped the tray of spoons. Eyjólfr had placed the sword that had been Gísli's between the wall and his legs. Þórdís recognised the sword and when she bent down for the spoons, she grabbed the hilt of the sword and lunged at Eyjólfr, wanting to hit him in the stomach. She did not notice that the guard was in the way and it caught on the table. She hit him lower than she had intended, cutting his thigh; it was a bad wound. [ch. 37]

Þórdís' husband Bǫrkr is not at all pleased and offers Eyjólfr full compensation for the wound, as if for a killing, on which Þórdís promptly declares herself divorced from her husband.

It is not unusual for a female character in a saga to demand vengeance for the death of her brother, but it is unusual for her to attempt to carry it out herself. But Þórdís was in an unusual, and difficult, position. She could not ask her husband to take vengeance, since it was he who was indirectly responsible for her brother's death in the first place. Gísli had killed her first husband, Þorgrímr, Bǫrkr's brother, and it was at her request that Bǫrkr successfully brought a case of outlawry against Gísli. Once Gísli was outlawed, he could be killed by anyone with impunity and Bǫrkr hired his cousin Eyjólfr for this purpose. Þórdís' situation is parallel to that of Guðrún in the poems of the *Edda*: her brother is responsible for the killing of her first husband, and she retaliates against her second husband for arranging the killing of her brother. What the author of *Gísla saga* did was to transplant this scenario to Iceland in the Saga Age and to devise a plot in which there was a connection between the two killings.

This parallel with Guðrún is made explicit by the author of the saga. Ch. 19 quotes a verse in which Gísli compares his sister to Guðrún – this is immediately after she has deduced that he killed her first husband Þorgrímr and instructed her second husband Bǫrkr to bring a court case against him:

> My inconstant sister had not the firm heart of wise Guðrún, Gjúki's daughter, in her breast.
> For that gold-adorned goddess, the necklace-bearer [Guðrún], caused her husband's death. Thus did Guðrún stoutly avenge her valiant brothers.

It was perhaps this taunt that stung Þórdís into her act of attempted vengeance when her brother is finally killed, but of course she does not go to the bloody lengths of Guðrún in her retaliation.

Although Gísli's verse (probably composed in the twelfth century and so antedating the saga, and used by its author as a source) contrasts Þórdís unfavourably with Guðrún, we get the strong impression that the thirteenth-century author and audience of the saga would have had more sympathy for her plight. The saga demonstrates the tensions between loyalty to blood kin and to relatives by love and marriage. The characters are torn in both directions and ultimately they all suffer.

The trouble starts (ch. 9) in a conversation between two women sitting and sewing, Gísli's wife Auðr and his brother Þorkell's wife Ásgerðr. Þorkell overhears the conversation and deduces from it (how correctly, we are never sure) that his wife still nourishes a youthful passion for Auðr's brother Vésteinn. Þorkell cannot kill his sister-in-law's brother with whom he has sworn brotherhood, so his brother-in-law Þorgrímr, husband of his sister Þórdís, does it secretly. Gísli kills his brother-in-law Þorgrímr (husband of his sister) in retaliation for the death of his brother-in-law Vésteinn (brother of his wife) and is protected by his own brother Þorkell who is uncomfortably caught between the two sides. When Þórdís guesses that her husband Þorgrímr was killed by her brother, she arranges for Gísli to be outlawed, as we have seen, and ultimately killed. Þorkell is meanwhile killed by the sons of Vésteinn, putting Gísli in a position where he ought to kill his wife's nephews to avenge the death of his brother. But she successfully gets them out of his way and he does not try to kill them, out of loyalty to her and the memory of Vésteinn. Finally, Gísli is killed by his brother-in-law (Bǫrkr)'s cousin, his wife Auðr having kept loyally on his side through many long years of outlawry.

Both Þorkell and Þórdís try to juggle the loyalties of both blood and marriage, whereas Gísli and his wife Auðr show most loyalty to their ties by marriage. The love and trust between these two is shown in a very favourable light, and we get a strong sense of weariness with the old heroic standards of honour and kin loyalty, and a new emphasis on loyalty based on strong emotions of love and friendship. Certainly, *Gísla saga* explores the tensions of married life and personal relationships in early Iceland in a way that no other saga does. It uses a literary model from the old heroic legends to question the very social structure expressed in that model and to demonstrate 'the conflict of loyalties into which incompatible social demands bring the individual'. Women, by reason of their double loyalty, are at the very heart of this conflict.

Laxdœla saga

Patterns of Icelandic womanhood

Gísla saga is not the only saga in which we sense that contemporary concerns about the role of women are projected onto its Viking Age characters. The development of Icelandic womanhood from the Viking Age to the medieval period is one of the themes of *Laxdœla saga*. Of all the sagas of Icelanders, it has the broadest range of female characters, all drawn to catch the reader's interest. In it we meet a pioneer settler of Iceland, a slave who turns out to be a princess, a sharp-tongued but loyal wife, a beauty who is desired by many men but loves only one, marries four times and in her old age becomes a nun, and many others. Not only does this saga have more female characters than any other, but they are so dominant, so much in control and so much more clearly individualised in a saga with many stock male characters, that it has been suggested that *Laxdœla saga*, if not written by a woman, was at least produced for a predominantly female audience.

Like *Gísla saga*, *Laxdœla saga* also has a female character trying to take her own vengeance with weapons. Auðr is married to a certain Þórðr, who takes a fancy to the heroine of the saga, Guðrún. In order to marry Guðrún, he divorces Auðr on the pretext that she is 'always in breeches', like a man. Auðr waits until Þórðr is alone at home one day and rides over, the narrator telling us that 'she was certainly in breeches then'. She attacks him in his bed-closet with a sword, wounding him severely. Þórðr will not hear of having her punished, saying 'she had done what she had to do'. [ch. 35]

When Guðrún's third husband, Bolli, has killed the man she had really wanted to marry, Kjartan, the duty of taking revenge falls on Kjartan's brothers. Their mother Þorgerðr (daughter of the saga hero Egill Skallagrímsson), in a stock goading scene, has to incite them to carry out this duty. She obviously has little faith in her sons, for she insists on accompanying them on their expedition to kill Bolli:

> they tried to prevent this and said it was not a journey for a woman. She insisted on going, 'because I know for sure, my sons, that you need the encouragement.' [ch. 54]

And indeed she is present throughout the fight, egging them on until Bolli is killed.

The other female characters in the saga may behave more in accordance with the way women were supposed to than Auðr and Þorgerðr, but are no less strong-minded and determined to get their way.

Setting the tone at the beginning of the saga is the Norwegian emigrant, Unnr the Deep-Minded. (Her sisters also have colourful if obscure nicknames: Horned-Þórunn and Jórunn Wisdom-Slope.) Unnr's whole family leaves Norway to escape the tyranny of King Haraldr Finehair (the usual thirteenth-century Icelandic explanation for the settlement of their country in the ninth century). While her two brothers and brother-in-law go straight to Iceland, Unnr goes to Scotland with her father Ketill. In Scotland Ketill and Unnr's son Þorsteinn the Red both die, and 'she realized that things would not improve for her there'. So Unnr has a ship built and gathers up all her valuables, her kin and her followers, and sets sail. The saga narrator is at pains to point out what an achievement this is:

> it is agreed that there is hardly another example of a woman who escaped from such unrest with so much wealth and so many companions. This shows what an exceptional woman she was. [ch. 4]

Þorsteinn the Red left a lot of daughters (*Laxdœla saga* mentions six) and Unnr has the task of finding husbands for them. Two of them are married off *en route*, one each in Orkney and the Faroes, and she finds good marriages for the others on arrival in Iceland.

The description in the saga of Unnr's settlement in Iceland elaborates its picture of her as an important and powerful woman. While sailing around Breiðafjörður to look for a place to settle, Unnr and her companions keep stopping at places which are afterwards known by a name associated with her. Thus, Dögurðarnes, 'Breakfast-ness', is the place where they stopped for breakfast, Kambsnes, 'Comb-ness', is where she lost her comb, and so on. She is so powerful that she is able to make large grants of land to her followers, and even frees some of her slaves and makes them substantial landholders, too.

Unnr's last task is to marry off her youngest grandchild and sole grandson, Óláfr feilan. Like most of the men in the saga, he does as he is told, and Unnr chooses the bride and arranges a splendid wedding-feast. This turns out to be her funeral feast as well, and that was clearly how she intended it. The manner of Unnr's dying befitted her living. When everyone had arrived at the feast, Unnr went down to welcome the guests and to announce that she was leaving everything to her grandson:

> Then Unnr got up and said she would go to the bed-closet she usually slept in. She told everyone to enjoy themselves in whatever way they pleased, and there would be ale for the enjoyment of everybody. People say that Unnr was both tall and well-built; she walked vigorously down the hall and it was said that she was still a stately woman. [ch. 7]

The next morning, she is found dead, 'sitting up against the pillows'.

Unnr's emigration to Iceland is not only emblematic of the whole early history of that country and its settlement from Norway and the British Isles, it also sets up the rest of the saga. The major characters of *Laxdæla saga* are all descended from Unnr or from one of her brothers. Thus, the cousins and foster-brothers Kjartan and Bolli are her great-great-great-grandsons, and Guðrún, over whom they come to blows, is great-great-granddaughter of Unnr's favourite brother Bjǫrn. Many of the minor characters in the saga are descended from her through her son Þorsteinn the Red. The tragedy of *Laxdæla saga* is thus not only a family tragedy in the widest sense, but also one that has national implications. But although the cast of characters in *Laxdæla saga* overlaps with those of other sagas, notably *Njáls saga*, *Egils saga*, *Gísla saga* and *Eyrbyggja saga*, it is *Laxdæla saga* which gives most prominence to women and their role in shaping events.

Guðrún, the heroine of the saga, does not appear until about halfway through the story and, when she does, she tends to eclipse the other women in the saga. Before her appearance, our interest is held by characteristic vignettes of other women, such as the two who are the mothers of the children of Hǫskuldr, great-grandson of Unnr. Hǫskuldr's wife is Jórunn, 'an attractive woman, but vain, and exceptionally intelligent' who 'was considered the best match in all the Vestfirðir'; she is clearly a worthy mate for the rich and handsome Hǫskuldr. They have a successful marriage and several children (including the Hallgerðr of *Njáls saga*). But Hǫskuldr feels 'his farm did not have such fine buildings as he would have wished' and he sails abroad for building materials, leaving Jórunn to look after his farm and the children.

Hǫskuldr seems to have felt that something else was lacking in his life for, even before getting his timber, he goes to a market in Scandinavia and first of all buys himself a concubine. From a man called Gilli, 'the wealthiest man in the guild of merchants', who had traded in the towns of Russia, he buys the most expensive slave-girl on offer. Gilli does not conceal that she has one fault: she is mute. Hǫskuldr clothes her, beds her and takes her home to Iceland. Jórunn accepts the speechless girl into her household, but her resentment grows when a baby boy is born, and even more when the slave is discovered talking to her son – in Irish! She claims to be an Irish princess called Melkorka. Eventually, Melkorka has to be established on a farm of her own, away from Jórunn's smouldering resentment.

Judging from the sagas, it was common for powerful men in Viking Age Iceland to have extramarital relationships and illegitimate children, and the medieval laws even make provision for such children. These relationships are rarely condemned, but *Laxdœla saga* recognises that such arrangements were not always conducive to happiness. Besides Jórunn's justified resentment (she had after all been looking after the farm while Hǫskuldr was cavorting abroad), there is the tragedy of Melkorka, kidnapped at fifteen, sold into slavery and shipped off to Iceland where she is treated as an outcast. Her life is only redeemed by the success of her son Óláfr the Peacock, who is more handsome and rich than his half-brothers. Óláfr's life story is a romantic one. He travels to Ireland to meet his grandfather, refuses his offer of an Irish kingdom, refuses high honour in Norway and returns to Iceland to marry Þorgerðr, the daughter of Egill Skallagrímsson. She at first refuses him as 'the son of a serving-woman', but is won over by his handsomeness and charm. Although Óláfr overcomes the adversities of his birth, tragedy visits in the next generation, when his son Kjartan falls in love with Guðrún. In Kjartan's absence in Norway, Guðrún marries his cousin Bolli instead (son of Hǫskuldr's legitimate son Þorleikr) and there is a feud which ultimately leads to the deaths of both Kjartan and Bolli. Thus were the sins of Hǫskuldr visited on a later generation.

Guðrún

Guðrún is the figure that holds the saga together and many have thought it ought really to be called 'Guðrún's saga', the only Saga of Icelanders to have a woman as its main character. It is interesting to compare Guðrún with her father-in-law's sister, Hallgerðr. Both are described as very beautiful and both marry four times. Both have a disastrous first marriage because they are not consulted. Both are ultimately responsible for the deaths of their third husbands. But Guðrún is much more likeable than Hallgerðr, and the author of *Laxdœla saga* is at pains to stress her intelligence and character. She is almost too good to be true, but we do get a glimpse of the baser side of her nature when she divorces her first husband. She deliberately makes him a low-cut shirt so that she can divorce him on the grounds of wearing effeminate clothing and, as we have already seen, so that she can marry Þórðr who has divorced his first wife on grounds of masculine dress.

When Þórðr is drowned, Guðrún is still a young woman and everyone expects she will marry the handsome Kjartan, son of Óláfr the Peacock. But this never happens. Kjartan, like many young men in Icelandic sagas, wants to go abroad for a while before settling down, and announces his decision to Guðrún rather suddenly. When he sees that she is upset, Kjartan offers to do whatever will make her happy. At this point, Guðrún makes the rather startling request that he take her with him. It was almost unheard of in the world of the sagas for women to accompany men on such voyages: they were usually undertaken by young men eager to make money by trading and raiding, to win renown at the Norwegian court, and generally to make a name for themselves before returning to Iceland and settling down. All the major male characters of *Laxdœla saga* make such a voyage and return to even more esteem than they left. But for a woman to go on such a voyage was unprecedented, especially an unmarried one. Guðrún's request to Kjartan must be interpreted as a coded proposal of marriage, for that was the only circumstance in which she could possibly accompany him, and it is a proposal he has unaccountably failed to make. Kjartan immediately backs off and rather patronisingly tells her to stay at home to look after her old father and her brothers, and to wait for him for three years.

Without the security of a betrothal, Guðrún naturally refuses to promise this and they part on bad terms.

An experienced saga-audience knows that this is a recipe for disaster. Kjartan does not return within the three years and when Bolli returns alone, without any message from Kjartan to Guðrún, and able to tell her that he has seen Kjartan flirting with the sister of the king of Norway, he is able to persuade Guðrún to marry him instead. She is not breaking any promises, but her heart is not in it. When Kjartan returns to Iceland, the jealousy between the two men is fomented by Guðrún, until she finally eggs on her five brothers and Bolli to ambush and kill Kjartan. From here, the saga follows a fairly standard feud pattern. Kjartan's brothers take revenge by killing Bolli. Guðrún waits many years until her two sons by Bolli grow up, and then they take revenge on the killers of Bolli. When all the feuding is out of the way, Guðrún marries, for the fourth time, the rich Þorkell Eyjólfsson. On his death, Guðrún becomes the 'first nun and anchoress in Iceland' and lives to a great age. The saga ends with her son Bolli asking her 'Which man did you love the most?' After some prevarication, Guðrún admits that 'I was worst to the one I loved the most', by which we have to understand Kjartan. Thus *Laxdœla saga* is unique among Icelandic sagas in telling the tragic story of an unfulfilled love, and in telling this love story from the point of view of the woman.

The audience of Laxdœla saga

Although the theme of love is not absent from other Sagas of Icelanders, in no other saga is it brought to the fore as it is in *Laxdœla saga*, and in no other saga are the destructive effects of jealousy explored in such detail. We are accustomed from more recent literature to see love as the motive force behind many human actions, but it is unusual to find this attitude in a saga. In the case of *Laxdœla saga*, this shows that its author and audience were well acquainted with the literary fashions of their time. In the early thirteenth century, at the same time as many Sagas of Icelanders were being written, works such as *Tristrams saga*, the well-known story of Tristan and Isolde, were being translated into Norse. *Laxdœla saga* represents the reinterpretation of native traditions in the light of the new literary interest in love. Such a literary interest in love unavoidably meant giving a greater prominence to female characters than in more traditional feud stories.

Are the female characters in *Laxdœla saga* only there for the love interest? Many critics have thought so, and have interpreted the saga according to the standard patterns of feud, counter-feud and reconciliation. But not only are there more female characters in this saga than in any other, they are also of a different type. From the pioneer Unnr to the proud Guðrún they are all strong and dominant. A close reading of the saga shows how often the action is forwarded at the instigation of a female character. The whole plot is set up by the emigration of Unnr to Iceland and by the marriages she arranges for her grandchildren, establishing the genealogical network within which all the action takes place. We have seen the decisive interventions of Auðr, Þorgerðr and Guðrún. There are other women who have things their own way throughout the saga. A woman called Vigdís defies her husband to shelter a kinsman of hers who is in trouble over a killing. Jórunn makes peace between her husband Hǫskuldr and his half-brother Hrútr in their quarrel over an inheritance. Melkorka marries a rich neighbour so that he will give her son Óláfr a good financial start in life, and enjoys the displeasure this gives Hǫskuldr. Kjartan's sister Þuríðr is the one who persuades him to marry Hrefna when Guðrún has married Bolli, and we are told that 'Kjartan and Hrefna came to love one another dearly.' Guðrún persuades Þorgils Hǫlluson to help her sons avenge their father Bolli by making him a false promise of marriage; when her ends have been achieved, she marries the wealthy Þorkell Eyjólfsson instead. At her own wedding-feast (paid for by herself) Guðrún defies Þorkell to give shelter and aid to a killer who had been sent to her for protection.

Laxdæla saga is a classic feud saga, made up of the same standard elements as other sagas being written at the same time, in the mid-thirteenth century. But this preponderance of strong female characters suggests that the conventional elements of the genre have been reinterpreted to appeal to an audience composed to a large extent of women. There is a certain amount of feminine wish-fulfilment in the saga, with slaves turning out to be princesses, wives who get the better of their husbands, and so on. It is not hard to imagine some women in the audience at a reading of the saga cheering when Auðr sinks her sword into her former husband.

Women's disenchantment with their limited role in society is symbolised by a scene in ch. 30, involving Þuríðr, daughter of Óláfr the Peacock. Her first marriage, to a Norwegian called Geirmundr, is not very happy. When he deserts her, leaving her with a one-year-old daughter, she follows him and bores his ship to slow his escape. Then she takes his sword and places the baby beside him in the hammock where he is sleeping. Ultimately, this tactic rebounds on her family, for Geirmundr puts a curse on the sword and it is the one with which Bolli kills Kjartan. But many a woman in the audience must have sympathised with Þuríðr's desire to make her husband take more responsibility for his offspring and her conviction that she was just as capable as he was of carrying out the male responsibilities symbolised by the sword.

But most of all, *Laxdœla saga* is the story of the terrible revenge taken by Guðrún on Kjartan for telling her to be a good little girl and stay at home to take care of her father and brothers. Even for the passionate Guðrún, self-respect came before love.

Like all Sagas of Icelanders, *Laxdœla saga* is anonymous. We can never know whether it was written by a woman. Nor do we really know who it was written for. But, as Peter Foote once wrote, 'the sagas themselves offer us prime information about the audiences who first heard and approved them'. The audience for whom *Laxdœla saga* was written was, socially and in terms of education, not unlike the audiences reflected in other sagas. But unlike these other sagas, *Laxdœla saga* was composed with the female members of that audience in mind.

Laxdœla saga *and the Viking Age*

Laxdœla saga can tell us much about the attitudes of the thirteenth century during which it was first written and it can show us the concerns of women in that period. Many of these concerns are shared by women at all periods in history, most notably the need to make successful relationships with men without losing self-respect. But *Laxdœla saga*, and some other Sagas of Icelanders, also show us what those thirteenth-century women thought of their female ancestors who lived in the Viking Age. A society so immersed in the past that much of their literary activity dealt with that past must have found something attractive in the lives of the women and men of the Viking Age. One attractive aspect of that past must have been the vision of women like Unnr and Guðrún who had some control over their own destiny. The fact that such women are not ubiquitous in the sagas, and that they are more prominent in some sagas than others, suggests that women did not normally have much control over their destiny in the world which consumed those sagas.

But can the Sagas of Icelanders tell us anything more than that the women of thirteenth-century Iceland thought their Viking Age predecessors were somehow more forceful than they could be? Can the sagas tell us anything about the Viking Age itself? After all, the thirteenth-

Viking-Age swords from Iceland.

century Icelanders were much closer to the Viking Age than we can ever be and they must have known more about it than we ever can.

Certainly, *Laxdœla saga* (and other sagas) could be used to confirm what we know from other sources. The world of the sagas is not so very different from the picture we get from archaeology and historical sources. There is always the danger of a circular argument (archaeologists, for instance, frequently use literary sources like the sagas to interpret their material), but the evidence does mount up.

Thus, it is likely that Unnr the Deep-Minded was a historical character and did settle in Iceland as the female leader of a band of followers. She is mentioned in a number of other sources, including at least one early, historically reliable one, *Íslendingabók* (where she is called Auðr; Auðr and Unnr are forms of what was originally the same name). There would have been good reason to remember her in medieval Iceland. Guðrún's fourth husband, Þorkell Eyjólfsson, was (like her third husband Bolli) a great-great-great-grandson of Unnr/Auðr. And their great-grandson was Ari Þorgilsson, author of *Íslendingabók*.

Archaeology, anthropology and anthroponymy suggest that at least some of the early population of Iceland came from the British Isles or had connections there. There is thus nothing improbable either in Unnr's sojourn in Scotland before settling in Iceland, or in anyone having an Irish slave as a mother. As for slaves, we do have other evidence that local inhabitants were captured in viking raids on Ireland. In the mobile world of the Viking Age, such captives could end up anywhere, but it is likely that quite a number of them ended up in Iceland.

The vignettes of women at work presented by the sagas, sewing or weaving, or serving at the table, are drawn from the real life of the thirteenth century, but such everyday tasks were not very much different in the Viking Age.

The Viking Age setting of the events described in the sagas is thus in its essentials not too far from the truth, in as much as we can find that out. But the interpretation of those events is characteristically thirteenth-century, as are the actions, motives and characters of the people involved in those events. To find out about the lives of women in the Viking Age, we have to shake off the spell of the romantic fictions bequeathed us by the medieval Icelanders and consider a much wider range of evidence.

Conclusion

The range of evidence presented in this multidisciplinary survey emphasises the variety and diversity of women's experience in the Viking Age. It is difficult to find an all-encompassing theme, a thread that runs right through the previous pages, and this is hardly surprising, given that the Viking Age lasted three centuries and given the geographical extent of its effects. It is also difficult to pronounce on whether Scandinavian or viking women were better or worse off than their contemporaries in other cultures, or their descendants in Christian medieval Scandinavia, or whether women in the Viking Age had the kind of control over their lives that we value so highly in the twentieth century. Such statements may provide answers to the questions that we, towards the end of the second millennium, like to ask, but at the risk of gross oversimplification of what was a complex historical period. Life in the Viking Age would probably not have appealed to those of us alive in the 1990s, any more than life in any other historical period when it was nasty, brutish and short, but apportioning praise or blame to people long dead seems especially futile.

If it is impossible to condense the history of women in the Viking Age into a snapshot or slogan easily digested by our three-minute culture, it is nevertheless possible to identify some general themes that not only tell us more about women but also provide new perspectives on the Viking Age in general.

Scandinavian women abroad

It is clear from a variety of evidence that, in the ninth and tenth centuries, large numbers of women were involved in the viking settlements of previously uninhabited, or relatively sparsely inhabited, areas, such as north and west Scotland, Faroe, Iceland and Greenland. Towards the end of this phase of settlement, they were also involved in voyages of exploration to North America, as indicated not only by Icelandic sagas but also by finds at the L'Anse aux Meadows site. Although most of these women will have travelled as members of a household headed by a man, there is some evidence to suggest that women could also play this role of pioneer, by organising the transport of their family and followers, and by making decisions on arrival at their destination.

Equally clear is that women accompanied men on trading and raiding voyages to more densely populated areas of Europe and elsewhere, although it is likely that they did this in smaller numbers than the North Atlantic colonists, whose primary purpose was to establish new and lasting settlements. The clearest picture is from England, where contemporary chronicles, archaeological finds, place names and other linguistic evidence demonstrate that the vikings who had such an impact on Anglo-Saxon England included women as well as men. There were few in the early raids in the ninth century, but more in the process of settlement that followed on from the vikings' military success. A similar picture can be discerned for Ireland and Normandy, while elsewhere in Frankia it is clear that women could accompany a travelling viking army, but not that any of them stayed behind. In Russia, there are again a variety of indications that the Rūs traders and warriors of Scandinavian origin included women. In all these instances, it is very likely that some of the women who accompanied these peripatetic vikings were not Scandinavian, but had been acquired *en route*, perhaps even captured as slaves, but the presence of typically Scandinavian female graves in all of these areas shows that some Scandinavian women found their way there too.

What the Viking Age did, compared to the period just before and just after, was to loosen the ties that bound people to their home districts and create new opportunities for travel, with all that meant for learning languages, acquiring wealth and being exposed to other cultures and customs. Women also had the chance of these new experiences and it is clear that many of them took advantage of the opportunities. When the dust had died down and the great movements of the Viking Age had subsided, it is likely that women led lives that were much more circumscribed by hearth and home, although in the Christian period the chance of going on pilgrimage was available to at least some women.

Scandinavian women at home

Of those women who stayed at home in Scandinavia, or who perhaps went abroad but returned, we know less, but even they could sometimes leave a mark. Our main source is archaeology, with additional information from runestones for the late Viking Age. Thus, a spectacular burial such as Oseberg and some of the Danish runestones demonstrate that aristocratic women could have great wealth and standing in the community. Other women left little or no mark, as the many simple, unaccompanied burials testify. Those graves in which women were buried with clothes, jewellery and domestic implements represent only a segment of the population, those with at least some status. As in so many other periods, the middle and upper classes are much more likely to figure in the historical and archaeological record.

The burials alone might suggest a static, conservative society, but the archaeology of settlements such Birka, Kaupang and Hedeby provides a more dynamic view of Viking Age Scandinavia. In these prosperous centres of trade and manufacture, with their national and international contacts, women are well represented. The numbers of female burials assume a natural proportion of the total. Both the organisation of the activities in these centres, and historical and archaeological evidence, suggest that women could also be merchants or craftspeople, working alone or as partners of their husbands. Again, the development of trade and industry in the Viking Age provided new opportunities for women, and there can be no doubt that some women took full advantage of them.

Another new opportunity was provided by Christianity. It cannot be a coincidence that the proportion of runic inscriptions mentioning women, especially those commissioned by women, rises toward the end of the Viking Age, particularly in the parts of the viking world where the inscriptions are overtly Christian. Although Christianity may eventually have turned out to be a mixed blessing for women, in the late Viking Age it meant that they could commission runic memorials, for their daughters as well as husbands and sons, build and repair bridges and causeways, and go on pilgrimage. The raising of runic memorials by ordinary men to their wives also seems closely connected to the spread of Christianity.

Women in masculine discourse

Archaeological and historical information provide a useful corrective to the view of the Viking Age that we get from its pictorial art, myth and legend, and poetry. Even without the problems of transmission and preservation of the verbal arts, and the general problem of referentiality in both verbal and pictorial art, it is clear that the cultural products of the Viking Age cannot be used as factual evidence about the lives of women in that period because they are the products of a predominantly masculine discourse throughout most of the Viking Age.

The little non-abstract art that survives is closely bound up with the mythological texts and can only be interpreted in connection with them. Since much of our knowledge of the mythology depends on the works of Snorri Sturluson and, ultimately, on his knowledge of skaldic poetry, it is no surprise that the preserved myths reflect the heroic, warrior society that was the primary context for this poetry. In this mythical world, females, whether goddesses, giantesses or ordinary women, are generally decorative and peripheral. The myths and poems (skaldic, and many Eddic) describe action that is almost always male action. Where women are involved in the action, it is often as catalysts for the conflicts that male action has to resolve, or if they are involved in a more positive way, it is as mythical figures of male fantasy, such as valkyries. Female figures are very occasionally allowed a quasi-masculine role, but then they are safely distanced by being a giantess (e.g. Skaði) or a heroine of the remote legendary past (e.g Guðrún).

Despite this, a few skaldic poems by female poets suggest that there was a tradition of poetry by women that was not preserved because it did not conform to the prevailing masculine discourse. The few extant poems by women skalds show them working within the mainstream skaldic tradition, but using this for their own ends.

In Eddic poetry we get a feeling, possibly of a female voice in some of the poems, almost certainly of an audience that also included women. The Eddic poems are designed to appeal to a wider cross-section of the population than the rather specialist creations of the skalds; even their anonymity, although it prevents us from discovering whether any were in fact composed by women, confirms this.

As the verbal artefacts of the Viking Age are preserved for us almost exclusively in medieval manuscripts, written down well after the end of the Viking Age, it is not surprising that the world view we detect in them is influenced by medieval attitudes, even if only in the selection of which aspects of Viking Age tradition were preserved.

Medieval attitudes (again, predominantly male) to women, whether historical or fictional, in the Viking Age, are clear in the writings of the Danish historian Saxo Grammaticus and of the anonymous authors of the Icelandic sagas. One particular interpretation of the female character which unites these medieval authors with those of some Viking Age texts is that which might be called 'the warring woman'. Descendants of the valkyries of Norse myth, combative, armed women appear in various guises in Scandinavian poetry and prose. The heroic fantasy of the armed female guardian spirit of the male warrior that we find in some Eddic poetry is hardly recognisable in Saxo, having given way to a cleric's misogynist fantasy of the female warrior as an aberration of the pagan period, to be tamed and turned into a 'real' woman. On a more realistic note, Guðrún, Skaði, and Þórdís in *Gísla saga* take up arms to avenge close relatives. Although only Guðrún succeeds in blood vengeance, the attempt is generally viewed with admiration. However, women who take up arms with less noble motives, such as Freydís, or Auðr in *Laxdæla saga*, are close to Saxo's misogynist myth of the virago, indicated by the fact that they wear men's clothes as well as carrying weapons. Even the more common vengeful female inciters of the sagas owe something to these concepts of warring women, although they restrict themselves to goading their male relatives and friends into violence.

In a saga like *Laxdæla saga*, and to some extent *Gísla saga*, we can find a more complex and even attractive view of women, suggesting that the saga authors and audience had a more sophisticated view than Saxo, and that the texts, like some of the Eddic poetry, were produced for a more varied audience. But despite suggestions of a female author for *Laxdæla saga*, the sagas remain another example of the masculine discourse that has helped form views of the Viking Age, right up to our own times.

Because the women of the Sagas of Icelanders are *not* portrayed primarily as objects of desire, many critics have been fooled into overlooking the stereotypical way in which they are portrayed. In 1936, C.S. Lewis wrote (in *The allegory of love*):

> The position of women in the Sagas is, indeed, higher than that which they enjoy in classical literature; but it is based on a purely commonsensible and unemphasized respect for the courage or prudence which some women, like some men, happen to possess. The Norsemen, in fact, treat their women not primarily as women but as people. It is an attitude which may lead in the fullness of time to an equal franchise or a Married Woman's Property Act, but it has very little to do with romantic love.

No doubt the authors of the Sagas of Icelanders also thought that they treated women with a 'commonsensible and unemphasized respect' but an analysis of their female characters suggests otherwise.

Women 'as women' or 'as people'?

The position of women in the Viking Age, or indeed in medieval Scandinavia, should not be romanticised. There is no doubt that women were treated 'as women' and suffered the physical perils of hard work, childbirth, male violence and slavery. The first three of these are hard to document from the available evidence, but are still the lot of many women around the world today. It is difficult to tell how much men, living in a violent age such as the Viking Age, would refrain from letting that violence affect women. However, historical sources indicate that women, in particular, were captured and enslaved. Some historical and archaeological evidence exists to suggest that women could be the victims of human sacrifice, and that such victims were most likely to have been slaves. A slave's lot cannot have been a happy one, whether male or female, for there is also evidence of male sacrifice. But the evidence for human sacrifice is limited and should probably not be exaggerated.

The Viking Age was, however, not all blood, sweat and tears, even for women. The Scandinavians' talents as seafarers, merchants and settlers, even their military talents, opened up new opportunities. At the end of the Viking Age, the introduction of Christianity brought yet more possibilities in its wake. Some women were able to take advantage of this window of opportunity and to make an impression outside the four walls of the home, leaving their mark on history. The history of the Viking Age is incomplete without them.

Notes

INTRODUCTION

p. 1 Alcuin is quoted from Whitelock 1955, 776. On the dates of the Viking Age, see Roesdahl 1991, 9–10, and Clarke and Ambrosiani 1991, 3.

p. 2 For *The Viking achievement*, see Foote and Wilson 1974. For the catalogue of the 1980 exhibition, see Graham-Campbell and Kidd 1980. The quotations are from p. 7.

p. 3 For books which do make mention of women, see Foote and Wilson, 1974, and Roesdahl 1982 and 1991.

p. 6 General books about the Viking Age which readers may find particularly useful include Foote and Wilson 1974, Graham-Campbell 1980b, Jones 1984, Roesdahl 1991 and P. Sawyer 1982. I am grateful to Hugh Goddard and Richard Perkins for advice on matters Arabic.

p. 8 For studies of the word 'viking', see Fell 1986 and 1987a, with further references.

CHAPTER I: LIFE AND DEATH – THE EVIDENCE OF ARCHAEOLOGY

The Westness woman

p. 9 The Westness finds are not yet fully published, but see Stevenson 1968, Kaland 1973 and Graham-Campbell 1980c, no. 312.

p. 10 For the Bjørke grave, see Bøe 1932 and Graham-Campbell 1980c, no. 309; and for insular material in Norwegian graves generally, Bakka 1963, C. Blindheim 1978 and Morris 1979.

The archaeology of burials

Studies referred to frequently in this section are the thorough analysis of some 1100 graves at Birka by Gräslund 1980 and the studies of burials in Sogn by Dommasnes 1978 and 1982.

p. 13 The Danish study referred to is Sellevold et al. 1984.

p. 15 For examples of women's jewellery, see Graham-Campbell 1980c, nos 108–75. For the textiles found at Birka, see Geijer 1979 and 1983, and Hägg 1969, 1971 and 1983. Some of the modifications to Hägg's reconstruction of women's dress at Birka suggested by Bau 1981 have been incorporated in the description here.

p. 17 The west Norwegian textile finds are analysed by Holm-Olsen 1975. The Haithabu excavations are summarised in Elsner.

p. 19 For examples of textile implements, see Graham-Campbell 1980c, nos. 66–91.

p. 21 For an example of a sickle from a female grave, see Graham-Campbell 1980c, no. 6. For the Santon Downham grave, see Evison 1969, 333, and Graham-Campbell 1980c, no. 117. The Gerdrup find is published in Christensen 1982. The Kaupang graves are catalogued in C. Blindheim et al. 1981a.

p. 22 For examples of crucifixes and Thor's hammers, see Graham-Campbell 1980c, nos. 522–32.

p. 24 The Pierowall cemetery is studied by Thorsteinsson 1968. For lapdogs, see Roesdahl 1982, 132, 165.

p. 25 It is likely that much of the material collected in Schetelig 1908–9 represents double burials rather than 'suttee'. The Hestehagen burials are described by Johansen 1981. For possible sacrifice in Danish graves, see Ramskou 1965. For the Gerdrup grave, see Christensen 1982. The Isle of Man graves are discussed in Bersu and Wilson 1966; see also Graham-Campbell 1980c, no. 509.

p. 27 For references to cooking equipment in male graves, see Graham-Campbell 1980c, nos. 42–8.

p. 29 For the cemeteries at Valsgärde and Tuna, see Stenberger 1956 and Schönbäck 1980.

p. 30 For further discussion of possible reasons for the distribution of male and female graves in Norway, see Hofseth 1988.

p. 31 The Oseberg burial is published in Brøgger et al. 1917–28, with English summaries.

p. 33 The Oseberg shoes are discussed in C. Blindheim 1959.

p. 34 *Heimskringla* is edited by Bjarni Aðalbjarnarson 1979 and there is an English translation by Monsen 1932. Ingstad 1981 argues that the younger woman buried at Oseberg was the Álfhildr of *Heimskringla*.

p. 35 For burials at Haithabu, see Elsner, 73–4.

p. 36 For Scandinavian burials in Russia, see Stalsberg 1984, and Avdusin and Puškina 1988. There is a general survey of viking colonial burials in Shetelig 1946. There is a map of Scandinavian burials in England in Wilson 1976 and they are critically discussed in Graham-Campbell 1980a. On the debate about the extent of Scandinavian settlement in England, see Fellows Jensen 1975.

p. 37 Crawford 1987, 116–27, discusses the Scandinavian burials in Scotland. For a survey of viking Orkney, see Morris 1985. The cemetery at Pierowall is discussed by Thorsteinsson 1965. The viking archaeology of the Isle of Man is discussed by Wilson 1974 and Cubbon 1983. The discovery of the 'pagan lady of Peel' is reported in Freke 1987. For viking Greenland, see Krogh 1967. The graves of Iceland are summarised in Shetelig 1937 and Eldjárn 1956.

Woman in her home environment

p. 38 For rural settlement sites in Scandinavia, see Bakka 1965, Becker et al. 1979. All the major urban sites are still in the process of being published, in the series: *Kaupang-funnene, Die Ausgrabungen in Haithabu, The archaeology of Lincoln, The archaeology of York, Medieval Dublin excavations 1962–81* and *Birka*. For a recent survey, see Clarke and Ambrosiani 1991. A popular introduction to York is provided by Hall 1984.

p. 40 For Borg, see Munch and Johansen 1988.

CHAPTER II: WOMEN'S LIVES IN RUNIC TEXTS

Runic inscriptions

p. 42 A brief introduction to runes is provided by Page 1987b, and Düwel 1983 is a useful bibliographical survey.

p. 45 For the Slemmedal hoard, see C. Blindheim et al. 1981b.

p. 46 For the Vä mount, the Lincoln comb-case, the Lindholm knife-haft and the Lund weaving-tablet, see Moltke 1985. For Rannveig's box, see Olsen and Liestøl 1941–80, V, 141–4, Graham-Campbell 1980c, no. 314, and M. Blindheim 1987. Translations are my own.

Memorial stones

p. 48 Hávamál is quoted from Neckel and Kuhn 1983, the translation is mine.

p. 49 The standard edition of Danish runic inscriptions is Jacobsen and Moltke 1941–2. More accessible, and containing inscriptions found since 1942, is Moltke 1985. Translations are my own. On the social implications of Danish runestones, see Randsborg 1980, 25–44.

p. 53 The standard edition (not yet complete, although the earliest volumes are now out of date) of Sweden's thousands of runic inscriptions is the series *Sveriges runinskrifter* (see Bibliography). Individual inscriptions are referred to by the name of the place in which they were found (and where they, in many cases, still stand) and are, to ease identification, classified with a letter or letters denoting the province in which they were found followed by a number. They can be traced in the appropriate volume of the series as follows:

Ög	=	Östergötland	(II)
Sö	=	Södermanland	(III)
Vg	=	Västergötland	(V)
U	=	Uppland	(VI–IX)
G	=	Gotland	(XI–XII)
Vs	=	Västmanland	(XIII)

New inscriptions continue to be found and are regularly published in the journal *Fornvännen*.

Transliterations of the inscriptions are taken from the standard edition, along with incidental information about the stones and, often, interpretations of the inscription. Translations into English are mine, although account has been taken of the translations into Swedish in the standard edition, as well as the selected translations (by Peter Foote) into English in Jansson 1987. This is a very useful introduction to the Swedish runic inscriptions, with excellent photographs (some in colour).

p. 55 An interpretation of runic inscriptions as 'declarations of property and inheritance', with special reference to women, is B. Sawyer 1988.

p. 58 The translation of the Ramsundsberget inscription assumes that Holmgeir was Sigrid's husband. The text is ambiguous and most commentators (e.g. the editors of *Sveriges runinskrifter*) have assumed that Holmgeir was Sigrid's father-in-law (for a fuller discussion, see Jesch 1991).

p. 60 The Högby inscription is discussed, and an attempt is made to relate it to other nearby memorial stones, by Selinge 1987. On verses in runic inscriptions, see Foote 1985.

p. 62 Women and poetic laments, including the Bällsta inscription, are discussed by Clover 1986b.

p. 66 Gräslund 1988–9 attempts to argue that the smaller number of daughters named in Swedish inscriptions is a result of the practice of female infanticide.

p. 69 On bridge-building, see Roesdahl 1990.

p. 70 The standard edition of Viking Age (and later) inscriptions in Norway is Olsen and Liestøl 1941–90 (in progress). Each inscription is referred to by the number given it in this edition. On some recently discovered stones, see Knirk 1987. Translations into English are mine, with account taken of the Norwegian translations in the edition.

p. 71 The iconography of the Norwegian runestones is discussed by Bjørn Hougen in Olsen and Liestøl 1941–90, I, 159–76, and Dynna is discussed in greater detail by Strömbäck 1970, Marchand 1975 and M. Blindheim 1977. See also ch. V, below.

p. 72 Manx runic inscriptions are covered most fully by Olsen in Shetelig 1940–54, VI, 151–232, but this should be supplemented by Page 1978–81 and 1983. The art of the crosses has been studied by Wilson 1970–73 and 1983, and Margeson 1983. The quotation is from Page 1983, 135.

CHAPTER III: FEMALE COLONISTS

The evidence of names

p. 75 This section is largely based on the collections of onomastic material made by von Feilitzen 1937 and Fellows Jensen 1968.

p. 76 For Scandinavian names outside the traditional areas of Scandinavian settlement, see Insley 1979, 1982 and 1985.

p. 77 On the Thorney names, see Whitelock 1937–45. For further comments on the onomastic evidence for Scandinavian women in Britain, see Fell 1984, 132–8. The long-standing scholarly controversy about the evidence for the extent and nature of Scandinavian settlement provided by place names is summarised by Fellows Jensen 1975. A detailed summary of the evidence for secondary migration is provided by Cameron 1985.

The settlement of Iceland

p. 79 Both *Íslendingabók* and *Landnámabók* are edited by Jakob Benediktsson 1968. *Íslendingabók* is translated in Halldór Hermannsson 1930. The *Sturlubók* version of *Landnámabók* is translated by Pálsson and Edwards 1974. All references are to chapter numbers of this version.

p. 80 Arnbjǫrg is in ch. 49 of *Sturlubók*.

p. 81 The passage about Geirmundr is in ch. 52 of *Sturlubók*. Eyvindr and his wife are in ch. 148 of *Sturlubók*. Ljót and her brothers are in ch. 349 of *Sturlubók*. Þorgerðr is mentioned in ch. 316 of *Sturlubók*. Ásgerðr is in ch. 341 of *Sturlubók*. The list of the noblest settlers in western Iceland is found in ch. 170 of *Sturlubók*. Auðr's career is recounted in chs 13 and 95–110 of *Sturlubók*. See also ch. VI below.

CHAPTER IV: FOREIGN VIEWS

International contact in the Viking Age

p. 85 A survey, with bibliography, of the variety of sources for the Viking Age can be found in P. Sawyer 1982. The quotation about Frankish annals is from P. Sawyer 1982, 24.

p. 88 For *Laxdæla saga*, see ch. VI. For al-Bakrī's account of a viking raid on the city of Nakūr (in present-day Morocco), in which two girls were kidnapped and ransomed, see Birkeland 1954, 64, and Melvinger 1955, 145.

Visitors to Scandinavia

p. 89 The *Vita Anskarii* is edited, with a parallel translation into German, by Trillmich and Buchner 1978. On the tendentious nature of the *Vita Anskarii*, see Wood 1987.

p. 90 On Dorestad, see Clarke and Ambrosiani 1991, 25–9. The quotation is from Wood 1987, 67.

p. 91 Adam of Bremen's *History* is edited, with a parallel translation into German, by Trillmich and Buchner 1978, and there is an English translation by Tschan 1959. Al-Qazwīnī's account of Ibrāhīm b. Ya'qūb's journey is translated into Norwegian in Birkeland 1954, 103–4. His life and diplomatic activities are discussed by el-Hajji 1970, 228–71, and Lewis 1982, 94–5, who quotes from his description of Schleswig on pp. 186, 262 and 286.

p. 92 The quotation about divorce comes from Foote and Wilson 1974, 114. On Muslim views of European women, see Lewis 1982, 284-93. Ibn Diḥya's account of al-Ghazāl's embassy is translated into Norwegian by Birkeland 1954, 83–8, and Swedish by Wikander 1978, 24–30, and is translated into English and discussed by both Allen 1958–61 and el-Hajji 1970, 166–203. The passages quoted are taken from the latter, except for Ibn Diḥya's comment on Andalusian poetry, (*p. 95*), which is from Allen 1958–61, 24–5. See also extracts and comment in Lewis 1982, 93–4, 284–6.

Viking women outside Scandinavia

p. 96 A translation into modern English of all the main versions of the *Chronicle*, together with a brief but invaluable introduction explaining the history of their composition, is provided by Whitelock et al. 1961. As the different versions of the *Chronicle* sometimes follow different dating conventions, or simply have mistakes, any dates given are the 'corrected' ones under which the entries are found in this translation.

p. 99 For a study of the Old English word *mann*, see Fell 1987b. A useful introduction to Cnut's reign is Christiansen 1986. An important, if tendentious, source for the life of Emma is the *Encomium Emmae reginae*, a laudatory text produced on her own instructions and probably representing how she wished to be remembered. Campbell 1949 provides an edition and translation of, and detailed (but somewhat out-of-date) commentary on this text.

p. 100 On Scandinavian personal names in Normandy, see Adigard des Gautries 1954. Page 1987a is an essay on some of the problems of using the later historians. Brief, translated extracts from Roger of Wendover, William of Malmesbury and Florence of Worcester can be consulted in Whitelock 1979.

p. 101 The passage from Roger of Wendover is quoted from Whitelock 1979, 257. For Florence of Worcester's account of the St Brice's day massacre, see Thorpe 1848–9, I, 156, translated in Forester 1854, 114.

p. 102 For William of Malmesbury's explanation of Swein Forkbeard's invasion, see Giles 1866, 185. The original text is edited by Stubbs 1887–9. Continental references to Cnut's daughter Gunnhild can be found in Trillmich and Buchner 1978 (see under *Chunihildis* in the index). The identification of the Gunnhild who was banished in 1044 as Cnut's sister was made by 'Florence' of Worcester, see Thorpe 1848–9, I, 199, translated in Forester 1854, 146.

p. 103 The Frankish annals and related sources quoted in this section are edited, and translated into German, by Rau 1968–9. There is an English translation of the *Annales regni Francorum* in Scholz 1970. A useful introduction to the sources for Carolingian history is McKitterick 1983, who also provides (pp. 228–36) a succinct summary of viking activities in the Frankish kingdoms.

p. 105 There is an edition, with translation into French, of Abbo's poem by Waquet 1942. This, with other Carolingian poetry mentioning vikings, is discussed by Andersson 1975.

p. 106 Hughes 1972 is a useful introduction to the Irish annals, although in some respects overtaken by recent research, notably the edition (with English translation) of the *Annals of Ulster* by Mac Airt and Mac Niocaill 1983, cited here. A general survey of this period of Irish history is Ó Corráin 1972. For a recent summary of archaeological evidence for vikings in Ireland, see Edwards 1990, 172–92.

p. 107 On Irish slaves, see Holm 1986. The translation of *Vita Findani* is quoted from Berry and Firth 1986, 284–7.

p. 108 For al-Bakrī's account of a viking raid on the city of Nakūr (in present-day Morocco) in which two girls were kidnapped and ransomed, see Birkeland 1954, 64, and Melvinger 1955, 145. The *Cogadh Gaedhel re Gallaibh* is edited and translated by Todd 1867 and its historical value dismissed by Ó Corráin 1972,

91–2. For the suggestion that Ota was Nūd, see Allen 1958–61, 46–8. Suggested identifications of the Red Maiden with legendary or semi- historical personages are summarised by Bugge 1905, 21–4, 37. On women warriors, see ch. VI below.

p. 109 An English translation of one version of the *Russian primary chronicle* is Cross and Sherbowitz-Wetzor 1953, quoted here, by permission of the Medieval Academy of America.

p. 111 On Scandinavian personal names in Russian sources, see Svane 1989, 25–6. The sixteenth-century *Life* of the Great Princess Olga is printed in Makarij 1889, I, 268–70. I am grateful to my colleague Dr Peter Herrity for providing me with a translation.

p. 114 On Olga as a saga heroine, see Chadwick 1946, 28–33. The quotation is from p. 30. Constantine's *De ceremoniis* is printed in the original Greek, with Latin translation, in Reiske 1829–30, I, 594–8, and translated into English in Leach 1946, 301–4. There is a useful summary of the relevant passages in Toynbee 1973, 504–5. L. Müller 1987 has the most up-to-date analysis of the various sources for the life of Olga, with particular reference to her conversion, and argues (p. 78) that her visit to Constantinople actually took place in 946.

p. 116 For *Laxdœla saga*, see ch. VI. For the Norse sources mentioning Yaroslav, see Cross 1929.

p. 117 Very few of the Arabic sources for vikings are available in English translation. For a bibliography, see Wikander 1976. Birkeland 1954 is a collection of extracts, including all the works referred to in this chapter, translated into and with commentary in Norwegian. For general works on the Arabs and Arabic literature, see Gibb 1963, Lewis 1966 and Dunlop 1971.

p. 118 There is a complete translation into English of Ibn Rusta's account in Macartney 1968, 213–15, which differs in a number of details from the version by Birkeland (1954, 14–17) followed here.

p. 119 For al-Iṣṭakhrī's account, see Birkeland 1954, 26–30. For al-Masʿūdī's account, see Birkeland 1954, 30–42, on him generally, Shboul 1979. For Ibn Miskawayh, see Birkeland 1954, 54–8, and Dunlop 1971, 123–5. Ibn Faḍlān's account of the Rūs is translated into English in Smyser 1965. A more reliable, but only partial, translation by J. M. Stern and Ralph Pinder-Wilson can be found in Foote and Wilson 1974, 408–11 (quoted here by permission except for some short passages not cited there, which are taken from Smyser). The whole of Ibn Faḍlān's book (and not just the section on the Rūs) is translated into Swedish by Wikander 1978, 31–72. For a study of his account as reportage, see Kowalska 1972–3.

CHAPTER V: ART, MYTH AND POETRY

Female figures in the art of the Viking Age

p. 124 The standard work on art in the Viking Age is Wilson and Klindt-Jensen 1980. A useful brief survey is Fuglesang 1981. There have been no detailed studies of the Oseberg tapestry (although it is often reproduced in books on the Viking Age) since Hougen 1940.

p. 126 The standard work on the picture stones of Gotland is Lindqvist 1941–2.

p. 128 An attempt at a more detailed interpretation of the pictures on the Ardre stone is Buisson 1976. A recent survey of the sources for the story of Thor's fishing expedition is Meulengracht Sørensen 1986b.

p. 129 The story of Hildr and the Everlasting Battle is told in Snorri's *Edda*, see Faulkes 1987, 122–3.

p. 131 The iconography of the Dynna stone has been discussed by Strömbäck 1970, Marchand 1975 and M. Blindheim 1977.

p. 133 On runic invocations to God's mother, see Gräslund 1987, 92.

Sexuality, wisdom and heroism: female figures in Norse myth and legend

p. 133 An elementary introduction to Norse mythology is provided by Page 1990.

p. 134 The complete *Poetic Edda* is edited by Neckel and Kuhn 1983. There are numerous translations into English, none of them entirely successful, but Bellows 1923 and Hollander 1962 are the most useful. (The translations of Eddic verse cited here are my own, unless noted otherwise.) There are general introductions to Eddic poetry in ch. 10 of Foote and Wilson 1974, more detailed in Turville-Petre 1953 (ch. 1) and Hallberg 1975. Harris 1985 is a bibliographical essay that provides an overview of recent Eddic research (which tends to the voluminous). Faulkes 1987 is a good modern translation of Snorri's *Edda*. All quotations from Snorri's *Edda* are given in my own translations. Faulkes 1982 is a useful student edition of the Prologue and *Gylfaginning* only. Other editions of the *Prose Edda* are primarily for specialists. For a bibliography of studies of the *Prose Edda*, see Lindow 1985. An important recent study is Clunies Ross 1987.

p. 140 Translations from *Lokasenna* are my own. Recent articles which explore the poem in some detail are McKinnell 1986–9 and Meulengracht Sørensen 1988.

p. 141 *Þrymskviða* is edited for students of Old Norse in Gordon 1957, 136–41. The sexual ambiguities of the poem are explored in Meulengracht Sørensen 1983, 23–4, and Perkins 1986–9.

p. 142 Translations from *Sigrdrífumál* are my own. For the interpretation 'healing runes', see G. Müller 1976, 359.

p. 143 A good introduction to *Vǫluspá* for those with some familiarity with the language is the student edition by Nordal 1978 and his general essays Nordal 1970–73. See also Jochens 1989.

p. 144 U. Dronke 1969 provides an edition and translation of, with detailed commentary on, *Atlakviða*. The poem is cited in her translation, by permission of Oxford University Press.

p. 148 The translation from *Vǫlundarkviða* is my own.

Women and skaldic poetry

p. 148 A good, brief introduction to the poetry of the Viking Age is ch. 10 in Foote and Wilson 1974. For those who read German, Foote 1985 is even better.

More detailed introductions to skaldic poetry which assume some familiarity with the language are by Turville-Petre 1976 and Frank 1978, and there is a survey of research in Frank 1985. The complete corpus of skaldic poetry is published in Finnur Jónsson 1912–15 and the texts on which this chapter is based are taken from there, except as noted below (in most cases where verses are preserved in Snorri Sturluson's *Heimskringla*, the texts are taken from Bjarni Aðalbjarnarson's edition). All translations of skaldic verse are my own, but reference is made to other translations where they exist and are easily accessible. My translations try to give a fairly close rendering of the content of the poems, reproducing the kennings as accurately as possible, while also trying to suggest the metre and rhyme structures of the originals. In this, they fall somewhere between the translations of Turville-Petre 1976 and Faulkes 1987, which give the sense very accurately, but do not attempt to reproduce the form, and Hollander 1945, who occasionally has to depart quite far from the meaning to reproduce the rhymes, alliterations and syllable count of the originals.

p. 149 The method of distinguishing genuine Viking Age skaldic poetry from later compositions is succinctly described by Foote 1978.

p. 150 The text of this poem and the translation on *p. 151* are based on Bjarni Aðalbjarnarson 1979, I, 281–2.

p. 152 Óttarr's verse is also translated in Faulkes 1987, 141. The translation of Þjóðólfr's poem is based on the text in Bjarni Aðalbjarnarson 1979, III, 141–3. There are English versions in Hollander 1945, 192–3, and Frank 1990, 73–4.

p. 154 The translation of Haraldr's last verse follows the text of Bjarni Aðalbjarnarson 1979, III, 188. Skúli's verse is also translated in Faulkes 1987, 138. The text of *Liðsmannaflokkr* follows Poole 1987, who also has a translation. The verses quoted here are also translated in Frank 1990, 71–2.

p. 155 The translation of Sigvatr's poem follows the text in Bjarni Aðalbjarnarson 1979, II, 140. There is a text with translation in Turville-Petre 1976, 83, and a translation in Hollander 1945, 156. See also Frank 1990, 72. Þjóðólfr's poem is in Bjarni Aðalbjarnarson 1979, III, 53.

p. 156 Sigvatr's poem in praise of Ástríðr is in Bjarni Aðalbjarnarson 1979, III, 5–7.

p. 157 Sigvatr's advice to Álfhildr is in Bjarni Aðalbjarnarson 1979, III, 20.

p. 158 Haraldr's ditty is in Bjarni Aðalbjarnarson 1979, III, 109. A companion verse to that by Óláfr about Ingigerðr is discussed by Frank 1978, 174. On the skald sagas, see Andersson 1979 and Bjarni Einarsson 1971.

p. 161 On the Niflung treasure, see Faulkes 1987, 100–104.

p. 162 *Eiríksmál* is edited for students of Old Norse in Gordon 1957, 148–9. For the *Fagrskinna* text, see Bjarni Einarsson 1984, 77–9. There is a text of Gunnhildr's poem in Bjarni Einarsson 1984, 75, but my translation takes account of some readings suggested by Kock (*Notationes norroenae* nos. 1926, 3046 and 3224).

p. 163 I have discussed Hildr's verse in some detail in Jesch 1989. The text follows Bjarni Aðalbjarnarson 1979, I, 123–4.

p. 164 My interpretation of Jórunn's difficult poem is explained in Jesch 1987, where the translation was first published.

p. 166 A slightly different text of Steinunn's poems is edited and translated in Turville-Petre 1976; the reasons for my choice of text and translation are given in Jesch 1987, where they were first published.

The audience of Viking Age poetry

p. 168 On women and Eddic poetry, see Gísli Sigurðsson 1986. The text of the Helgi poems follows the edition by Neckel and Kuhn 1983; translations are my own. For general comments on the Helgi poems, with translations of selected verses, see Hallberg 1975, 64–70, and Jónas Kristjánsson 1988, 51–5.

p. 170 On 'the dead lover's return', see P. Dronke 1976.

CHAPTER VI: WARRIOR WOMAN TO NUN – LOOKING BACK AT VIKING WOMEN

Warrior women

p. 176 Saxo's History is edited by Olrik and Ræder 1931, and Books 1–9 are translated with detailed commentary by Fisher and Davidson 1979–80 (quoted here by permission). The quotation about women warriors is from Fisher and Davidson 1979–80, I, 212. For Sela, see Fisher and Davidson 1979–80, I, 83. The quotation about Lathgertha is from Fisher and Davidson 1979–80, I, 280.

p. 177 The quotations from Saxo's account of the battle of Brávellir are from Fisher and Davidson 1979–80, I, 238–44. A related account of the battle of Brávellir can be found in the Icelandic text Sǫgubrot, edited in Bjarni Guðnason 1982, 46–71. On this text, see Jónas Kristjánsson 1988, 353. The quotation about Rusila is from Fisher and Davidson 1979–80, I, 246. The quotation about Stikla is from Fisher and Davidson 1979–80, I, 150. The quotations about Alvild are from Fisher and Davidson 1979–80, I, 211–12. The quotation about Gurith is from Fisher and Davidson 1979–80, I, 225.

p. 178 For a study of female figures in Saxo, see Strand 1980. The quotation about Camilla is from Knight 1958, 200. The quotations from Saxo's preface are from Fisher and Davidson 1979–80, I, 5. On maiden warriors in Icelandic literature, see Clover 1986a.

p. 179 The quotations about Hagbarth and Signe are from Fisher and Davidson 1979–80, I, 214. Helgakviða Hundingsbana II is edited in Neckel and Kuhn 1983, 150–61, the translation is my own. The quotation about Lathgertha is from Fisher and Davidson 1979–80, I, 282–3.

p. 180 The passage about 'forest maidens' is quoted from Fisher and Davidson 1979–80, I, 69.

Old Norse literature

p. 180 There are many general introductions to Old Norse literature, or to aspects of it. A recent one is Jónas Kristjánsson 1988, with excellent photographs. See also Turville-Petre 1953, Hallberg 1962 and 1975, and Schach 1984. Meulengracht Sørensen 1977 is recommended to those who read Danish.

Clover and Lindow 1985 provide a detailed bibliographical survey of most branches of Old Norse literature. Jesch 1989 is a survey of work on women in Old Norse literature, with a bibliography. The quotation about Icelandic writings is from the *First grammatical treatise*, see Haugen 1972, 13.

p. 181 Saxo on Icelanders is from Fisher and Davidson 1979–80, I, 5.

Women in the sagas of Icelanders

p. 182 Grœnlendinga saga and *Eiríks saga* are edited by Einar Ól. Sveinsson and Matthías Þórðarson 1935, and have been translated into English many times, e.g. by Magnus Magnusson and Hermann Pálsson 1965.

p. 183 For the Norse discovery of North America and the excavations at L'Anse aux Meadows, see Ingstad and Ingstad 1985.

p. 185 Njáls saga is edited by Einar Ól. Sveinsson 1954 and translated by Magnus Magnusson and Hermann Pálsson 1960. Many books and articles have been written about this saga, see the bibliography in Clover 1985.

p. 189 Many have written about female inciters in the sagas, but see particularly Heller 1958, 98–122, who emphasises their purely literary nature. The suggestion that the literary motif represents women's actual participation in feudal behaviour by instigating vengeance has been made by Ólafía Einarsdóttir 1983, 235 and Clover 1986b (who examines the Hildigunnr episode in detail). Gunnar Karlsson 1986, 70–72, reiterates the literary nature of female inciters.

p. 191 Gísla saga is edited by Björn K. Þórólfsson 1943 and translated by Johnston 1963. An important essay on the saga is Meulengracht Sørensen 1986a, which refers to most earlier studies of the saga.

p. 192 The translation of Gísli's verse is taken from Turville-Petre 1972, 126–7.

p. 193 The quotation is from Meulengracht Sørensen 1986a, 262. *Laxdœla saga* is edited by Einar Ól. Sveinsson 1934 and translated by Magnus Magnusson and Hermann Pálsson 1969. A useful study of the female bias in the saga is Kress 1980: many of her insights have been incorporated into my argument.

p. 196 On concubinage in early Norse sources, see Karras 1990.

p. 200 The quotation is from Foote 1974, 19.

p. 201 For a discussion about the extent of the British Isles contribution to Icelandic emigration, see Saugstad et al. 1977. For the capture of slaves in Ireland, see Holm 1986.

Bibliography

Scandinavian and other characters are alphabetised as follows:

å	=	aa
ä	=	ae
ð	=	d
ö,ø	=	oe
þ	=	th
ü	=	ue

Other diacritics are ignored.
Icelandic authors are listed under their patronymics.

Åhlén, Marit. 'Sex vikingatida släkter i Mälardalen', *Släkthistorisk forum* 1/86 (1986), 2–7.

Aðalbjarnarson, Bjarni (ed.). *Snorri Sturluson: Heimskringla I-III*. (Íslenzk fornrit, 26–8). Reykjavík: Hið íslenzka fornritafélag, 1979 (2nd ed.).

Adigard des Gautries, Jean. *Les noms de personnes scandinaves en Normandie de 911 à 1066*. (Nomina Germanica, 11). Lund: Carl Blom, 1954.

Allen, W.E.D. 'The poet and the spae-wife: an attempt to reconstruct al-Ghazal's embassy to the vikings', *Saga-Book* 15 (1958–61), 149–258. [also published as a monograph, Dublin 1960]

Andersson, Theodore M. 'Skalds and troubadours', *Mediaeval Scandinavia* 2 (1969), 7–41.

Andersson, Theodore M. 'The viking image in Carolingian poetry'. In: *Les relations littéraires franco-scandinaves au Moyen Age*. Bibliothèque de la Faculté de Philosophie et Lettres de l'Université de Liège 208 (1975), 217–46.

Avdusin, D.A. and T.A. Puškina. 'Three chamber graves at Gniozdovo', *Fornvännen* 83 (1988), 20–33.

Bakka, Egil. *Some English decorated metal objects found in Norwegian viking graves*. (Årbok for Universitetet i Bergen. Humanistisk serie, 1963/1). Bergen: Norwegian Universities Press, 1963.

Bakka, Egil. 'Ytre Moa. Eit gardsanlegg frå vikingtida i Årdal i Sogn', *Viking* 29 (1965), 121–45.

Bau, Flemming. 'Seler og slæb i vikingetid: Birka's kvindedragt i nyt lys', *Kuml* 1981 [publ. 1982], 13–47.

Becker, C.J. et al. 'Viking-age settlements in western and central Jutland: recent excavations', *Acta archaeologica* 50 (1979), 89–208.

Bellows, Henry Adams. *The poetic Edda, with introduction and notes*. New York: American-Scandinavian Foundation, 1923.

Benediktsson, Jakob (ed.). *Íslendingabók, Landnámabók*. (Íslenzk fornrit, 1). Reykjavík: Hið íslenzka fornritafélag, 1968.

Berry, R.J. and H.N. Firth (eds). *The people of Orkney*. (Aspects of Orkney, 4). Kirkwall: Orkney Press, 1986.

Bersu, Gerhard and David M. Wilson. *Three viking graves in the Isle of Man*. London: Society for Medieval Archaeology (Monograph Series, 1), 1966.

Birkeland, Harris (ed.). *Nordens historie i middelalderen etter arabiske kilder*. (Skrifter utgitt av det Norske Videnskaps-Akademi i Oslo, II. Historisk-Filosofisk Klasse, No. 2). Oslo: Jacob Dybwad, 1954.

Blindheim, Charlotte. 'Vernesfunnene og kvinnedrakten i Norden i vikingtiden', *Viking* 9 (1945), 143–62.

Blindheim, Charlotte. 'Osebergskoene på ny', *Viking* 23 (1959), 71–86.

Blindheim, Charlotte. 'Trade problems in the Viking Age: some reflections on insular metalwork found in Norwegian graves of the Viking Age'. In: *The Vikings: proceedings of the symposium of the Faculty of Arts of Uppsala University, June 6–9, 1977*. Ed. Thorsten Andersson and Karl Inge Sandred. Uppsala: Almqvist & Wiksell, 1978, pp. 166–76.

Blindheim, Charlotte, Birgit Heyerdahl-Larsen and Roar L. Tollnes. *Kaupangfunnene* I. (Norske oldfunn, 11). Oslo: Universitetets oldsaksamling, 1981.

Blindheim, Charlotte, Kolbjørn Skaare and Aslak Liestøl. 'Slemmedal-skatten', *Viking* 45 (1981) [publ. 1982], 5–48.

Blindheim, Martin. 'A Norwegian eleventh-century picture stone: the journey of the Magi to Bethlehem', *Journal of the British Archaeological Association* 130 (1977), 145–56.

Blindheim, Martin. 'The Ranuaik reliquary in Copenhagen: a short study'. In: *Proceedings of the Tenth Viking Congress; Larkollen, Norway, 1985*. Ed. James E. Knirk. (Universitetets Oldsaksamlings Skrifter, Ny rekke, 9). Oslo: Universitetets Oldsaksamling, 1987, pp. 203–18.

Bøe, Johs. 'An Anglo-Saxon bronze mount from Norway', *The antiquaries journal* 12 (1932), 440–2.

Brøgger, A.W., H. Falk and H. Schetelig. *Oseberg-fundet* I–IV. 1917–28.

Bugge, Alexander (ed.). *On the Fomorians and the Norsemen*. Christiania: Det Norske Historiske Kildeskriftfond, 1905.

Buisson, Ludwig. *Der Bildstein Ardre VIII auf Gotland*. (Abhandlungen der Akademie der Wissenschaften in Göttingen, philologisch-historisch Klasse, dritte Folge, 102.) Göttingen: Vandenhoeck & Ruprecht, 1976.

Cameron, Kenneth. 'Viking settlement in the East Midlands: the place-name evidence'. In: *Gießener Flurnamen-Kolloquium*. Ed. Rudolf Schützeichel. Heidelberg: Carl Winter, 1985, pp. 129–53.

Campbell, Alistair (ed.). *Encomium Emmae reginae*. (Camden Third Series, 72). London: Royal Historical Society, 1949.

Chadwick, N. K. *The beginnings of Russian history: an enquiry into sources*. Cambridge: Cambridge University Press, 1946.

Christensen, Tom. 'Gerdrup-graven', *Årbog for Roskilde Museum* 2 (1982), 19–28.

Christiansen, Eric. 'Canute and his world', *History today* 36 (November 1986), 35–9.

Clarke, Helen, and Björn Ambrosiani. *Towns in the Viking Age*. Leicester: Leicester University Press, 1991.

Clover, Carol J. 'Icelandic family sagas (*Íslendingasögur*)'. In: *Old Norse-Icelandic literature: a critical guide*. Ed. Carol J. Clover and John Lindow. (Islandica, 45). Ithaca, NY: Cornell University Press, 1985, pp. 239–315.

Clover, Carol J. 'Maiden warriors and other sons', *Journal of English and Germanic philology* 85 (1986), 35–49.

Clover, Carol J. 'Hildigunnr's lament'. In: *Structure and meaning in Old Norse literature*. Ed. John Lindow et al. Odense: Odense University Press, 1986, pp. 141–83.

Clover, Carol J. and John Lindow (eds). *Old Norse-Icelandic literature: a critical guide*. (Islandica, 45). Ithaca: Cornell University Press, 1985.

Clunies Ross, Margaret. *Skáldskaparmál: Snorri Sturluson's ars poetica and medieval theories of language*. (Viking Collection, 4). Odense: Odense University Press, 1987.

Crawford, Barbara E. *Scandinavian Scotland*. (Scotland in the early middle ages, 2). Leicester: Leicester University Press, 1987.

Cross, Samuel Hazzard. 'Yaroslav the Wise in Norse tradition', *Speculum* 4 (1929), 177–97.

Cross, Samuel Hazzard, and Olgerd P. Sherbowitz-Wetzor. *The Russian primary chronicle: Laurentian text*. Cambridge, Mass.: The Medieval Academy of America, 1953.

Cubbon, Marshall. 'The archaeology of the Vikings in the Isle of Man'. In: *The Viking Age in the Isle of Man*. Ed. Christine Fell et al. London: Viking Society for Northern Research, 1983, pp. 13–26.

Dommasnes, Liv Helga. 'Et gravmateriale fra yngre jernalder brukt til å belyse kvinners stilling', *Viking* 42 (1978) [publ. 1979], 95–114.

Dommasnes, Liv Helga. 'Late Iron Age in western Norway: female roles and ranks as deduced from an analysis of burial customs', *Norwegian archaeological review* 15 (1982), 70–84.

Dronke, Peter. 'Learned lyric and popular ballad in the early Middle Ages', *Studi medievali* ser. 3, no. 17 (1976), 1–40.

Dronke, Ursula (ed.). *The poetic Edda. Volume I: heroic poems*. Oxford: Clarendon, 1969.

Düwel, Klaus. *Runenkunde*. Stuttgart: Metzler, 1983 (2nd ed.)

Dunlop, D.M. *Arab civilization to A.D. 1500*. London: Longman, 1971.

Edwards, Nancy. *The archaeology of early medieval Ireland*. London: Batsford, 1990.

Einarsdóttir, Ólafía. 'Kvindens stilling i fristatstidens Island: sociale og økonomiske betragtninger.' In *Historica IV: Föredrag vid det XVII Nordiska historikermötet, Jyväskylä 1981*. (Studia Historica Jyväskyläensia, 27). Jyväskylä: Jyväskylän Yliopisto, 1983, pp. 227–38.

Einarsson, Bjarni. 'The lovesick skald: a reply to Theodore M. Andersson', *Mediaeval Scandinavia* 4 (1971), 21–41.

Einarsson, Bjarni (ed.). *Ágrip af Nóregskonunga sǫgum. Fagrskinna – Nóregs konunga tal*. (Íslenzk fornrit, 29). Reykjavík: Hið íslenzka fornritafélag, 1984.

Eldjárn, Kristján. *Kuml og haugfé úr heiðnum sið á Íslandi.* Akureyri: Norðri, 1956.

Elsner, Hildegard. *Wikinger Museum Haithabu: Schaufenster einer frühen Stadt.* Kiel: Archäologisches Landesmuseum der Christian-Albrechts-Universität, ca. 1989.

Evison, Vera I. 'A viking grave at Sonning, Berks.', *The antiquaries journal* 49 (1969), 330–45.

Faulkes, Anthony (ed.). *Snorri Sturluson: Edda. Prologue and* Gylfaginning. Oxford: Clarendon, 1982.

Faulkes, Anthony (trans.). *Snorri Sturluson: Edda.* London: Dent, 1987.

von Feilitzen, Olof. *The pre-Conquest personal names of Domesday Book.* (Nomina Germanica, 3). Uppsala: Almqvist & Wiksell, 1937.

Fell, Christine. *Women in Anglo-Saxon England.* London: British Museum, 1984.

Fell, Christine. 'Old English *wicing*: a question of semantics', *Proceedings of the British Academy* 72 (1986), 295–316.

Fell, Christine E. 'Modern English *Viking*', *Leeds studies in English* 18 (1987), 111–23.

Fell, Christine. 'Old English semantic studies and their bearing on rune-names'. In: *Runor och runinskrifter.* (Kungl. Vitterhets Historie och Antikvitets Akademien, Konferenser 15). Stockholm: Almqvist and Wiksell, 1987, pp. 99–109.

Fellows Jensen, Gillian. *Scandinavian personal names in Lincolnshire and Yorkshire.* (Navnestudier udgivet af Institut for navneforskning, 7). Copenhagen: Akademisk forlag, 1968.

Fellows Jensen, Gillian. 'The vikings in England: a review', *Anglo-Saxon England* 4 (1975), 181–206.

Fisher, Peter and Hilda Ellis Davidson (trans. and ed.). *Saxo Grammaticus: History of the Danes I-II.* Cambridge: D.S. Brewer, 1979–80.

Foote, Peter. 'The audience and vogue of the Sagas of Icelanders – some talking points.' In: *Iceland and the medieval world: studies in honour of Ian Maxwell.* Ed. Gabriel Turville-Petre and John Stanley Martin. Melbourne: University of Melbourne, 1974, pp. 17–25. [reprinted in Foote, Peter. *Aurvandilstá. Norse studies.* Odense: Odense University Press, 1984, pp. 47–55.]

Foote, Peter. 'Wrecks and rhymes.' In: *The Vikings: proceedings of the symposium of the Faculty of Arts of Uppsala University, June 6–9, 1977.* Ed. Thorsten Andersson and Karl Inge Sandred. Uppsala: Almqvist & Wiksell, 1978, pp. 57–66. [reprinted in Foote, Peter. *Aurvandilstá. Norse studies.* Odense: Odense University Press, 1984, pp. 222–35.]

Foote, Peter. 'Skandinavische Dichtung der Wikingerzeit'. In: *Europäisches Frühmittelalter.* Ed. Klaus von See. (Neues Handbuch der Literaturwissenschaft, 6). Wiesbaden: AULA-Verlag, 1985, pp. 317–57.

Foote, Peter, and David M. Wilson. *The viking achievement.* London: Sidgwick and Jackson, 1974 (2nd ed.).

Forester, Thomas (trans.). *The chronicle of Florence of Worcester with the two continuations.* London: Bohn, 1854.

Frank, Roberta. *Old Norse court poetry: the* dróttkvætt *stanza.* (Islandica, 42). Ithaca NY: Cornell University Press, 1978.

Frank, Roberta. 'Skaldic poetry.' In: *Old Norse-Icelandic literature: a critical guide.* Ed. Carol J. Clover and John Lindow. (Islandica, 45). Ithaca, NY: Cornell University Press, 1985, pp. 157–96.

Frank, Roberta. 'Why skalds address women'. In: *Poetry in the Scandinavian Middle Ages. Atti del 12° Congresso Internazionale di Studi sull'alto medioevo.* Spoleto: Centro Italiano di Studi sull'alto medioevo, 1990, 67–83.

Freke, David. 'Pagan lady of Peel', *Archaeology today* 8/1 (February 1987), 40–45.

Fuglesang, Signe Horn. 'Vikingtidens kunst.' In: *Norges kunsthistorie I.* Ed. Knut Berg et al. Oslo: Gyldendal, 1981, pp. 36–138.

Geijer, Agnes. 'The textile finds from Birka', *Acta archaeologica* 50 (1979), 209–22.

Geijer, Agnes. 'The textile finds from Birka'. In: *Cloth and clothing in medieval Europe. Essays in memory of Professor E.M. Carus-Wilson.* Ed. N. B. Harte and K.G. Ponting. (Pasold studies in textile history, 2). London: Heinemann, 1983, pp. 80–99.

Gibb, H.A.R. *Arabic literature: an introduction.* Oxford: Clarendon Press, 1963 (2nd ed.).

Giles, J.A. (trans.). *William of Malmesbury's chronicle of the kings of England.* London: Bell & Daldy, 1866.

Gordon, E.V. *An introduction to Old Norse.* Oxford: Clarendon, 1957 (2nd ed., revised by A.R. Taylor).

Gräslund, Anne-Sofie. *The burial customs: a study of the graves on Björkö.* (Birka, 4). Stockholm: Kungl. Vitterhets och Antikvitets Akademien, 1980.

Gräslund, Anne-Sofie. 'Pagan and Christian in the age of conversion'. In: *Proceedings of the Tenth Viking Congress; Larkollen, Norway, 1985.* Ed. James E. Knirk. (Universitetets Oldsaksamlings Skrifter, Ny rekke, 9). Oslo: Universitetets Oldsaksamling, 1987, pp. 81–94.

Gräslund, Anne-Sofie. ' "Gud hjälpe nu väl hennes själ": om runstenskvinnorna, deras roll vid kristnandet och deras plats i familj och samhälle', *Tor* 22 (1989–90), 223–44.

Graham-Campbell, James. 'The Scandinavian Viking-Age burials of England – some problems of interpretation'. In: *Anglo-Saxon cemeteries 1979. The fourth Anglo-Saxon symposium at Oxford.* Ed. Philip Rahtz et al. (British Archaeological Reports, British Series, 82). Oxford: Council for British Archaeology, 1980, pp. 379–82.

Graham-Campbell, James. *The Viking world.* London: Frances Lincoln, 1980.

Graham-Campbell, James. *Viking artefacts: a select catalogue.* London: British Museum, 1980.

Graham-Campbell, James and Dafydd Kidd. *The Vikings.* London: British Museum, 1980.

Guðnason, Bjarni. *Danakonunga sǫgur.* (Íslenzk fornrit, 35). Reykjavík: Hið íslenzka fornritafélag, 1982.

Hägg, Inga. 'Die wikingerzeitliche Frauentracht von Birka. Einige Bemerkungen zur Hemdform', *Tor* (1969), 13–25.

Hägg, Inga. 'Mantel och kjortel i vikingatidens dräkt', *Fornvännen* 66 (1971), 141–53.

Hägg, Inga. 'Viking women's dress at Birka: a reconstruction by archaeological methods'. In: *Cloth and clothing in medieval Europe. Essays in memory of Professor E.M. Carus-Wilson.* Ed. N. B. Harte and K. G. Ponting. (Pasold studies in textile history, 2). London: Heinemann, 1983, pp. 316–50.

el-Hajji, Abdurrahman Ali. *Andalusian diplomatic relations with western Europe during the Umayyad period (A.H. 138–366 / A.D. 755–976): an historical survey.* Beirut: Dar al-Irshad, 1970.

Hall, Richard. *The viking dig.* London: The Bodley Head, 1984.

Hallberg, Peter. *The Icelandic saga.* Lincoln: University of Nebraska Press, 1962.

Hallberg, Peter. *Old Icelandic poetry: Eddic lay and skaldic verse.* Lincoln: University of Nebraska Press, 1975.

Harris, Joseph. 'Eddic poetry.' In: *Old Norse-Icelandic literature: a critical guide.* Ed. Carol J. Clover and John Lindow. (Islandica, 45). Ithaca, NY: Cornell University Press, 1985, pp. 68–156.

Haugen, Einar (ed.). *First grammatical treatise: the earliest Germanic phonology.* London: Longman, 1972 (2nd ed.).

Heller, Rolf. *Die literarische Darstellung der Frau in den Isländersagas.* (Saga: Untersuchungen zur nordischen Literatur- und Sprachgeschichte, 2). Halle (Saale): Max Niemeyer, 1958.

Hermannsson, Halldór (ed.). *The book of the Icelanders.* (Islandica, 20). Ithaca, N.Y.: Cornell University Library, 1930.

Hofseth, Ellen Høigård. 'Liten tue velter. . . Problemer knyttet til manns- og kvinnegravenes fordeling i Nord-Rogaland'. In: *Artikkelsamling II.* Ed. Einar Solheim Pedersen. (AmS-Skrifter, 12). Stavanger: Arkeologisk museum, 1988, pp. 5-38.

Hollander, Lee M. *The skalds: a selection of their poems with introduction and notes.* New York: The American-Scandinavian Foundation, 1945. [reprinted 1968]

Hollander, Lee M. *The poetic Edda, with introduction and explanatory notes.* Austin: University of Texas Press, 1962 (2nd ed.).

Holm, Poul. 'The slave trade of Dublin, ninth to twelfth centuries', *Peritia* 5 (1986), 317–45.

Holm-Olsen, Inger Marie. 'Noen gravfunn fra vestlandet som kaster lys over vikingtidens kvinnedrakt'. *Viking* 39 (1975) [publ. 1976], 197–205.

Hougen, Bjørn. 'Osebergfunnets billedvev', *Viking* 4 (1940), 85-124.

Hughes, Kathleen. *Early Christian Ireland: introduction to the sources.* London: Hodder and Stoughton, 1972.

Ingstad, Anne Stine. 'Osebergdronningen – hvem var hun?' *Viking* 45 (1981) [publ. 1982], 49–65.

Ingstad, Anne Stine and Helge Ingstad. *The Norse discovery of America I–II.* Oslo: Universitetsforlaget, 1985.

Insley, John. 'Regional variation in Scandinavian personal nomenclature in England', *Nomina* 3 (1979), 52–60.

Insley, John. 'Some Scandinavian personal names from south-west England', *Namn och bygd* 70 (1982), 77–93.

Insley, John. 'Some Scandinavian personal names in south-west England from post-Conquest records', *Studia anthroponymica scandinavica* 3 (1985), 23–58.

Jacobsen, Lis and Erik Moltke. *Danmarks runeindskrifter*. Copenhagen: Ejnar Munksgaard, 1941–2.

Jansson, Sven B.F. *Runes in Sweden*. Stockholm: Gidlunds, 1987.

Jesch, Judith. 'Women poets in the Viking Age: an exploration,' *New comparison* 4 (1987), 2–15.

Jesch, Judith. 'Frauen in der altnordischen Literatur.' In: *Auf-Brüche: uppbrott och uppbrytningar i skandinavistisk metoddiskussion*. Ed. Julia Zernack et al. (Artes et litterae septentrionales, 4). Leverkusen: Literaturverlag Norden Mark Reinhardt, 1989, pp. 152–80.

Jesch, Judith. 'Who was hulmkir? Double apposition in the Ramsund inscription', *Arkiv för nordisk filologi* 106 (1991), 125–36.

Jochens, Jenny. '*Vǫluspá*: Matrix of Norse womanhood', *Journal of English and Germanic philology* 88 (1989), 344–62.

Johansen, Øystein. 'En dobbeltgrav fra vikingtid i et "funnfattig" område', *Viking* 45 (1981) [publ. 1982], 66–80.

Johnston, George (trans.). *The saga of Gisli*. London: Dent, 1963.

Jones, Gwyn. *A history of the Vikings*. Oxford: OUP, 1984 (rev. ed.).

Jónsson, Finnur (ed.). *Den norsk-islandske skjaldedigtning*. 4 vols. Copenhagen: Gyldendal, 1912–15.

Kaland, Sigrid Hillern Hanssen. 'Westnessutgravningene på Rousay, Orknøyene', *Viking* 37 (1973), 77–102.

Karlsson, Gunnar. 'Kenningin um fornt kvenfrelsi á Íslandi', *Saga* 24 (1986), 45–77.

Karras, Ruth Mazo. 'Concubinage and slavery in the Viking Age', *Scandinavian studies* 62 (1990), 141–62.

Knight, W.F. Jackson (trans.). *Virgil: the Aeneid*. Harmondsworth: Penguin, 1958.

Knirk, James E. 'Recently found runestones from Toten and Ringerike'. In: *Proceedings of the Tenth Viking Congress; Larkollen, Norway, 1985*. Ed. James E. Knirk. (Universitetets Oldsaksamlings Skrifter, Ny rekke, 9). Oslo: Universitetets Oldsaksamling, 1987, pp. 191–202.

Kock, Ernst Albin. *Notationes norroenae: anteckningar till Edda och skaldediktning*. (Lund Universitets årsskrift, n.s., sec. 1). Lund: Gleerup, 1923–44.

Kowalska, Maria. 'Ibn Fadlan's account of his journey to the state of the Bulgars', *Folia orientalia* 14 (1972–3), 219–30.

Kress, Helga. 'Meget samstavet må det tykkes deg: om kvinneopprör og genretvang i Sagaen om Laksdölene', *Historisk tidskrift (Stockholm)* 100 (1980), 266–80.

Kristjánsson, Jónas. *Eddas and sagas. Iceland's medieval literature*. Reykjavík: Hið íslenska bókmenntafélag, 1988.

Krogh, Knud J. *Viking Greenland*. Copenhagen: The National Museum, 1967.

Leach, Henry Goddard. *A pageant of Old Scandinavia*. Princeton: Princeton University Press, 1946.

Lewis, Bernard. *The Arabs in history*. London: Hutchinson, 1966 (4th ed.).

Lewis, Bernard. *The Muslim discovery of Europe*. London: Weidenfeld and Nicolson, 1982.

Lindow, John. 'Mythology and mythography'. In: *Old Norse-Icelandic literature: a critical guide*. Ed. Carol J. Clover and John Lindow. (Islandica, 45). Ithaca, NY: Cornell University Press, 1985, pp. 21–67.

Lindqvist, Sune. *Gotlands Bildsteine I-II*. (Kungl. Vitterhets historie och antikvitets akademien, monografier 28). Stockholm: Wahlström & Widstrand, 1941–2.

Mac Airt, Seán and Gearóid Mac Niocaill. *The Annals of Ulster*. Dublin: Institute for Advanced Studies, 1983.

Macartney, C.A. *The Magyars in the ninth century*. Cambridge: Cambridge University Press, 1968 (reprint of 1930 ed.).

McKinnell, John. 'Motivation in *Lokasenna*', *Saga-Book* 22 (1986-9), 234–62.

McKitterick, Rosamond. *The Frankish kingdoms under the Carolingians, 751–987*. London: Longman, 1983.

Magnusson, Magnus and Hermann Pálsson (trans.). *Njal's saga*. Harmondsworth: Penguin, 1960.

Magnusson, Magnus and Hermann Pálsson (trans.). *The Vinland sagas: the Norse discovery of America*. Harmondsworth: Penguin, 1965.

Magnusson, Magnus and Hermann Pálsson (trans.). *Laxdæla saga*. Harmondsworth: Penguin, 1969.

Makarij [Metropolitan of Moscow]. *Istorija russkoj cerkvi 12 tomach*. St Petersburg, 1889. (reprinted Düsseldorf, 1968).

Marchand, James W. 'A note on the Epiphany in runic art', *Arv* 31 (1975), 109–23.

Margeson, Sue. 'On the iconography of the Manx crosses'. In: *The Viking Age in the Isle of Man*. Ed. Christine Fell et al. London: Viking Society for Northern Research, 1983, pp. 95–106.

Melvinger, Arne. *Les Premières incursions des Vikings en Occident d'après les sources arabes*. Uppsala: Almqvist & Wiksell, 1955.

Meulengracht Sørensen, Preben. *Saga og samfund*. Copenhagen: Berlingske forlag, 1977.

Meulengracht Sørensen, Preben. *The unmanly man. Concepts of sexual defamation in early Northern society*. Odense: Odense University Press, 1983.

Meulengracht Sørensen, Preben. 'Murder in marital bed. An attempt at understanding a crucial scene in *Gísla saga*. In: *Structure and meaning in Old Norse literature. New approaches to textual analysis and literary criticism*, ed. John Lindow et al. Odense: Odense University Press, 1986, pp. 235–63.

Meulengracht Sørensen, Preben. 'Thor's fishing expedition.' In: *Words and objects: towards a dialogue between archaeology and the history of religion*. Ed. Gro Steinsland. Oslo: Norwegian University Press, 1986, pp. 257–78.

Meulengracht Sørensen, Preben. 'Loki's *Senna* in Ægir's hall.' In: *Idee, Gestalt, Geschichte. Festschrift Klaus von See*. Ed. Gerd Wolfgang Weber. Odense: Odense University Press, 1988, pp. 239–59.

Moltke, Erik. *Runes and their origin: Denmark and elsewhere*. Copenhagen: Nationalmuseets forlag, 1985.

Monsen, Erling (trans.). *Heimskringla: or the lives of the Norse kings by Snorre Sturlason*. Cambridge: W. Heffer & Sons Ltd, 1932.

Morris, C.D. 'The Vikings and Irish monasteries', *Durham University journal* 71/2 (1979), 175–85.

Morris, Christopher D. 'Viking Orkney: a survey'. In: *The prehistory of Orkney*. Ed. Colin Renfrew. Edinburgh: Edinburgh University Press, 1985, pp. 210–42.

Müller, Gunter. 'Zur Heilkraft der Walküre: Sondersprachliches der Magie in kontinentalen und skandinavischen Zeugnissen', *Frühmittelalterliche Studien* 10 (1976), 350–66.

Müller, Ludolf. *Die Taufe Rußlands*. Munich: Erich Wewel, 1987.

Munch, Gerd Stamsø and Olav Sverre Johansen. 'Borg in Lofoten – An inter-Scandinavian research project', *Norwegian archaeological review* 21 (1988), 119–26.

Neckel, Gustav, and Hans Kuhn. *Edda: die Lieder des Codex Regius nebst verwandten Denkmälern*. Heidelberg: Carl Winter, 1983 (5th ed.).

Nordal, Sigurður. 'Three essays on Völuspá', *Saga-Book* 18 (1970-73), 79–135.

Nordal, Sigurður (ed.). *Vǫluspá*. Durham and St Andrews Medieval Texts, 1. Durham: Department of English Language and Medieval Literature, 1978.

Ó Corráin, Donncha. *Ireland before the Normans*. Dublin: Gill and Macmillan, 1972.

Olrik, J. and H. Ræder (eds). *Saxonis Gesta Danorum*. Copenhagen: Levin & Munksgaard, 1931.

Olsen, Magnus, and Aslak Liestøl (eds). *Norges innskrifter med de yngre runer*. Oslo: Norsk Historisk Kjeldeskrift-Institutt, 1941–90 [in progress].

Page, R.I. 'Some thoughts on Manx runes', *Saga-Book* 20 (1978–81), 179–99.

Page, R.I. 'The Manx rune-stones'. In: *The Viking Age in the Isle of Man*. Ed. Christine Fell et al. London: Viking Society for Northern Research, 1983, pp. 133–46.

Page, R.I. *'A most vile people: early English historians on the vikings*. London: Viking Society, 1987.

Page, R.I. *Runes*. (Reading the past). London: British Museum, 1987.

Page, R.I. *Norse myths*. (The legendary past). London: British Museum, 1990.

Pálsson, Hermann and Paul Edwards (eds). *The book of settlements*. Manitoba: University of Manitoba Press, 1972.

Perkins, Richard. '*Þrymskviða*, stanza 20, and a passage from *Víglundar saga*', *Saga-Book* 22 (1986–9), 279–84.

Poole, Russell. 'Skaldic verse and Anglo-Saxon history: some aspects of the period 1009–1016.' *Speculum* 62 (1987), 265-98.

Ramskou, Thorkild. 'Vikingerne ofrede mennesker', *Nationalmuseets arbejdsmark* 1963–5 (1965), 79–86.

Randsborg, Klavs. *The Viking Age in Denmark: the formation of a state*. London: Duckworth, 1980.

Rau, Rheinhold. *Quellen zur karolingischen Reichsgeschichte I–III*. Darmstadt: Wissenschaftliche Buchgesellschaft, 1968–9.

Reiske, J. J. *Constantini porphyrogeniti imperatoris De Ceremoniis Aulae Byzantinae*. Bonn: Weber, 1829–30.

Roesdahl, Else. *Viking Age Denmark*. London: British Museum, 1982.

Roesdahl, Else. 'At bygge bro – om det ældste brobyggeri i Norden'. In: *Gulnares hus*. Ed. A. Bistrup et al. Copenhagen: Samleren, 1990, pp. 23–8.

Roesdahl, Else. *The Vikings*. Harmondsworth: Allen Lane, 1991.

Saugstad, Letten Fegersten et al. 'The settlement of Iceland', *Norwegian archaeological review* 10 (1977), 60–83.

Sawyer, Birgit. *Property and inheritance in Viking Scandinavia: the runic evidence.* Alingsås: Viktoria Bokförlag, 1988.

Sawyer, P. H. *Kings and vikings: Scandinavia and Europe AD 700-1100.* London: Methuen, 1982.

Schach, Paul. *Icelandic sagas*. Boston: Twayne, 1984.

Schetelig, Haakon. 'Traces of the custom of "suttee" in Norway during the Viking Age', *Saga-Book* 6 (1908–9), 180–208.

Schönbäck, Bengt. 'Båtgravskicket'. In: *Vendeltid*. Ed. Ann Sandwall. Stockholm: Statens historiska museum, 1980, pp. 108–22.

Scholz, Bernhard Walter. *Carolingian chronicles.* Ann Arbor: University of Michigan Press, 1970.

Selinge, Klas-Göran. 'The rune stones, barrow, village and church at Högby, Östergötland'. In: *Runor och runinskrifter* (Kungl. Vitterhets Historie och Antikvitets Akademien, Konferenser 15). Stockholm: Almqvist and Wiksell, 1987, pp. 255–80.

Sellevold, Berit Jansen, Ulla Lund Hansen and Jørgen Balslev Jørgensen. *Iron Age man in Denmark.* (Nordiske fortidsminder, B 8). Copenhagen: Det kongelige nordiske oldskriftselskab, 1984.

Shboul, Ahmad. *Al-Mas'udi and his world.* London: Ithaca Press, 1979.

Shetelig, Haakon. 'Islands graver og oldsaker fra vikingetiden', *Viking* 1 (1937), 205–19.

Shetelig, Haakon (ed.). *Viking antiquities in Great Britain and Ireland I–VI.* Oslo: Aschehoug, 1940–54.

Shetelig, Håkon. 'Gravskikk og religion i norrøne vikingebygder', *Viking* 10 (1946), 161–76.

Sigurðsson, Gísli. 'Ástir og útsaumur: umhverfi og kvenleg einkenni hetjukvæða Eddu', *Skírnir* 160 (1986), 126–52.

Smyser, H.M. 'Ibn Fadlan's account of the Rus, with some commentary and some allusions to Beowulf'. In: *Medieval and linguistic studies in honor of Francis Peabody Magoun, Jr.* Ed. Jess B. Bessinger and Robert P. Creed. London: Allen and Unwin, 1965, pp. 92–119.

Stalsberg, Anne. 'Skandinaviske vikingetidsfunn fra Russland med særlig vekt på kvinnefunnene', *Unitekst* 6 (1984), 86–103.

Stenberger, Mårten. 'Tuna in Badelunda: a grave in central Sweden with Roman vessels', *Acta archaeologica* 27 (1956), 1–21.

Stevenson, Robert B. K. 'The brooch from Westness, Orkney'. In: *The Fifth Viking Congress.* Ed. Bjarni Niclasen. Tórshavn: Føroya Landsstri, 1968, pp. 25–31.

Strand, Birgit. *Kvinnor och män i Gesta Danorum.* Lindome: Kompendiet, 1980.

Strömbäck, Dag. *The Epiphany in runic art: the Dynna and Sika stones.* London: University College London, 1970.

Stubbs, W. (ed.). *Willelmi Malmesbiriensis de Gesti Regum I–II.* (Rolls series, 90). London: HMSO, 1887–9.

Svane, Gunnar. 'Vikingetidens nordiske låneord i russisk'. In: *Beretning fra Ottende tværfaglige vikingesymposium.* Ed. Torben Kisbye and Else Roesdahl. Aarhus: Hikuin, 1989, pp. 18–32.

Sveinsson, Einar Ól. (ed.). *Laxdœla saga.* (Íslenzk fornrit, 5). Reykjavík: Hið íslenzka fornritafélag, 1934.

Sveinsson, Einar Ól. (ed.). *Brennu-Njáls saga.* (Íslenzk fornrit, 12). Reykjavík: Hið íslenzka fornritafélag, 1954.

Sveinsson, Einar Ól. and Matthías Þórðarson (eds). *Eyrbyggja saga.* (Íslenzk fornrit, 4). Reykjavík: Hið íslenzka fornritafélag, 1935.

Sveriges runinskrifter. Stockholm: Kungl. Vitterhets historie och antikvitets akademien, 1900–.

I.	Ölands runinskrifter. Ed. Sven Söderberg and Erik Brate. 1900–06.
II.	Östergötlands runinskrifter. Ed. Erik Brate. 1911–18.
III.	Södermanlands runinskrifter. Ed. Erik Brate and Elias Wessén. 1924–36.
IV.	Smålands runinskrifter. Ed. Ragnar Kinander. 1935–61.
V.	Västergötlands runinskrifter. Ed. Hugo Jungner and Elisabeth Svärdström. 1940–1971.
VI–IX.	Upplands runinskrifter. Ed. Elias Wessén and Sven B.F. Jansson. 1940–1958.
XI–XII.	Gotlands runinskrifter. Ed. Sven B.F. Jansson, Elias Wessén and Elisabeth Svärdström. 1962–78.
XIII.	Västmanlands runinskrifter. Ed. Sven B.F. Jansson. 1964.
XIV.	Närkes runinskrifter. Värmlands runinskrifter. Ed. Sven B.F. Jansson. 1975–78.
XV.	Gästriklands runinskrifter. Ed. Sven B.F. Jansson. 1981.

Þórólfsson, Björn K. (ed.). *Vestfirðinga sǫgur.* (Íslenzk fornrit, 6). Reykjavík: Hið íslenzka fornritafélag, 1943.

Thorpe, Benjamin (ed.). *Florentii Wigorniensis monachi chronicon ex chronicis I–II.* London: English Historical Society, 1848–9.

Thorsteinsson, Arne. 'The viking burial place at Pierowall, Westray, Orkney'. In: *The Fifth Viking Congress.* Ed. Bjarni Niclasen. Tórshavn: Føroya Landsstri, 1968, pp. 150–73.

Todd, James H. (ed.). *The war of the Gaedhil with the Gaill.* London: Rolls series (48), 1867.

Toynbee, Arnold. *Constantine Porphyrogenitus and his world.* London: Oxford University Press, 1973.

Trillmich, Werner, and Rudolf Buchner (eds). *Quellen des 9. und 11. Jarhunderts zur Geschichte der hamburgischen Kirche und des Reiches.* Darmstadt: Wissenschaftliche Buchgesellschaft, 1978 (5th ed.).

Tschan, Francis J. (ed.). *Adam of Bremen: History of the Archbishops of Hamburg-Bremen.* New York: Columbia University Press, 1959.

Turville-Petre, G. *Origins of Icelandic literature.* Oxford: Clarendon, 1953.

Turville-Petre, Gabriel. *Nine Norse studies*. London: Viking Society for Northern Research, 1972.

Turville-Petre, E.O.G. *Scaldic poetry*. Oxford: Clarendon, 1976.

Waquet, Henri (ed.). *Abbon: Le siège de Paris par les Normands*. Paris: Société d'édition 'Les belles lettres', 1942.

Whitelock, Dorothy. 'Scandinavian personal names in the Liber Vitae of Thorney Abbey', *Saga-Book* 12 (1937–45), 127–53.

Whitelock, Dorothy (ed.). *English historical documents c. 500–1042*. (English historical documents, 1). London: Eyre & Spottiswoode, 1979 (2nd ed.).

Whitelock, Dorothy, David C. Douglas, and Susie I. Tucker. *The Anglo-Saxon chronicle*. London: Eyre and Spottiswoode, 1961.

Wikander, Stig. 'Bibliographia Normanno-Orientalis', *Bibliography of Old Norse-Icelandic studies* 1974 (1976), 7–16.

Wikander, Stig. *Araber, vikingar, väringar*. Lund: Svenska humanistiska förbundet, 1978.

Wilson, D.M. 'Manx memorial stones of the Viking period', *Saga-Book* 18 (1970–73), 1–18.

Wilson, David M. *The Viking Age in the Isle of Man: the archaeological evidence*. Odense: Odense University Press, 1974.

Wilson, David M. 'The Scandinavians in England'. In: *The archaeology of Anglo-Saxon England*. Ed. David M. Wilson. London: Methuen, 1976, pp. 393–403.

Wilson, David M. 'The art of the Manx crosses of the Viking age'. In: *The Viking Age in the Isle of Man*. Ed. Christine Fell et al. London: Viking Society for Northern Research, 1983, pp. 175–87.

Wilson, David M. and Ole Klindt-Jensen. *Viking art*. London: George Allen and Unwin, 1980 (2nd ed.).

Wood, Ian. 'Christians and pagans in ninth-century Scandinavia'. In: *The Christianization of Scandinavia*. Ed. Birgit Sawyer et al. Alingsås: Viktoria bokförlag, 1987, pp. 36–67.

Index

Index

Index